Will Draftsman's

C000190290

Related titles by Law Society Publishing

Probate Practitioner's Handbook

General Editor: Lesley King
1 85328 831 4

Elderly Client Handbook

General Editors: Caroline Bielanska and Martin Terrell
Consultant Editor: Gordon R. Ashton
1 85328 872 1

Drafting Confidentiality Agreements, 2nd edn

Mark Anderson and Simon Keevey-Othari
1 85328 937 X

Drafting Employment Contracts

Gillian Howard
1 85328 906 X

All books from Law Society Publishing can be ordered through good bookshops or direct from our distributors, Marston Book Services, by telephone 01235 465656 or email law.society@marston.co.uk. Please confirm the price before ordering.

For further information or a catalogue, please contact our editorial and marketing office at publishing@lawsociety.org.uk.

Will Draftsman's Handbook

8th Edition

Robin Riddett

The Law Society

All rights reserved. No part of this publication may be reproduced in any material form, whether by photocopying, scanning, downloading onto computer or otherwise without the written permission of the Law Society and the author except in accordance with the provisions of the Copyright, Designs and Patents Act 1988. Applications should be addressed in the first instance, in writing, to Law Society Publishing. Any unauthorised or restricted act in relation to this publication may result in civil proceedings and/or criminal prosecution.

The views expressed in this publication should be taken as those of the author only unless it is specifically indicated that the Law Society has given its endorsement.

The author has asserted the right, under the Copyright, Designs and Patents Act 1988, to be identified as author of this work.

© Robin Riddett 2004

ISBN 1–85328–826–8

Published in 2004 by the Law Society
113 Chancery Lane, London WC2A 1PL

Typeset by J&L Composition, Filey, North Yorkshire

Printed by TJ International Ltd, Padstow, Cornwall

IN MEMORIAM

DONALD MICHAEL PETTITT

30 April 1928–13 December 2003

Without whose erudite collection of will precedents
the first edition of this book would never have happened

Large streams from little fountains flow
Tall oaks from little acorns grow

Contents

Preface

In the nine years since the previous edition of this book two significant statutory changes to the law and practice relevant to wills and the will draftsman have occurred.

The Trustee Act 2000 is the first major piece of trust legislation since the property legislation of 1925. Based on the Law Commission Report, *Trustees' Powers and Duties* (Law Commission No.260) the Act received Royal Assent on 23 November 2000 and came into force on 1 February 2001. It is primarily designed to give trustees powers to enable them to administer trusts in modern day circumstances. Despite its title the Act applies ' . . . in relation to personal representatives administering an estate . . .'. The Act is retrospective in that it applies to wills and trusts created before the commencement date. It generally operates on a 'default' basis so that for many professionally drafted trust instruments containing very wide powers for the trustees there will be little need to rely upon the powers available under the Act.

Among the implied provisions are:

(a) the power for trustees to invest as if 'beneficial owners';
(b) the power to acquire land for various purposes including 'occupation by a beneficiary';
(c) a new set of provisions permitting agents to carry out trustees' 'delegable functions'; and
(d) improved provisions relating to remuneration of trustees and insurance of trust property.

In addition a duty of care applicable to only certain of the statutory provisions is introduced so leaving the pre-existing law to apply in all other situations.

The dual system of strict settlements under the Settled Land Act 1925 and trusts for sale for successive interests in land came under scrutiny by the Law Commission in its 1989 Report, *Transfer of Land, Trusts of Land* (Law Commission No.181). It concluded that the benefits of simplified trusts of land were worthwhile and so recommended it become impossible to create new strict settlements while permitting existing settlements to continue. Such was the position implemented by the Trusts of Land and Appointment of Trustees Act 1996 (TOLATA 1996) with effect from 1 January 1997. Although essentially concerned with land transactions TOLATA 1996 nevertheless had considerable implications for the will draftsman.

As a consequence, for the draftsman the dichotomy of the Settled Land Act 1925 on the one hand and the mutually exclusive 'trust for sale' on the other is no longer as significant as it once was. Although future use of the trust for sale remains a possibility should particular circumstances require it, no longer is it a necessary feature of drafting in the vast majority of cases where land is to be limited in succession by the will. In future it is merely necessary for property to be given 'upon trust' to the trustees. Overall this represents a major simplification of the task of the draftsman when considering trusts where land is involved. Use of a trust for sale of land could, in narrow circumstances, remain useful and is addressed within the pages that follow along with various other provisions of TOLATA 1996 that have a bearing on will drafting. In particular, beneficiaries with an interest in possession in a trust of land are given the right to be consulted by the trustees as to their wishes as well as having the right to occupy the land itself in certain circumstances (unless in either case such rights are excluded by the trust instrument).

TOLATA 1996 contains power (if not expressly excluded by the trust instrument) for beneficiaries of full age and capacity entitled together to the trust property to direct the appointment and retirement of trustees. By its nature such provision is not available to beneficiaries of discretionary trusts nor can it be exercised if there is any living nominee within the trust instrument for appointing trustees.

Beyond the Trustee Act 2000 and TOLATA 1996 it is worthy of note that the inheritance tax (IHT) and capital gains tax (CGT) legislation for the variation or disclaimer of gifts by will post-death, and the provisions permitting use of discretionary trusts in wills designed to allow flexible appointment by trustees, remain available to the draftsman. There have been many occasions when a repeal of these provisions has been considered imminent but, to date, apart from minor alterations to the legislation no substantial changes have occurred.

The pre-budget statement by the Chancellor of the Exchequer in December 2003 proposed that from 6 April 2004 the trust tax rate paid on income and gains increase from 34 per cent to 40 per cent (the dividend trust rate correspondingly increasing from 25 per cent to 32.5 per cent). Such increases will affect the decisions testators must reach when considering whether to leave contingent or vested interests to minor beneficiaries in particular. How the balance of advantage between such gifts has altered is discussed within Chapter 4 of Part I: Preliminary Notes where the effects of taxation are dealt with generally. Additionally the Chancellor outlined proposals:

(i)   to introduce anti-avoidance measures to protect tax revenues where individuals enjoy free continuing use of assets they once owned – the 'tax treatment of pre-owned assets';
(ii)   to deny CGT gift relief for disposals to a 'settlor interested settlement'; and
(iii) to modernise trust income tax and CGT legislation.

Although some of these proposals may have an impact upon issues discussed within the following pages it is probable their impact will be at a minimum in a book whose main theme is will drafting rather than tax planning schemes.

Recent years have seen a marked increase in negligence litigation surrounding, in particular, the making of wills for testators. Many of the judgments have been decisions in favour of beneficiaries against the professional who prepared the will.

It would seem that the litigious attitude of beneficiaries renders it all the more necessary that extreme care be taken when receiving instructions for the will and when subsequently drafting in accordance with those instructions.

Throughout this book the masculine pronoun is used in order to be concise and is intended to be neutral.

Table of cases

Table of statutes

Page references in **bold** indicate that the legislation has been set out in part or in full in the Appendices.

Table of statutory instruments

Page references in **bold** indicate that the legislation has been set out in part or in full in the Appendices.

Abbreviations

AEA 1925	Administration of Estates Act 1925
AJA 1982	Administration of Justice Act 1982
CA 1989	Children Act 1989
CGT	capital gains tax
F(No.2)A 1987	Finance (No.2) Act 1987
FA 1986	Finance Act 1986
FA 1988	Finance Act 1988
FLRA 1987	Family Law Reform Act 1987
I(PFD)A 1975	Inheritance (Provision for Family and Dependants) Act 1975
ICTA 1988	Income and Coporation Taxes Act 1988
IEA 1952	Intestates' Estates Act 1952
IHT	inheritance tax
IHTA 1984	Inheritance Tax Act 1984
IT	income tax
LPA 1925	Law of Property Act 1925
LR(S)A 1995	Law Reform (Succession) Act 1995
PET	potentially exempt transfer
SLA 1925	Settled Land Act 1925
TA 1925	Trustee Act 1925
TA 2000	Trustee Act 2000
TCGA 1992	Taxation of Chargeable Gains Act 1992
TOLATA 1996	Trusts of Land and Appointment of Trustees Act 1996
VTA 1958	Variation of Trusts Act 1958
WA 1837	Wills Act 1837

PART I

Preliminary Notes

1

Introduction

The purpose of this book is to provide the professional will draftsman with essential material from which he may readily prepare the draft of a will appropriate to the circumstances of most clients. Where the estate is very substantial and complex trusts are envisaged, or perhaps existing trusts have to be taken into consideration, more sophisticated precedents may be required: if so, they are available elsewhere, and this book makes no claim to supersede them. In cases where specialised material is not called for, the standard collections of precedents will often be found inconveniently full for regular use, and sometimes not wholly apt to modern conditions. Usually, there is no real need for a will to be complex – clients understandably dislike complexity – and it should be possible to give effect to the wishes of most clients in reasonably simple and straightforward terms. The forms in this book are intended to help the draftsman to do so, in a convenient and economical manner.

The precedent clauses in Part II have been arranged in such a way as will facilitate the selection of what is required; in the more straightforward cases the arrangement may be found to offer what is in itself virtually an outline scheme for the draft. The process of selection should also serve to draw attention to matters on which clients ought to give specific instructions, while relying heavily on their advisers.

For increasing numbers of practitioners who use word-processing techniques, the accompanying CD-Rom containing these precedent clauses will permit a draft will to be readily assembled from whichever of the clauses may be appropriate to the particular circumstances.

All the clauses are accompanied by individual notes by way of commentary on some of their more important implications. While they cannot be exhaustive, it is hoped that these notes will be of some assistance to draftsmen of varying experience; they are however purely auxiliary and the clauses are intended to stand on their own.

The clauses are followed by a series of appendices (Part III) embodying for ready reference some of the more important of the statutory provisions bearing on the draftsman's work.

In Appendix 8 and on the CD-Rom there will be found a short series of three complete will precedents. These are introduced as offering more or less standard provisions for the needs of many clients disposing of comparatively small estates, and also illustrate the ease with which a draft may be compiled or adapted from individual clauses, to meet the circumstances of any particular case.

Many clients will be concerned about the impact of taxation, and especially of capital taxation. The need for careful planning of the dispositions of an estate, so as to give effect to the client's wishes and thus minimise the burden of tax, imposes a considerable responsibility on the draftsman to give effect to the client's instructions and to assist the client in formulating them. Tax considerations are of great importance, but so are a number of other considerations which may arise when instructions are taken; for example, matters of law or drafting, and matters which may affect the way in which the will is planned and prepared. Ease of drafting depends mainly on the care with which instructions have been taken; these instructions in turn depend on the advice which has been offered, in the light of the relevant law and of the particular circumstances of the individual client. The chapters which follow in Part I: Preliminary Notes are concerned with various aspects of this essential preliminary process.

2

Law of intestacy:
some comparisons

When considering the possible dispositions of a testator's estate, it is sometimes useful to consider how this would have devolved in the event of intestacy. The comparison is instructive, not only as to the effect of the statutory provisions, but also as to the terms in which these are drawn. The more important of these provisions are reproduced in Appendix 1.

Entitlement of an intestate's spouse to inherit under the intestacy law is in all cases dependent on survival by 28 days; failure to do so causes the intestate's estate to be distributed as though the spouse had predeceased the intestate (Administration of Estates Act 1925 (AEA 1925), s.2A inserted by the Law Reform (Succession) Act 1995 (LR(S)A 1995) in respect of deaths occurring on or after 1 January 1996). Subject to this, the following points are of particular significance:

1. If the intestate leaves issue, the entire residuary estate (excluding succession assets which are not regulated by English law; see *Re Collens (deceased)*; *Royal Bank of Canada (London)* v. *Krough* [1986] Ch 505) passes to a surviving husband or wife in so far as (exclusive of personal chattels) it does not exceed £125,000 (Family Provision (Intestate Succession) Order 1993, SI 1993/2906 (deaths on or after 1 December 1993)). As to any excess over that amount, the estate is divided. One half is held on trust, as to income only, for the surviving spouse for life, and, subject thereto, as to capital, on the statutory trusts for issue. The income and capital of the other half are held on the statutory trusts for issue.

2. In the larger estates, the entitlement of a surviving spouse to capital can be increased by exercise of the right to call for the life interest to be capitalised under the Intestate Succession (Interest and Capitalisation) Orders 1977 and 1983 and redeemed under AEA 1925, s.47A (reproduced in Appendix 1). Under the Intestates' Estates Act 1952 (IEA 1952), s.5 and Sched.2 a surviving spouse may also call for appropriation of the intestate's interest in any dwelling house in which the spouse was resident at the time of death, in or towards any absolute interest of the spouse in the estate (on payment of equality money, if necessary: *Re Phelps* [1980] Ch 275). These are valuable rights: there seems to be no obvious reason why corresponding rights should not be conferred (in appropriate cases) by will instead of leaving the spouse

to be dependent on the sympathetic exercise of whatever discretions may be given to the trustees or on a family arrangement. Precedent clauses F15.1 and F15.2 might be considered for this purpose.

3. If the intestate leaves no issue, but other close relatives survive, the entire residuary estate passes to a surviving husband or wife in so far as it does not exceed £200,000 (Intestate Succession (Interest and Capitalisation) Orders 1977 and 1983). As to any excess over that amount, the estate is again divided, but in this case one half of the excess passes to the surviving spouse absolutely. The other half is held absolutely for the parent or parents; or if neither survives, then upon the statutory trusts for any brothers and sisters of the whole blood. Only if there is no surviving parent, brother, sister, or issue of a deceased brother or sister, does a surviving spouse take the whole estate.

4. If the estate under consideration is so comparatively small that, on intestacy, it would pass entirely to a surviving wife or husband, the question may be asked: Is any purpose served by making a will? It is often said that, all other considerations apart, the real advantage of making a will is that the estate will be administered by an executor of the testator's choice. In this situation, however, the spouse, who would be the most natural choice for executor would equally have the best right to apply for letters of administration on intestacy (under the Non-Contentious Probate Rules 1987, SI 1987/2024 (L.10), r.22) and although an administrator is in some circumstances at a disadvantage as compared with an executor (in that his or her appointment is not, for most purposes, retrospective), there is no practical difference where the whole estate passes to that person as sole beneficiary.

Perhaps the most convincing reason for advising that a will should be made even in such circumstances is, quite simply, that circumstances (and, in particular, the nominal values of assets) may change, and that the change may pass unnoticed. If an estate now worth less than the amount of the spouse's 'statutory legacy' were to increase above that amount in nominal value, it seems very unlikely that a well-advised testator would think it right for any part of the estate to pass away from the spouse unless the increase were, in real terms, a substantial increase, or unless the spouse had other substantial means. The practical considerations referred to in Chapter 4 are equally relevant here.

Although the statutory rules for intestate succession were enacted in the light of a thorough analysis of many actual wills, and so represent an attempt to arrive at something like an 'average' series of dispositions, and although, over the years, their effect has been modified by increases in the amount of a surviving spouse's 'statutory legacy' (e.g., the original figure where issue survive of £1,000 increased to £40,000 in March 1981, to £75,000 in 1987 and for deaths on or after 1 December 1993 is £125,000) it would seem to be little more than irresponsible, in modern conditions, to allow an estate to devolve (in any case where a spouse is likely to survive) on a basis so unfavourable to the spouse. For possible further reform of the intestacy law see *Family Law, Distribution on Intestacy* (Law Commission No.187).

Unless a *new* will is made, an intestacy or partial intestacy may also result from the effect upon an existing will of marriage, or of divorce, with perhaps equally undesirable results (see Wills Act 1837 (WA 1837), ss.18 and 18A (as substituted by Administration of Justice Act 1982 (AJA 1982), s.18 and by LR(S)A 1995, s.3).

3

Law of family provision

Since, in those cases to which it applies, the Inheritance (Provision for Family and Dependants) Act 1975 (I(PFD)A 1975) empowers the court, in effect, to re-make the testator's will, its provisions must always be borne in mind in any case where the dispositions which the testator wishes to make do not self-evidently make 'reasonable' financial provision for any person who is a potential applicant under I(PFD)A 1975. For convenience of reference, the I(PFD)A 1975 (as amended by LR(S)A 1995[1]) is reproduced in Appendix 2.

The provisions of most immediate concern to the draftsman are those of I(PFD)A 1975, ss.1–3, which define the circumstances in which the jurisdiction of the court can arise, its powers, and the matters to which it should have regard in exercising those powers. Among subsequent provisions of I(PFD)A 1975, perhaps the most important are those which define what property is available for financial provision (should this be ordered), those which confer special powers on the court in relation to transactions intended to defeat applications for financial provision, and those concerning the liability of personal representatives.

Since the main purpose of I(PFD)A 1975 is to put right something which has gone wrong (or may be supposed to have done so), a detailed discussion of its provisions would clearly be inappropriate in a book on will drafting. However, as I(PFD)A 1975 may also be seen as putting testators on notice of the fact that testamentary freedom has its limits, there will be occasional cases where it will be part of the duty of the draftsman to offer some guidance to his client as to its effects. Happily, these will be comparatively few. It will therefore suffice to mention briefly the cases where special care may be required. In terms of I(PFD)A 1975, s.1, these are cases where:

(a) the testator's marriage is not stable; or
(b) a former wife or husband is alive[2,3] and has not remarried,[4] or
(c) the testator has a cohabitee at the time of his or her death; or
(d) there are children, whether of the present or of any other marriage, who are the testator's own children; or
(e) there are children who are treated by the testator[5] as children of the family in relation to any marriage to which the testator was ever a party; or
(f) there is any person for whose maintenance the testator has assumed some

responsibility[6] and who at the time of death was being wholly or partly maintained by the testator.[7]

If an application should be made under I(PFD)A 1975 by or on behalf of any such dependant, it would be the task of the court to strike a balance between the needs and resources of the applicant, and those of the various beneficiaries, and perhaps also between those of one applicant and another. The difficulty of this task lies usually in the fact that there are probably insufficient resources to provide for them all. The draftsman who is aware of a potential conflict of this kind faces precisely the same difficulty: but if with his guidance the testator has genuinely tried to do the best he can, an applicant may well be deterred.

When advising a client about the effect of I(PFD)A 1975, the draftsman may find himself called upon to attempt some estimate of the nature and extent of the provision which, in the event of an application, the court might be expected to order. Since the court is given a very wide discretion, it will be extremely difficult to make more than a very approximate estimate, even in relation to the circumstances as they are known to exist at present. Note that the court must take into account the facts as known at the date of the hearing (I(PFD)A 1975, s.3(5). In this respect, it is possible to give only general guidance, by drawing attention to the fact that I(PFD)A 1975 establishes two different standards of provision.

In the case of a surviving husband or wife,[8] the standard is 'such financial provision as it would be reasonable in all the circumstances of the case for a husband or wife to receive, *whether or not* that provision is required for his or her maintenance' (see *Re Besterman* [1984] Ch 458, showing that the court is not limited to the concept of maintenance; and see *White* v. *White* [2000] 3 WLR 1571). In assessing this, the court is directed to have regard (*inter alia*) to the provision which the applicant might reasonably have expected to receive if the marriage had ended by divorce instead of by death (see I(PFD)A 1975, s.1(2)(a), read in conjunction with s.3(2); but this is not a *maximum* (see *Re Bunning* [1984] Ch 480)). Such provision will be likely to include a substantial transfer of capital, perhaps to the extent of making up the capital of the applicant to a third or even half of the total capital assets of the parties. In particular, it may involve the transfer to the applicant of some interest in the matrimonial home.

In the case of other applicants, the standard is based upon reasonable provision for *maintenance*, according to the circumstances (I(PFD)A 1975, s.1(2)(b)). The question is, what would have been *reasonable* from an objective view (see *Re Hancock (dec'd)* [1998] 2 FLR (CA) showing that an adult, self-supporting, child needs 'a factor of great weight' to succeed not necessarily a 'moral obligation' or 'other special circumstance', as in *Re Coventry* [1980] Ch 461.)? The provision to be made is to meet recurring expenses of living, of an income nature, at whatever standard of living is appropriate to the applicant. However, this need not necessarily be by way of income payments: in some cases a lump sum may be appropriate.

In all cases, some further guidance as to what the court might consider reasonable is to be found in the generalised but quite detailed provisions of s.3 as to the matters to which the court is to have regard in exercising its powers under I(PFD)A 1975.

It should also be borne in mind that although the testator's reasons for doing what he did, or refrained from doing, are not in themselves directly relevant to the question of what would have been reasonable, an oral or written statement by the testator is nevertheless admissible as evidence of fact, by virtue of I(PFD)A 1975, s.21. Where there are clear and specific reasons for cutting down or omitting what would otherwise have seemed to be the appropriate provision for a spouse, or any other potential applicant, a contemporaneous written and signed statement should always be placed with the will. This can provide important evidence which otherwise might not be available. Since the terms of such a statement must depend entirely on the particular circumstances, no precedent form is suggested in this book.

In such a situation, the testator may well decide to proceed as he thinks fit, and leave it to the court to make an order if so advised. If based on a careful estimate of the probabilities, this may be the only practical course to take. In some cases, however, the testator might be better advised to make some provision *beyond* what he had in mind, in the hope that an application might at least be discouraged. The facts must be faced, in the interests of the beneficiaries under the will, that even an application which has little merit may have a considerable nuisance value, and that the executors might find themselves under some pressure to compromise it.

For IHT purposes, property affected by an order under the Act is deemed to have devolved subject thereto (Inheritance Tax Act 1984 (IHTA 1984), s.146). This is also the case where an order is made by consent (IHTA 1984, s.146(8)).

CHAPTER NOTES

1 LR(S)A 1995, s.2 adds cohabitees living for a period of two years with the deceased as husband or wife as a category of applicant for financial provision and introduces factors for the court to take into account when considering an order.

2 A claim on which no order has been made during the lifetime of a surviving spouse cannot be continued by his or her personal representatives: *Whytte* v. *Ticehurst* [1986] Fam 64.

3 The court may on divorce order the former spouse not to apply under s.15 of the LR(S)A 1995.

4 An application will be entertained only in exceptional circumstances if the parties have settled their financial affairs on divorce with legal advice: *Re Fullard* [1981] 3 WLR 743.

5 But not necessarily by both parties to the marriage: *Re Leach* [1986] Ch 226 (CA).

6 In terms of I(PFD)A 1975, s.3(4); and see *Re Beaumont* [1980] Ch 444, and *Jelley* v. *Iliffe* [1981] Fam 128 (CA).

7 By 'substantial contribution in money or money's worth towards the reasonable needs of that person', otherwise than for full valuable consideration (see I(PFD)A 1975, s.1(3)). As to 'consideration', see, by way of example, *Jelley* v. *Iliffe* above and *Bishop* v. *Plumley* [1991] 1 All ER 236.

8 And also, should death occur within 12 months of decree absolute, a former wife or husband, if an application for a financial provision order or a property adjustment order has not already been made, or determined (see I(PFD)A 1975, s.14).

4

Effect of taxation

4.1   Estate planning

In the planning of a will, due weight must always be given to taxation considerations, but these should never be decisive. This book is mainly concerned (as are most practitioners) with the testator who is providing for his or her immediate family. In planning a will for such a client, the first responsibility of a professional adviser is to give effect to the client's wishes as making the best possible provision for these beneficiaries. In many cases there will be only one practicable way to do this. Only where the available resources are such as to allow a measure of choice will taxation considerations bear directly upon the planning of the will; though where choices are open, these considerations will assume great importance.

It is a fact that IHT represents a significant burden on only a comparatively small proportion of all deaths, but it does bear upon a much larger proportion of all professionally drawn wills. Accordingly, the draftsman will need to be ready to advise as to the bearing of taxation on the real value of the intended beneficial interests, in relation to all but the smallest of the estates with which he is concerned. Taxation bears very differently upon different estates, and upon different dispositions of the same estate. In relation to any particular disposition, while IHT considerations will usually be paramount, it may also be necessary to consider the effects of CGT and sometimes of income tax (IT).

Since no two cases are ever quite alike, the relevance of taxation considerations and the weight to be attached to them will depend entirely on the practical situation. Accordingly, in this book, taxation considerations (like any other) are seen as far as possible in their practical aspects. Attention is therefore drawn to particular points in the context of particular dispositions in the notes to those precedent clauses to which they may seem to be specially relevant.

It is not the purpose of this book to offer any comprehensive or systematic treatment of the law relating to IHT, CGT or IT: it would not be appropriate to do so within the compass of a book of this kind nor is it necessary, in view of the number of standard works available for reference. However by way of introduction to the precedent clauses, the present note is included in order to draw attention to various considerations of general importance, relating mainly to IHT and CGT which will commonly be in view when instructions are taken and when the draft will is prepared.

4.2   Mitigation of tax – transfer on death: spouse exemption and nil rate of tax

In the great majority of cases, where the testator is a married man or woman, he or she will not be disposing of a sufficiently large estate for any real choice of dispositions to arise. Where this is the case, a simple will in favour of the surviving spouse will usually be the most appropriate from the tax viewpoint, at least in the short term. Whatever the theoretical possibilities may be, it is not in practice open to the testator to take the longer view unless the combined resources of the spouses are substantial enough for there to be no short-term problem.

If it may be assumed that the first concern of the testator is to preserve for his or her spouse, so far as possible, a standard of living comparable with that at present enjoyed by the family, the real difficulty lies in estimating (in a marginal case) the amount of capital which may be expected to be required for this purpose. In relating this estimate to the probable value of the testator's estate (which in itself is usually very much of an unknown quantity), it is plainly necessary to make a generous allowance for the probability of continuing inflation, and the strong possibility of erosion of real capital values with the passage of time, particularly where the survivor is likely to outlive the testator for any considerable number of years. Many wives are younger than their husbands, and women tend on average to live longer than men. As to what allowance should be made for this contingency, it is impossible to generalise: there are too many variable and unknown factors. In particular, much will depend on the nature and likely composition of the particular estate, as well as on the view taken of prevailing and prospective social, economic and political considerations. At best, any judgment on such matters must be based to some extent on speculation. Erring on the side of caution, it is usually considered unwise to leave anything away from a surviving spouse unless the present value of the combined estates is at least £450,000. Usually, moreover, the capital of the fund will not be wholly income producing. The family house may account for a substantial proportion, and few widows will be likely to think of the undoubted value of their beneficial occupation as income. The actual income of the rest of the fund cannot necessarily be expected to retain its real value.

By way of contrast, a fairly modest estimate of the needs of a surviving spouse appears to be implied by the statutory provisions as to intestate succession (see Chapter 2) under which, where issue survive, the estate becomes divisible in so far as (disregarding personal chattels) its value exceeds £125,000, the spouse receiving that amount absolutely, but only a life interest in half the surplus. Even where no issue survive the spouse cannot expect to receive more than the first £200,000; plus one half of any excess, if there are surviving parents, brothers, sisters, nephews or nieces. While in the case of a small estate the result of these dispositions may be that where issue survive, little or no IHT may be payable on the death of either spouse, this result is obtained by confining the spouse to what may, in effect, be little more than the probable value of the matrimonial home.

Whatever the amount which, in the particular circumstances, is thought to be appropriate by way of provision for a surviving spouse, the short-term effect of the spouse exemption, as to that amount, is to postpone any liability for IHT until the death of the spouse. The whole of the testator's capital is thereby made available without reduction during the lifetime of the spouse; in addition the spouse is enabled, if sufficient funds are available, to make lifetime transfers within the usual annual and other lifetime exemptions, without any liability at all for IHT.

Hitherto, where the spouse exemption has been fully utilised, it has been seen as a potentially adverse consideration, that when the property passing through the estate of a surviving spouse was eventually taxed as part of the estate passing on his or her death its aggregation with the free estate of the spouse, or perhaps with settled property in which the spouse was interested, might have led to a higher rate of tax being incurred than the property in question would have attracted on its own. Under the system of graduated rates of tax which has hitherto prevailed, for purposes of estate duty, capital transfer tax and IHT, this was a consideration of real importance, and it has always been one of the purposes of estate planning to avoid, so far as possible, the aggregation of values in the same taxable estate, in order to avoid the resultant inflation of the effective rate of tax chargeable on each constituent part.

The introduction of a flat rate of charge to IHT, by the Finance Act 1988, s.136, has the effect of removing this difficulty. It can now be said that, in general terms, not only is there no fiscal penalty attaching to the gift of an estate to the testator's surviving spouse within the IHT spouse exemption; but indeed there is a positive fiscal incentive to take full advantage of that exemption, in that any liability for payment of tax is thereby postponed, without any risk that a higher rate of tax will be incurred on the survivor's death as a result.

This generalisation must however be qualified in one important respect. In principle, although they might become aggregated in the hands of the survivor, the estates of husband and wife are regarded for IHT purposes as separate estates with each entitled to its own exemptions and reliefs. The benefit of the nil rate band, or threshold exemption, is thereby available in relation to transfers by each spouse, whether during their lives or on death. However, in relation to the death of the first of the spouses to die, the benefit of the nil rate can attach only to property on which tax is chargeable at that time; or, in terms of this discussion, on property which is left outside the spouse exemption. Therefore if the whole estate of the first to die is left to or in trust for the survivor, there can be only one application of the nil rate: in the estate of the survivor. If, on the first death, part of the estate had been left to children or otherwise outside the spouse exemption, then the nil rate would have been applicable on the first death, in relation to that property; and again on the second death, in relation to the estate of the survivor. Accordingly, if the children benefit under each will, the net value of their combined entitlements will then be greater than it would have been if their entitlements had arisen only under the will of the survivor. However, the estate available in the meantime for the support of the survivor will naturally have been reduced in value by the amount given to the children under the will of the first to die. In conclusion, the full benefit of the nil rate can be obtained in each estate if each will gives to or in trust for children, or other non-exempt beneficiaries, an amount up to the nil rate band at the time of death (as in Precedent clause E3.1 in this book); residue being given to or in trust for the spouse if he or she is the survivor, and otherwise to the children. If in the circumstances it is not practicable or desirable to give such an amount to the children, the benefit of the nil rate band of tax can still be secured to a lesser extent by giving such amount as may be appropriate.

Where lifetime transfers have already been made and are not exempt or only potentially exempt (see para.4.3), the amount of the non-exempt gift by will should not exceed the unused balance of the nil rate of tax: Precedent clause E3.1 anticipates this.

Formerly, when tax was chargeable at progressive rates, similar considerations applied in relation to the possible application of lower rates of tax in one estate in comparison with higher rates in the other. Since under that system the overall burden of tax was minimised where the taxable dispositions by each spouse were almost equal, it was a general principle of estate planning that the spouses should be placed in a position to make transfers as equal as possible by arranging the ownership of their combined estates in such a way that the values of their estates should themselves be almost equal.

In this respect also, the introduction of a uniform, flat rate of tax results in a welcome simplification. It is no longer necessary to advise that estates should be equalised on fiscal grounds alone, except to such extent as may be necessary to obtain the benefit of the nil rate of tax in each estate. To this extent, it is still important that each should possess a separate estate and dispose of it separately; or as much so as possible without detriment to the survivor. Shared ownership of the family house usually goes a long way towards this (but see further at para.4.8): for this purpose, the house should be held by the spouses as tenants in common and not as joint tenants. Any lifetime transfers between the spouses which facilitate any of these arrangements will be made within the spouse exemption in the ordinary way: as long as they are not made under any explicit agreement, or arrangement, there should be no danger that the Inland Revenue would invoke the anti-avoidance rules against associated operations.

In order to obtain the full benefit of the nil rate of tax in each estate, it is sufficient for the wills of both spouses to be drawn in reciprocal terms, so that a non-exempt gift to children (or others) will take effect on the first death. For many testators this will be the only acceptable way to make such provision. Although the unavoidable effect is that the amount in question will cease to be available for the support of the survivor (unless made so by way of a 'mini' discretionary trust, as under Precedent clause E4.1 in this book), that amount will at least have been available to the spouse during their joint lives, when perhaps they may have been reliant upon it. However, if the amount of the resources available to the spouses exceeds what is necessary for their support, the opportunity is opened for them to consider making transfers *inter vivos*, either within the standard IHT exemption or by way of potentially exempt transfers. If this can be done, the benefit may be considerable. Transfers which are exempt at the time when they are made, or which become so during the lifetime of the transferor, will not form part of the estate of the transferor at his or her death and will therefore not be subject to IHT at all. Further, the benefit of the nil rate of tax will continue to be available upon death, except to such extent as it may have been taken up by any lifetime transfer which was a chargeable transfer.

It is the general policy of IHT legislation to encourage lifetime gifts (and especially the transfer *inter vivos* of business and agricultural assets); and these should therefore be considered whenever the available resources permit.

4.3 Mitigation of tax – lifetime transfers: exempt and potentially exempt transfers

For most testators the opportunity to make lifetime gifts will arise most often within the standard exemptions. These are familiar but, perhaps for lack of professional advice, may not always be used as fully as they could be. This would be unfortunate for the amount of an exempt transfer will bear no IHT at all, even though the death of the transferor should occur within seven years afterwards, and the transferor should have reserved some benefit to himself.

Whenever any question of estate planning comes under review, it will be appropriate to verify at the outset that the available exemptions (IHTA 1984, as variously amended) have been utilised as fully as possible. In this context, the annual exemption (IHTA 1984, s.19) with its option to carry forward an unused balance to the following year and the exemptions for gifts in consideration of marriage (IHTA 1984, s.22) will be particularly in view. Also of considerable importance and sometimes overlooked, are the provisions whereby 'dispositions for maintenance of family' (IHTA 1984, s.11) are not in terms exempt but removed from the scope of the tax altogether: these include provision for the maintenance, education or training of children; and reasonable provision for the care or maintenance of a 'dependent relative' of the transferor, including his or her mother or mother-in-law if widowed separated or divorced, and of any relative of either spouse who is incapacitated by old age or infirmity. Other relieving provisions of which it will be important to take the fullest advantage, are the valuation reliefs in respect of business and agricultural property (IHTA 1984, ss.103–24). However, where a transfer of such property is potentially exempt (see below), it may be important to appreciate that under IHTA 1984, ss.113A, B and 124A, B (as amended), relief will only be available on the death of the transferor within seven years if the conditions for relief still continue to be satisfied at that time; but relief will not be lost by reason of a disposal of the property if similar qualifying property is acquired within 12 months.

For taxpayers disposing of surplus assets beyond the scope of the general exemptions, the opportunity exists to make absolute or (in certain cases) settled gifts, which may qualify for exemption from IHT to an unlimited extent, if made within the requirements for potentially exempt transfers in the Finance Act 1986 (FA 1986), s.101 and Sched.19, as extended by Finance (No.2) Act 1987, s.96 and Sched.7. They were introduced with the stated intention of allowing family businesses and farms to be passed on to the next generation without a possibly crippling charge to IHT. The benefit of these provisions is not restricted to business assets, but is of quite general application. To qualify as potentially exempt, a transfer must in principle be one made by an individual on or after 18 March 1986 in favour of another individual, or else into an accumulation and maintenance settlement (see para.4.7) or a disabled trust. As a relaxation of this general principle (by the Finance (No.2) Act 1987), a transfer into a settlement under which an individual has an interest in possession can qualify as potentially exempt; so can the termination of an interest in possession, where either an individual becomes entitled to any of the settled property, or else it becomes subject to an accumulation and maintenance settlement or disabled trust.

A transfer which qualifies as potentially exempt will become so in fact if and when the transferor has survived the transfer by seven years. In the meantime, it is 'assumed' that the transfer will prove to be an exempt transfer, and accordingly no charge to tax arises when the transfer is made, nor can it have any effect on any other transfer.

A transfer into any other kind of settlement (meaning, for all practical purposes, transfer into a discretionary trust) can never qualify as a potentially exempt transfer. Such a transfer is chargeable as a transfer into settlement, though at half the death rate (and with the benefit of the usual exemptions and reliefs), the settled property would thereafter be subject to the normal ten-yearly charge and 'proportionate' or exit charge, under the provisions of IHTA 1984, Part III, Chapter III. By the effect of provisions in IHTA 1984, ss.54A and 54B (inserted by Finance (No.2) Act 1987, Sched.17), an anti-avoidance charge to tax is incurred if any of the settled property should become subject to discretionary trusts within seven years after a potentially exempt transfer into an interest in possession trust, and during the lifetime of the original transferor.

Although a transfer into a settlement on discretionary trusts will always be a chargeable transfer, it will not necessarily be a taxable transfer. In particular it may be made within the nil rate of tax. Because of the great flexibility of such trusts, a discretionary settlement within the nil rate may sometimes be recommended for inclusion in a will, for the reasons discussed in the notes to Precedent clause E4.1. For very similar reasons, an *inter vivos* settlement within the nil rate may be considered. For different reasons, the introduction of short-term discretionary trusts into a will may be recommended to facilitate any future variation of the dispositions of the estate, as discussed in the notes to Precedent clause G1.1.

Apart from these special applications, it is usually considered that a settlement on discretionary trusts should no longer be recommended. However, as a generalisation, it could be misleading. The flexibility which discretionary trusts provide will sometimes be important to the welfare of the beneficiaries; and this consideration may sometimes be of sufficient importance to outweigh the impact of tax charges on the settled property. Although these tax charges are generally considered to be onerous, the fact is that if estimates are made, they may in the long term seem less so than those which would be likely to arise over a similar period under other dispositions. Where it is material, this question should be considered in relation to the actual circumstances, and with an open mind.

Where a potentially exempt transfer has been made, and the transferor dies within seven years thereafter, the transfer is then treated as a chargeable transfer, but with only partly retrospective effect. Tax is charged by reference to values at the date when the transfer was actually made, but is computed by reference to the rate (or rates) of tax chargeable at the date of the transferor's death. In the context of this and other provisions discussed in this book, the introduction of a uniform flat rate of tax in place of a progressive scale of rates gave rise, in transition, to some anomalies.

On a transfer becoming chargeable, the usual exemptions and reliefs would normally become available although special provisions apply in relation to the application of the annual exemption under rules in relation to potentially exempt transfers to be found in FA 1986, Sched.19. The contingent liability to tax in respect of a potentially exempt transfer may usually be covered by insurance without undue expense. Not only does this protect the beneficiary but it may also provide a valuable and reasonable safeguard to the transferor's personal representatives, who are contingently but nevertheless personally liable to the Inland Revenue for payment of any tax unpaid by the beneficiary (see para.4.4).

Just as a transfer into or out of an interest in possession settlement can be potentially exempt, so does a corresponding charge to tax arise if the life tenant of an interest in possession settlement should die within seven years after termination of the life interest. If death occurs within seven years after the partial termination of a life interest, as where there has been an advancement of capital to a remainderman, a tax charge arises in respect of that part. It is usually possible to obtain insurance to cover any contingent liability in this respect; it will be as well if the trustees have been given express power to effect such insurance.

The favourable treatment of potentially exempt transfers is subject to an important limitation, in the shape of the anti-avoidance provisions in relation to gifts with reservation in FA 1986, s.102 and Sched.20. These provisions are intended to prevent a taxpayer from obtaining exemption in respect of a gift of property from which he nevertheless continues to derive some kind of benefit during his lifetime; for example, by continuing to live in a house which he had given away.

The effect of these provisions is that the estate of a transferor at his death is deemed to include any property which, immediately before his death, is 'property subject to a reservation' (FA 1986, s.102). Any such property is thereby taxed on his death as if it were still his own. For this purpose, property is 'subject to a reservation' if 'possession and enjoyment' of the property is not 'bona fide assumed by the donee' at least seven years before the donor's death; or if at any time in that seven-year period 'the property is not enjoyed to the entire exclusion, or virtually to the entire exclusion, of the donor and of any benefit to him by contract or otherwise'.

Provision is made in FA 1986, s.102(4) for the case where there is a gift subject to a reservation and then the reservation is later released or otherwise comes to an end. There is deemed to be a potentially exempt transfer at the time when the property ceases to be subject to the reservation. This might happen at any distance of time after the original gift was made.

Although these provisions of FA 1986 had no counterpart in the legislation relating to capital transfer tax (nor have they now any application to those transfers which are fully exempt), they do closely resemble provisions which were long established and well known in the law of estate duty, and embodied in FA 1894,

s.2(1)(c). Accordingly, it may be anticipated that the considerable body of authority on the interpretation of the estate duty legislation will prove to be of great
assistance in the construction of the provisions of FA 1986.

As well as setting out a number of detailed rules supplemental to FA 1986,
s.120, Sched.20 contains relieving provisions which cover two exceptional cases.
First, under para.6(1)(a), the retention or assumption of a benefit is disregarded
if full consideration is given. So, for example, the grant of a lease back of property to the donor may represent consideration, if the lease is granted on fully com-
mercial terms. Second, under Sched.20, para.6(1)(b), there is an exception with
regard to interests in land where following an unforeseen change in circumstances,
reasonable provision is made for the care and maintenance of a relative who has
become unable to maintain himself through old age, infirmity or otherwise.

Further anti-avoidance provisions are contained in FA 1986, s.103, whereby
certain debts are disallowed as deductions in valuing the estate of a deceased person for tax purposes. Debts to which s.103 applies are broadly those where the
consideration for the debt consists of property derived directly or indirectly from
the deceased. The enforceability of such debts as between the parties would not,
of course, normally be affected by their disallowance for tax purposes; the existence of such a debt might however clearly affect the balance of the beneficial
dispositions.

Because, by the effect of FA 1986, s.103, otherwise in certain comparatively
unusual circumstances, the possibility exists that property might be chargeable to
tax both in relation to an *inter vivos* disposition and also in relation to the death
of the disponer, FA 1986, s.104 empowers the Board of the Inland Revenue to
make regulations for avoiding such double charges. They have done so, by the
Inheritance Tax (Double Charges Relief) Regulations 1987, SI 1987/1130.

4.4   Burden of tax

The balance of the beneficial dispositions under a will may sometimes depend as
much on the incidence of liabilities of the estate – and in particular of tax liabilities – as upon the beneficial dispositions themselves. In planning the will, it is
therefore important to make the best possible evaluation of the prospective liabilities, and of the statutory provisions as to their incidence; and where appropriate to consider whether the effect of those provisions may need to be varied or
compensatory dispositions made by the terms of the will. Precedent clause D10.1
provides a framework within which this can be done.

Of no less importance is the consideration that whenever personal representatives will or may incur a liability to tax, which will be a personal liability on their
part, they should be placed in a position to discharge that liability out of the
estate, and with the least possible disturbance to the beneficial dispositions. This
aspect of the matter assumes particular importance, and may present particular
difficulties where the testator has made lifetime transfers, or might do so in the
future, without the personal representatives (or perhaps even his advisers) necessarily knowing anything about them.

The primary liability of personal representatives for IHT on death arises under

IHTA 1984, s.200. Under IHTA 1984, s.211, in relation to deaths on or after 26 July 1983, and subject to any contrary intention shown in the will, IHT on death for which personal representative are liable in respect of unsettled property in the UK which vests in them is to be treated as part of the general testamentary and administration expenses of the estate. Furthermore, IHT paid by personal representatives which is not a testamentary expense (including, for example, IHT on jointly owned property) is repayable to them by the person in whom the property becomes vested (IHTA 1984, s.211(3)). Although in this respect the subsection does not expressly so provide, it is clearly open to the testator to vary this provision by express provision in the will. An example of such a direction may be found in Precedent clause F4.1.

Where an estate is partly exempt, as in the case where it is disposed of partly for the benefit of a surviving husband or wife (or by some other exempt disposition), and partly for the benefit of children (or by some other non-exempt disposition), the allocation of exemptions as between different gifts must be determined by reference to rules embodied in IHTA 1984, ss.36–42, considered in para.4.5. These rules affect not only the liability (or otherwise) to tax, but also its incidence. In particular, s.41 establishes two rules. First, no tax is to fall on any specific (i.e. non-residuary) gift in so far as that gift is exempt. Second, no tax attributable to residue is to fall on any exempt share of residue. It seems unlikely that anyone would wish to vary these particular rules; but this in fact cannot be done.

Quite apart from their primary liability for tax on the estate of the deceased, it is most important that personal representatives should be aware of the effect of IHTA 1984, s.199 (as amended), under which they are secondarily liable for any tax chargeable in respect of lifetime transfers; that is, on the value of any potentially exempt transfer which has become chargeable, or of any other chargeable transfer made within seven years of the transferor's death, and which would not have been payable if the transferor had not died within seven years after the transfer. The liability on the part of personal representatives arises, by virtue of s.204(6) (as amended), should tax remain unpaid 12 months after the death.

Like jointly owned property in which the deceased had a share (in relation to which similar difficulties can possibly arise), property comprised in an *inter vivos* gift by the deceased is in no way under the control of the personal representatives. Indeed, they might not even know that a gift had been made. It is also possible that an unscrupulous beneficiary might perhaps delay payment of tax for which he was liable, knowing that if the personal representatives were assessed they would have to meet the liability. It cannot be too strongly emphasised that although only secondary, the liability of a personal representative is a personal liability, to which distribution of the estate is no answer. Before distributing, therefore, personal representatives should make careful enquiries; in some cases they might wish to protect themselves by insurance (for solicitors, personal representative professional indemnity cover may be available), or by taking an indemnity or other appropriate security. In the present context however the most important point of all is that the incidence and effect of prospective liabilities to tax in relation to lifetime transfers, and the possible need or special provision to meet such liabilities, ought to be properly anticipated at the time when the transfers themselves are under consideration.

Where, in conjunction with a potentially exempt transfer, there is an agreement that the donee should bear any tax in the event of the transferor's death within seven years, it is the official view that this agreement would not bring into play the gift with reservation provisions of FA 1986, s.102: see correspondence published in [1987] *Gazette*, 8 April, 1041.

A further secondary liability is faced by personal representatives under IHTA 1984, s.204(9) in respect of unpaid tax chargeable under FA 1986, s.102 on a gift with reservation. Similar or greater difficulties may arise in that the personal representatives may not be aware that the gift had been made or of the possibility of a reservation, the existence of which may be a difficult question of law.

4.5   Partial exemption

In cases where part of the estate is left within the spouse exemption (or the charity and related exemptions) and part is not, the precise amount of tax payable in respect of the non-exempt gift, and its incidence as between the beneficiaries, is governed by the partial exemption rules in IHTA 1984, Part II, Chapter III. For more detailed explanation of these rules see Chapter 11 of the Inheritance Tax Manual available on the Inland Revenue's website **www.inlandrevenue.gov.uk**.

The immediate and practical result of these rules, so far as the will draftsman is concerned, is that normal pecuniary legacies, preceding an exempt gift of residue, will rarely attract any tax at all. Tax-free legacies of a specified amount can be given up to the amount of the unused balance of the testator's nil rate band. At the planning stage, therefore, the amount and incidence of any tax liability in respect of non-exempt gifts need enter into the draftsman's calculations only if the amount of any legacies is unusually large, or if the non-exempt gift is not a legacy but a share of residue, the balance of which is given under an exempt gift.

The most usual case is the tax-free gift made immediately to children, preceding an exempt gift of residue to the surviving spouse. Here, the point which will usually concern the draftsman is that for the purpose of calculating the amount of tax attracted by such a gift, its tax-free value to the legatee must be grossed at the appropriate rate, as explained below.

If the amount is at all substantial however the draftsman will also be concerned with the rules as to the incidence of tax, which take effect notwithstanding any provision in the will. These depend upon the nature of the non-exempt gift. If the gift is a 'specific' gift (a gift of particular assets or a specified amount) the relative tax is payable out of residue; it reduces the value of residue in the hands of the widow. If however, the non-exempt gift comprises a share of residue, the relative tax is payable wholly out of the non-exempt share and does not reduce the value of the exempt share of residue. This rule is mandatory, and may lead to an unexpected result. If, for example, residue is given on trust to discharge debts and funeral and testamentary expenses, and to hold the balance in equal moieties for the widow and the children, it would be natural to suppose that IHT would be payable out of the general fund of residue, along with other liabilities, leaving a balance to be divided into two equal shares. That would be incorrect; despite the direction in the will, the exempt share of the widow must not suffer any of the tax, which is therefore taken wholly from the children's share. This result has to be accepted, even if it is undesired.[1] Any attempt to achieve actual equality, by way of additional gift to the children, would be likely to lead to an increase in the amount of tax payable, and should be avoided.

In either case, the amount of tax payable depends upon the gross value of the non-exempt part of the estate. It is computed according to the statutory rules, the main effect of which may be shortly summarised as follows:

1. *Specific tax-free gifts.* Where the only non-exempt gifts are specific gifts (as above) on which the tax is payable out of residue, the value of such gifts, for the purpose of apportioning the value of the estate as between exempt and non-exempt gifts, must be calculated by grossing the net amount at the rate appropriate to a transfer comprising only those gifts. Hence, normal legacies within the nil rate band are grossed at the nil rate; they attract no tax. Whether or not a gift bears its own tax depends upon the terms of the will or, if this is silent, on the general law. IHT attributable to unsettled property in the UK which vests in the personal representative is declared by IHTA 1984, s.211 to be a testamentary expense. The burden of IHT attributable to a gift of such property, whether it is realty or personalty, will not thereby fall upon the specific beneficiary, unless the will directs that it should do so; see further para.4.4, and also Precedent clauses D10.1 and F4.1, and notes thereto. IHT paid by personal representatives on other property is repayable to them by the person in whom the property becomes vested, unless the will directs otherwise. For an example of such a direction, see Precedent clause F4.1.

2. *Specific gifts bearing their own tax.* When the tax on such a gift falls on the legatee, the amount given is the gross value of the gift for the purposes of these rules.

3. *Taxable share of residue.* Where the only non-exempt gift is a share of residue, the chargeable part of the estate is the amount apportionable to the non-exempt beneficiary or beneficiaries. If there is any preceding exempt specific gift (whether to the spouse, or to charity, etc.), this is first deducted (see footnote 1).

4. *Different chargeable gifts.* Where, in addition to tax-free specific gifts, there is also any specific gift which bears its own tax or a non-exempt gift of a share in residue, it is again necessary to calculate the gross value of the chargeable part of the estate on which tax is payable. In order to find the true estate rate of tax at which to gross net values however, it is necessary to make a preliminary calculation in order to find the true relative values of the exempt and chargeable parts of the estate. These calculations are somewhat complex. Suffice it to say here that their purpose is simply to produce the fairest overall result in relation to a will including any such combination of gifts, and that in the somewhat unlikely event of the draftsman being instructed to prepare such a

will, the complexity of the calculations which may have to be made on the
distribution of the estate need not deter him from so doing.

The above rules may have some further significance at the planning stage in
that if the estate is substantial, it may be necessary to consider whether some further tax might be saved by reversing the usual order of dispositions. Thus if a specific (exempt) gift were made to the spouse with residue (non-exempt) left to
children, grossing would be avoided, in that the chargeable estate would be the
actual balance remaining after deducting the exempt specific gift. Alternatively,
instead of making any specific gift, the will might give residue in whatever might
be thought to be appropriate shares between the children and spouse. Again, the
chargeable part of the estate would be reckoned without grossing (see footnote
1). In another alternative, there might be a specific gift to the spouse, followed by
a gift of residue in shares.

Whether the saving of tax which might result from any of these somewhat
unusual dispositions would be sufficient in amount to outweigh their evident
practical disadvantages can be determined only by making comparative estimates
in the light of the particular circumstances. While it is difficult to generalise, it
seems unlikely that in any normal estate the benefit would be more than marginal; and probably much less than the margin of error to which all such calculations are unavoidably subject.

In one respect the manner (or order) in which beneficial gifts are made can
actually assume considerable importance. Where a partly exempt estate includes
property eligible for business or agricultural relief, the incidence of such relief
depends upon the provisions of FA 1986, s.105. This section substantially alters
the previous rules, with results which may substantially affect the value of the
relief to the beneficiaries. Where property attracting business or agricultural relief
is disposed of by way of specific gift, the relief attaches to the property itself (FA
1986, s.105). However, in any other case the relief has to be allocated on a proportional basis between the exempt and chargeable parts of the estate, with the
result that the benefit of the relief is realised only in part. It follows that the maximum benefit can be derived from the relief only where the business or agricultural property is the subject of a specific gift to or for the benefit of non-exempt
beneficiaries. From this point of view therefore, in the normal family situation,
business or agricultural property should, if possible, be given to or in trust for
children, with any loss to a surviving spouse being compensated in some other
way. It should not be given to the spouse.

4.6   Survivorship conditions

In order to guard against the possibility that the deaths of the testator and of an
intended beneficiary might occur in a common disaster, or else that a beneficiary
might survive the testator for a nominal period only, it is common practice to
make beneficial gifts in a will subject to a 'survivorship clause'. In one form or
another, the effect of such a clause is to make any particular beneficial disposition, or perhaps all such dispositions, subject to the condition precedent that the

intended beneficiary should survive the testator by some stipulated period of time, commonly 28 or 30 days. Where this is done, it is of course necessary to make further provision, by way of gift over, for the contingency that the primary beneficiary might fail to survive the period of the condition.

For tax purposes, provision is made by IHTA 1984 in relation to each of these possible situations.

The possibility of contemporaneous deaths is dealt with by IHTA 1984, s.4(2), which provides that 'where it cannot be known which of two or more persons who have died survived the other or others they shall be assumed to have died at the same instant'. The effect of this provision is that property passing on one death can never, for tax purposes, be treated as passing through the estate of another person who was not actually the survivor, even though the second person may have to be treated for purposes of the law of succession as having notionally survived the first, by virtue of being the younger. This presumption for succession purposes is embodied in the well-known provisions of Law of Property Act 1925 (LPA 1925), s.184 which serves to establish the actual beneficial entitlements to the property, having regard to the occurrence of the contemporaneous deaths, in any case where its ultimate devolution has not been secured by will.

In a case where LPA 1925, s.184 operates (necessarily in the absence of a survivorship condition) it will follow that the combined estates will devolve according to the will or intestacy of the notional survivor. In a case where, outside LPA 1925, s.184, the beneficiary does actually survive for a short time only, and where likewise the interest of that beneficiary was not subject to a survivorship condition, the result will be the same. This may or may not be what the parties intended. Where they are husband and wife, in particular, it may be the case that appropriate wills have been made by each, perhaps in reciprocal terms, which will cover the position. It may nevertheless be considered less than satisfactory that either estate could devolve in any way outside the terms of the testator's own will. It may also be considered a practical inconvenience that if assets in one estate do in fact devolve as part of the other, separate grants will be required.

It may therefore be suggested as a generalisation that if beneficial gifts are made subject to a survivorship condition, all difficulties of this kind will have been prevented. The dispositions of each estate will then depend entirely on the will of the testator concerned, whether an intended beneficiary should unfortunately predecease or suffer death in a common disaster or survive only for a short period, or whether the beneficiary should in fact survive to take the benefit in the manner intended.

The consequences of a survivorship condition for IHT purposes are governed by IHTA 1984, s.92, according to the outcome. It is provided, in effect, that the estate is to be treated for tax purposes as if the property in question had passed directly under whatever dispositions actually take effect, having regard to the operation of the condition. It follows that, as between husband and wife, if the surviving spouse actually survives the period of the survivorship condition (not being more than six months), the spouse exemption is given in the estate of the spouse who first died, in the normal way. If the spouse failed to survive that period (or at all), no spouse exemption is available in relation to either estate. It could have been otherwise if the survivorship condition had been omitted, where one spouse did actually survive the other, or for succession purposes was deemed to do so; but the practical difficulties already discussed would not have been resolved.

In the case of a gift outside the spouse exemption to a non-exempt beneficiary, the inclusion of a survivorship condition serves to exclude the possibility of a double charge to tax, if the same property were to pass through two taxable estates. The same result would normally be achieved however by virtue of the relief for 'successive charges' under IHTA 1984, s.141.

4.7   Minority and contingent interests

If residue or any other part of the estate is held in trust for one or more beneficiaries who are minors or whose entitlement is contingent, the property so held will be settled property for IHT purposes (IHTA 1984, s.43), and in the case of contingent (but not vested) entitlements, for CGT purposes also (Taxation of Chargeable Gains Act 1992 (TCGA 1992), s.68, in conjunction with s.60).

Accordingly, if the terms of the will are such that a minority or contingent interest may arise, whether in favour of the testator's own children or grandchildren, or of children of the testator's brothers or sisters, or indeed of anyone, it is necessary to bear in mind the special charging and relieving provisions applicable to settled property for the purposes of each of these taxes. Although the testator is unlikely to alter the substance of his instructions on this account, the taxation implications should always be considered; in some cases these may prompt some modification of the instructions, to ensure that tax charges are not incurred unnecessarily.

IHT: accumulation and maintenance trusts

For IHT purposes, if the terms of the will are such that the beneficial trusts are 'accumulation and maintenance' trusts within IHTA 1984, s.71 while tax will have been chargeable on the testator's death in the normal way, the fund will not suffer the tax charges normally imposed on discretionary trusts[2] either when a minor attains majority, or when a contingent interest vests, or in the meantime. It is therefore important to ensure that nothing in the terms of the will can infringe the requirements of IHTA 1984, s.71. In the case of what may be termed a normal family will, under which the beneficial entitlements of children (or perhaps of grandchildren or others) are governed by s.31 of TA 1925 (reproduced in Appendix 4), compliance with these requirements should be virtually certain, for they are framed with this type of trust primarily in view. In any other case (and perhaps especially in relation to an *inter vivos* settlement, with which this book is not directly concerned), care is needed. If the requirements are not satisfied, then (in so far as no beneficiary has become entitled to an interest in possession) the settled property will be subject to the ten-year anniversary and proportionate charges imposed by IHTA 1984, Part III, Chapter III. These tax charges may not necessarily prove unduly burdensome, and in some circumstances might be considered an acceptable price for the greater flexibility of a true discretionary trust. In other circumstances, the limited use of a discretionary trust might well be considered: see para.4.3, *passim,* and Precedent clauses E4.1 and G1.1, and notes thereto. Should IHTA 1984, s.71 cease to apply to the property (or should the trustees make a disposition depreciating its value), in circumstances other than a beneficiary becoming beneficially entitled to it within the terms of the section, or dying before obtaining the specified age (IHTA 1984, s.71(4)), it will be subject to a flat rate exit charge (IHTA 1984, s.71(3), in conjunction with s.70(2)). The rate of charge depends on the duration of the settlement and ranges from 0.25 per cent per quarter for the first 40 quarters to an overall maximum of 30 per cent after 50 years. The terms of IHTA 1984, s.71 are thus of such special importance that this section is reproduced in Appendix 5.

The requirements for application of the section are well known, but nevertheless call for comment. The primary requirement embodied in s.71(1)(a) is that . . . 'one or more . . . beneficiaries will, on or before attaining a specified age not exceeding 25, become beneficially entitled to [the settled property] or to an interest in possession in it'.

As to the age of vesting, no difficulty should normally arise. Beneficial interests need not be absolute: an interest in possession will suffice. By virtue of TA 1925, s.31(1)(ii) a beneficiary whose interest is contingent on attaining an age greater than the age of majority will obtain the necessary interest in possession at majority, since he then becomes entitled to receive the income as of right until his entitlement to capital vests or fails. If it is desired to defer not only the vesting of capital, but also the entitlement to income,[3] the income entitlement must arise by the age of 25 at the latest, to satisfy IHTA 1984, s.71. However, this entitlement should not normally be deferred beyond the age of 21, because of the next requirement of s.71, that income not applied for maintenance or the like is to be accumulated. In the present context, accumulations cannot be directed for a period longer than 21 years after the testator's death (LPA 1925, ss.164–165).

It has to be accepted that once an interest in possession has arisen in this way, a charge to tax would arise in the event of the death of the beneficiary (not, of course, under IHTA 1984, s.71, but under ss.51–53) even if this happened before he had attained a vested interest in capital (the exemption in s.71(4)(b) only prevents a charge under s.71(3)) but the amount of such a liability is unlikely to be considerable, unless the estate is very large, or the beneficiary has entitlements under other trusts; the possibility of premature death will hardly influence the choice of age for entitlement to income.

This choice may, however, be influenced by the consideration that once an entitlement to income has arisen, the effect for IT purposes is that the income ceases to be income of the trustees, in whose hands it was liable at the Schedule F trust rate (dividends, currently 32.5 per cent) or the rate 'applicable to trusts', i.e. currently 40 per cent (under ICTA 1988, s.686 (as amended)); it becomes income of the beneficiary, and as such fully available to support a repayment claim against any unused personal reliefs.

There is another aspect of the first requirement of IHTA 1984, s.71 which may give rise to difficulty in certain cases. This concerns the degree of certainty that one or more persons 'will' become entitled, on or before attaining the specified age (s.71(1)(a)). That provision has been construed as meaning that the subsection will not be satisfied unless it can be said that if the person or persons in question attain an age not exceeding 25 they will be *bound* to become entitled (see *Lord Inglewood v. IRC* [1983] 1 WLR 366 (CA)). If a settlement contains any power (whether express or incorporated by statutory provision) which is capable of exercise in such a way as could prevent such an entitlement from arising, the settlement is deprived of the protection of s.71 from the outset. The existence of a power of revocation would have this result (*Inglewood*), as would the existence of a power of appointment, unless this were exercisable only in such a way as to comply with the requirements of s.71. For published views of the Inland Revenue see *Law Society's Gazette* of 11 June 1975 [1975] BTR 436 and 8 October 1975 [1975] BTR 437 and Statement of Practice of 19 January 1976 [1976] BTR 406.

This may affect precedent clauses in fairly common use, and, in particular, two which appear in this book. Thus, under the overriding discretionary trusts in Precedent clause G1.1 (as they stand) the powers to effect a variation of the will, which it is the purpose of the clause to facilitate, could possibly be so exercised as to defeat beneficial entitlements, or property could possibly be appointed in terms outside IHTA 1984, s.71; equally, the common form power of appointment in Precedent clause F11.1 (as this stands) could possibly be exercised in such a way. It is suggested that these clauses, and a power of appointment in any form, should be adopted only in conjunction with Precedent clause H15.1, or with the addition of provisions to the like effect: this clause is intended to restrict the exercise of any such power to purposes within s.71.

Similar considerations may sometimes apply in relation to powers of advancement, in that such a power (whether it is the statutory power under s.32 of TA 1925, or an express power) may properly be exercised by declaring trusts of the property advanced (see *Pilkington v. IRC* [1964] AC 612); trusts could be so declared in terms outside IHTA 1984, s.71. It is however settled (as the law stands under *Inglewood*) that a settlement will not be excluded from s.71 merely because it contains the statutory power[4] (even if this is extended from a moiety to the whole of the beneficiary's share as in *Inglewood*), though presumably if an advance were actually made in such a way as could contravene the requirements of the section, an exit charge to tax under s.71(3) would be incurred. If the will substitutes an express power, as under Precedent clause H8.3, the position is less clear: it is suggested that these clauses also should be adopted only in conjunction with Precedent clause H15.1.

The second and third requirements are contained in IHTA 1984, s.71(1)(b): no interest in possession subsists in the settled property, and the income from the settled property is to be accumulated, so far as not applied, for the maintenance, education or benefit of a beneficiary.

If there is a subsisting interest in possession, the settled property is treated for IHT purposes as part of the estate of the person who enjoys that interest. So, if a testator leaves property on trust for his widow for life, and after her death for children at 25, the settled property is not held on accumulation and maintenance trusts until after the widow's death (when IHT will have been charged on the termination of her interest), and then only if any child is still under 25. Conversely, if the trust is an immediate trust for children at 25 and one of them attains that age, his share then ceases to be held on accumulation and maintenance trusts (though no IHT is chargeable under IHTA 1984, s.71(4)), but the shares of any younger children continue to be so. If a child is born into the class, diminishing the shares of those already in being, a charge to IHT will arise in respect of the diminution in value of the share of any who has already attained an interest in possession, though it seems unlikely that any tax would normally be payable, unless the estate was very large.

The second requirement of IHTA 1984, s.71(1)(b), as to accumulation of surplus income, is automatically satisfied in any case to which s.31 of TA 1925 is applicable, since that section expressly requires it. However, accumulations under s.31 cease at 18, and so if a later vesting age is required, either the beneficiary must be allowed to take an interest in possession at that age under TA 1925, s.31(1)(ii), or else the application of s.31 (including the duty to accumulate) must be extended by substituting a later age for the age of 18, as in Precedent clause H7.1, para.(iii). As explained above, the substituted age should not be greater than 21. If the age at which capital vests is later than 21, beneficiaries should nevertheless be allowed to take interests in possession by 21. If, for some reason, accumulations are dealt with by express provision and not by reference to TA 1925, s.31, this provision must impose a *direction* to accumulate surplus income; a mere *power* to accumulate is not sufficient.

The last condition for the establishment of accumulation and maintenance trusts is in IHTA 1984, s.71(2), and is in the alternative. Either not more than 25 years must have elapsed since the creation of the settlement or since the statutory requirements became satisfied (IHTA 1984, s.71(2)(a)), or else all the persons who are or have been beneficiaries are or were grandchildren of a common grandparent; or children, widows or widowers of such a person who has died before becoming entitled (IHTA 1984, s.71(2)(b)). While limiting accumulation and maintenance trusts to a single generation, this second alternative allows *inter alia* the usual substitutional gift in favour of children of a deceased child. The terms of the trust should not however be framed for the benefit of a mixed class of children and issue (or simply of issue) as original beneficiaries. For this purpose, children include illegitimate children, adopted children and stepchildren.

Reference is made in para.4.10 to the opportunity which arises under certain conditions, to vary the dispositions of a will after death, without penalty in terms of IHT or CGT. See also Precedent clause G1.1 which provides alternative machinery.

Subject to the reservation that (unless entirely in their favour) a variation affecting the rights of minor and possible unborn beneficiaries must be sanctioned by the court, there is no reason in principle why accumulation and maintenance trusts should not be declared retrospectively by way of variation of the will. It should be borne in mind that for IT purposes, a variation can be caught by the 'settlement' provisions of ICTA 1988, s.660B, so that a parent making a variation in favour of children could find that he or she was assessable to IT (at all rates) on some or all the income arising. If a similar disposition in favour of the children had been included in the will itself, these provisions could not apply. The income would have been income of their trustees for IT purposes, and so while it would have attracted the rate applicable to trusts under ICTA 1988, s.686, in the hands of the trustees, it would have been available to support a repayment claim against unused personal allowances of the children, in so far as it was applied for their benefit and not accumulated.

CGT: vesting of contingent interests

For CGT purposes, as has been noticed, property held in trust for beneficiaries whose entitlement is contingent is settled property; though property held for minors who would be absolutely entitled but for their minority is not. When a contingent entitlement vests and a beneficiary becomes absolutely entitled as against the trustees, there is a notional disposal and re-acquisition of that property at its current market value (TCGA 1992, ss.71 and 73); and any resulting gain (after allowance for the relevant acquisition costs, any available indexation allowance, taper relief and also the trustees' annual exemption, if unused) is chargeable against the trustees, unless the absolute entitlement arises by reason of the death of a life tenant (TCGA 1992, s.73). The notional re-acquisition provides a new acquisition cost for purposes of any future disposal by the beneficiary.

If desired, a gain arising from the notional disposal could, until 14 March 1989, be held over to the beneficiary (at the joint election of the trustees and the beneficiary)(FA 1982, s.82), in which case the beneficiary's acquisition cost is reduced by the amount of the held-over gain. Tax on the held-over gain which is therefore postponed remains prospectively payable on any future disposal by the beneficiary. The FA 1989, while not affecting the principles of liability where a beneficiary becomes absolutely entitled against the trustees, severely restricts the occasions where holdover relief is available. Apart from cases involving business assets (where gains may still be held over) in this context only gains arising on the vesting of contingent entitlement at the age of 18 may be held over (TCGA 1992, s.260), since if only an interest in possession arises at that time the later vesting of the capital will not attract relief. Typically if a testator wishes to provide that capital should vest beyond the end of the accumulation period, he should be advised that the notional disposal then occurring will not attract holdover relief. The result of these provisions is that, in terms of CGT, a contingent interest is treated unfavourably as compared with a vested interest. This fact may prompt the question whether it is desirable to modify the traditional view that the beneficial interests of children ought to be contingent upon attaining whatever may be considered to be the age of responsibility, thereby also avoiding the risk that a share might pass as part of the beneficiary's estate in the event of premature death. This view undoubtedly reflects what most testators would consider to be in the best interests of their children. Need this natural preference be disturbed? When it is considered that if the children are young, the trust might continue for an extended period, and that in an estate of any size, substantial gains might accrue before an absolute entitlement arises, it is clear that a substantial tax liability might be involved if beneficial interests are contingent. However, there are three mitigating factors.

1. Although allowed at only half the rate available to individuals, the annual exemption allows trustees to realise tax-free gains (where these exist) on a regular basis during the life of the trust, so reducing the build-up of gains at the time of distribution.
2. Revision of the base date, the indexation allowance and (since April 1998) taper relief, should go a long way towards eliminating purely inflationary gains on future disposals.
3. The possibility of holding over gains at distribution to the beneficiary, while it provides no exemption, does at least allow a deferment of liability, which is valuable.

An absolute beneficiary, holding the same investments for the same period, would have anticipated the future taxation of similar unrealised gains, although he would have enjoyed the full amount of annual exemption in the meantime.

It is a decision for the testator to make, but in most cases the advice will probably be that despite the charge to tax on distribution, the availability of the indexation allowance, taper relief and the possibility of holdover relief may sufficiently mitigate the burden of CGT to leave the contingent interest as an acceptable form of disposition, where this is preferred (as invariably it is) on personal grounds. A charge to CGT may similarly arise where, by the exercising of a power of appointment or advancement, new trusts are declared in respect of settled property in such a way as to constitute a new settlement.[5] The prospect of this CGT charge in addition to the probable IHT charge (upon the settled property ceasing to be held on accumulation and maintenance trusts) would normally discourage the trustee from making a resettlement. The inclusion in the will of a clause in terms of Precedent clause H15.1 is intended to avoid an additional charge to IHT by preventing any resettlement outside the requirements for an accumulation and maintenance settlement; it should also serve, in most cases, to prevent a resettlement from incurring a charge to CGT.

IT: treatment of income where beneficial interests are contingent or vested

Until the pre-Budget report on 10 December 2003, contingent interests were generally supposed to be treated unfavourably for purposes of IT, in that income in the hands of trustees for persons contingently entitled to capital was taxed at 25 per cent (Schedule F dividend rate) or 34 per cent (rate applicable to trusts under ICTA 1988, s.686 (as amended)). If the beneficial interest had been vested, the same income would have been taxed at the basic rate only, though (where appropriate) it would have fallen to be grossed up as part of the total income of the beneficiary for purposes of the higher rate of tax.

In reality however income attributable to a contingent interest was effectively

taxed at the trust rate only to the extent that the income exceeded the beneficiary's unused personal allowance, or was accumulated. Income applied towards
the beneficiary's maintenance was available to support a repayment claim on his
behalf covering tax at the 34 per cent rate. Where trust income was needed and
applied, for maintenance, tax at that rate was commonly recoverable. The only
disadvantage lay in the fact that the trustees would have suffered the tax in the
first place (see ICTA 1988, s.687 which may impose a charge on payments made
at the trustees' discretion) and that some administrative expense will have been
incurred.

The position differed in cases where a surplus of income arose, whether
because the trust income was greater in amount than the current needs of the
beneficiaries, or perhaps because other funds were available for their maintenance. Any such surplus, when accumulated, represents new capital formed out
of income that has been taxed at the trust rate; and the tax so suffered was irrecov-
erable. However, two points arose. First, although the accumulated income had
suffered IT at the trust rate, it never suffered the higher rate of IT, because it never
formed part of the total income of an individual beneficiary for IT purposes.
Second, while accumulated income became (in effect) capitalised, the accumulations nevertheless passed eventually from the trust without liability to IHT, so
long as the requirements for an accumulation and maintenance settlement
remained satisfied. Investments representing the accumulations were, like any
other, subject to CGT. Thus, in relation to family trusts where there was in fact
surplus income available to accumulate, these benefits (in particular the freedom
from higher rate IT) could be seen as establishing an important advantage in
many cases, as compared with the position where vested interests were given.
Surplus income (grossed up) would have been treated, for higher rate purposes,
as part of the total income of a beneficiary with a vested interest, were they
applied for his benefit, or accumulated under TA 1925, s.31 (reproduced in
Appendix 4). Where an interest was contingent, income did not bear higher rate
tax, unless actually applied under TA 1925, s.31.

It has sometimes been suggested that the disparity in the treatment of giving
vested and contingent interests can be avoided, with advantage, by the device of
giving a contingent interest in capital, coupled with a vested interest in income.
This can be done simply by varying the application of TA 1925, s.31 in such a
way as to provide that accumulations of income are to be held in trust for individual beneficiaries in any event. If the age at which contingent interests are to
vest is over 18, a correspondingly higher age (but not over 25) may also be substituted for 18 for purposes of the statutory entitlement to income under
s.31(1)(ii): see above, under the heading 'IHT: accumulation and maintenance
trusts'. That approach has not been adopted in any of the forms in this or any
earlier edition; the position must be carefully evaluated (in those comparatively
few cases where the question is relevant) in relation to the particular circumstances. In such a case, in addition to the considerations outlined above, it will
be in view that if a vested interest in income were given, this would amount to
an interest in possession for IHT purposes. On the premature death of a beneficiary, this would result in a possible IHT charge on the full capital value of the

beneficiary's share under the trust, even though his entitlement to capital might still be contingent.

From April 2004 the pre-Budget report proposes an increase in the tax rate applicable to trusts to 40 per cent and the corresponding Schedule F trust rate to 32.5 per cent thus bringing income tax rates for trustees and beneficiaries more into line. While it continues to remain just as necessary to evaluate the tax and non-tax comparisons of contingent and vested interests, it is apparent that the proposed increases in the trust income tax rates renders the retention of accumulated income attributable to contingent interests less desirable. Such income will, when the proposals become law, suffer an irrevocable 40 per cent of tax. If applied, the income will support repayment at that rate where appropriate to the beneficiary's circumstances.

4.8   The family home

It is a well-known fact that the family home represents the most important asset in the estates of many, if not most, testators and potential testators. Not surprisingly, its disposal for the benefit of the family is of corresponding importance to them. It is not always appreciated however that in case the existing family home might not pass into the absolute ownership of a surviving spouse, or where it proves unsuitable for some reason, it may be of equal or greater importance to ensure that provision is made by the will to enable a new home to be acquired for the benefit of the family.

Absolute gifts

It may be assumed that, in most cases, testators making provision for a surviving spouse will wish the family home to pass to the spouse outright. Where residue as a whole is given to the spouse, the usual general gift of residuary realty and personalty will suffice to include the interest of an absolute owner, tenant in common of freehold or leasehold land; or that of a joint tenant, should the beneficial joint tenancy be severed during the testator's lifetime.

Gifts in trust

A trust will necessarily arise where the spouse is restricted to a limited interest or, more commonly, where an outright gift to the spouse is followed by an alternate gift to children or issue (in case the spouse is not living at the testator's death, or fails to survive for some stipulated period), and the interests of children or issue are themselves contingent on attaining majority, or some other age. Further, by express provision the family home (or the testator's interest in it) may be subject to discretionary trusts.

Traditionally where land was to be held in trust the choice was between the machinery of the Settled Land Act 1925 (SLA 1925) in relation to settled land and the alternative machinery of the trust for sale. The issues surrounding the choice and subsequent decision are no longer relevant following the abolition of new strict settlements under the SLA 1925 after the commencement of TOLATA 1996 (with effect from 1 January 1997). Use of a trust for sale remains possible and there is implied power despite any provision to the contrary for the trustees to postpone the sale (TOLATA 1996, s.4(1)).

Trustees have implied powers to purchase land by way of investment, for occupation by a beneficiary or for any other reason (Trustee Act 2000 (TA 2000), s.8(1); and by s.8(3) have powers of an absolute owner when exercising their functions in relation to land). Similar express provision will normally be conferred on them, for example under Precedent clause D8.1 or more usually Precedent clause H5.1.

Limited interest

In those cases where a life or other limited interest is given to the spouse (whether by way of specific gift or as part of residue), the main question for consideration is whether the responsibility for maintaining the home, for deciding whether and when a sale is desirable and in that event what new purchase should be made, should rest with the trustee or the spouse. This is entirely a matter for the testator and express instructions ought to be taken. While it may be assumed that the trustees will have been chosen for their ability to act in the best interests of the family as a whole, it does not by any means follow that the testator would wish to see his or her spouse in the position of being dependent on their discretion in this respect despite their statutory obligation to consult, and to give effect to the wishes of the life tenant i.e., the beneficiary with an interest in possession, 'so far as consistent with the general interest of the trust' (under TOLATA 1996, s.11(1) (formerly LPA 1925, s.26(3))) unless excluded (s.11(2)(a))). Further, such beneficiaries have a right of occupation of land held for the purposes of the trust (s.12) although this may be excluded by express provision.

Terms of occupation: IHT and CGT

If the surviving spouse becomes absolute owner of the family home, whether as surviving joint tenant or by an absolute gift in the will, it will form part of the estate of the spouse for IHT purposes, and when the spouse dies or otherwise disposes of the beneficial interest by way of gift, its value at that time will accordingly attract IHT. On the other hand, any increase in value since the death of the testator will not be chargeable to CGT where the conditions for the 'owner-occupier' exemption are satisfied (TCGA 1992, s.222), nor in any case upon death (TCGA 1992, s.62).

Where the spouse occupies under an express provision, the position will be exactly the same. If the trustees are directed to allow the spouse to occupy (as Precedent clauses D8.1 and F3.1) the spouse will have an interest in possession for IHT purposes. For CGT purposes the trustees will be entitled to the exemption because the spouse was 'entitled to occupy under the terms of the settlement'

(TCGA 1992, s.225). Alternatively, if the spouse with an interest in possession occupies by reason of that interest, the position will again remain the same. Unless expressly excluded by the will, such a beneficiary has a right to occupy the land if the purpose of the trust includes making land available for him or other beneficiaries or if the trustees hold land which is available for that purpose (TOLATA 1996, s.12(1)).

If the trustees are simply empowered to *permit* the spouse (or anyone else) to occupy (as in Precedent clause H5.1), the position is at first sight less clear, because as a matter of property law, the exercise of such a power by the trustees creates no more than a licence in favour of the spouse, and in principle this would seem not to create a sufficiently exclusive right to amount to an interest in possession. It is, however, the practice of the Inland Revenue to treat the exercise by trustees of such a power as giving rise to an interest in possession, if the power is wide enough to cover the creation of an exclusive or joint right of residence and is exercised with the intention of providing a particular beneficiary with a permanent home (see Inland Revenue Statement of Practice SP10/79). If the official practice accords with the law, the position for IHT purposes is the same as in the previous examples. The CGT exemption remains available (see *Sansom v. Peay* [1976] 1 WLR 1073).

It is perfectly possible to give the spouse a secure right of occupation without giving rise to an interest in possession. For example, the trustees could be authorised to grant a lease or tenancy, and if this were done for full consideration and without creating an assured tenancy and so that no loss to the estate resulted, IHT could be saved. Other means could be devised to achieve the same result. However, such a saving could be achieved only at a high and probably unacceptable price: the benefit of the CGT exemption would almost certainly be lost, for there would no longer be occupation 'under the terms of the settlement'.

In most cases, the benefit of the CGT exemption will be likely to outweigh the burden of IHT. The practical choice seems to lie between absolute ownership and an entitlement to occupy trust property, or perhaps occupation under licence granted by the trustees. As between these possibilities, the choice can and should be governed by personal rather than tax considerations.

Can the family home be kept out of the survivor's estate?

In many estates, the family home is a very substantial asset; in some, the most substantial. Its value may give rise to an IHT liability on the death of the surviving spouse which, in relation to the value of the whole estate, may be most unwelcome; without it there might even be no liability at all. It is therefore natural to ask whether this prospective liability might be reduced or avoided altogether by dividing the beneficial ownership in some way between the spouse and the children. Plainly, if this could be done without detriment to the spouse, such an arrangement might provide a valuable saving, for the ultimate benefit of the children. Where there is little or no opportunity to plan for such a saving by the careful disposition of other assets, attention is directed all the more closely to the family home.

The question is, then, can the family home, or a substantial part of its value, ever be kept out of the estate of the surviving spouse? The immediate answer is that this is certainly possible. For one thing, the property could simply be given directly to children, relying upon them to ensure that occupation of the surviving spouse remains undisturbed for so long as he or she wishes. Another possibility, allowing more security, would be to create a tenancy in common as between husband and wife, enabling each to dispose of the undivided share by will to the children. The survivor, as tenant in common, has a right to occupy the entirety (although this is not an exclusive right since the children have an equivalent right to occupy based on their undivided share). The survivor is then more secure. No longer is there an implied trust for sale; the survivor as surviving trustee of a trust for land has all the powers of an absolute owner (TOLATA 1996, ss.5, 6(1)). This arrangement does provide the surviving spouse with real security, but almost certainly it also destroys the possibility of saving tax: it seems to amount to a settlement of the children's share, under which the survivor has an interest in possession (see *IRC v. Lloyds Private Banking Ltd* [1998] STC 559 and see *Woodhall v. IRC* [2000] STC 558).

Other possibilities can be imagined, but where a lifetime transfer is contemplated, it is necessary to be alert for anything which might amount to a 'reservation', within the anti-avoidance provisions of FA 1986, s.102. These provisions do not however apply to gifts which are themselves exempt transfers.[6] They do not apply in so far as full consideration is given for any reserved benefit. Part consideration might then be received in the form of a lease back (on appropriate terms); but apparently only at the cost of loss of CGT reliefs. The general conclusion seems always to be that if the survivor has security, no tax is saved, whereas if tax is saved, this will have been achieved only by placing the security of the survivor at risk to some extent.

In a united family the risk to the survivor's security may seem not to be very real. This may be a dangerous assumption to make. However united the family may seem to be, the fact is that if ownership of the house is shared, that security will have been weakened; tension could arise in the event of remarriage; there could be difficulties if a child died; the survivor's freedom to move house might be curtailed; difficulties might arise over repairs; there might be other unforeseen difficulties. These possible difficulties might be compounded if the testator had been married before and had two families or perhaps stepchildren to provide for. Moreover, even if IHT were saved on the value of the half share given to the children, the price of this saving would seem to be the loss of the CGT exemption on that half of any gain, either on a sale or gift of the house or when the survivor dies.

With one possible exception, discussed in the note to Precedent clause E5.1, the sensible conclusion seems to be that the family home ought not to be made an instrument of tax planning.

4.9   The family business

If the estate includes a business, or a substantial interest in a business, its disposal
will call for careful consideration. Possibly, though comparatively unusually,
where the testator is sole proprietor and insists upon remaining so until his death,
the assets of the business may fall to be disposed of by specific gift,[7] or pass as
part of residue. If anything but a simple outright gift is contemplated, considerable difficulties may arise: continuity of management must somehow be secured,
and the differing needs and expectations of those members of the family who
depend on the business must be reconciled and provided for. Suitable trustees
must be found. They may have to be asked to accept a considerable responsibility, for which special powers would be needed. Even if they are relieved of personal responsibility, it is notoriously (and understandably) difficult to find
trustees who will undertake the management or close supervision of any business
unless they are themselves its beneficial owners. If such a case should arise (and
it is suggested that it should not normally be allowed to arise) the nature of the
provisions which would be required for the disposal of the business by will must
depend so much on the particular circumstances that the draftsman would need
to consult those standard works which include a wide range of precedents. See
for example those in *Encyclopaedia of Forms and Precedents* (5th ed.), vol. 42(1),
title 'Wills' at pp.467 et seq.

If there is no prospect of the business being continued after the testator's death,
it will have to be wound up or disposed of. This will normally be dealt with in the
ordinary course of administration unless the testator has already disposed of it
during his lifetime, perhaps upon retirement.

Where there is a possibility that the business will continue because other members of the family are willing and able to manage it in the general interest, there
may already be some degree of active participation on their part, for practical and
fiscal reasons alike. In this, the most usual case, it is therefore more likely than
not that the interest of the testator in his business will be that of a controlling
shareholder, or senior partner. In either case, the transmission of his interest
should present few if any difficulties for the draftsman.

If the business is incorporated, this will allow much flexibility in that shares
can be passed on to individuals, or settled, by way of lifetime transfer or by will
at any time and in any proportions. If a controlling shareholding is left in the
hands of the trustees, as part of residue, it is normally necessary only to ensure
that the trustees are given sufficiently wide powers to act effectively (see, for
example, Precedent clause H11.1).

If the business has not already been incorporated, the likelihood is that it will
already be managed by some kind of family partnership. If it is not, and if eventual family participation is envisaged, serious consideration should be given to
the possibility of forming such a partnership, either at the present time, or as soon
as circumstances allow. Where there are children who are at present too young,
they could always be admitted at a later time to a partnership formed initially,
between the testator and his wife. Apart from its taxation advantages, the partnership represents an even more flexible instrument for the division of ownership,

functions and income within the family than does the company. The partnership agreement can and should provide not only for these matters, but also for the succession to the share of any partner who retires or dies. Where this accrues as of right to the continuing or surviving partners, under provisions which represent full consideration by each (by analogy with *A-G v. Boden* [1912] KB 539), it is often possible for the interest of the testator to be passed on with little or no liability either for IHT or for CGT. The transfer of shares in a company, by contrast, will normally attract both liabilities though, as to IHT, with the benefit of the valuable relief for business property (IHTA 1984, ss.103–111 as amended).

Under an appropriate partnership agreement, therefore, the testator's interest in his business can be excluded from his estate, and its proper devolution secured outside the terms of his will.

4.10   Possibility of future arrangements

In view of the many uncertainties surrounding any attempt to minimise the burden of capital taxation, it is of some comfort to those advising the testator to know that if a miscalculation should prove to have been made, or if there is a material change of circumstances, there will be opportunities to vary the dispositions of his estate before or during the period of two years following his death. For the most part however this will be possible only if the testator has a united family, and conflicts of interest can be avoided.

While a full discussion of the relative statutory provisions lies somewhat outside the scope of a book on will drafting, the draftsman is bound to be influenced to some extent by their existence, and a brief summary of their main features may be useful.

Variation or disclaimer

If within two years after the death, any of the dispositions, by will or on intestacy, of property comprised in the estate of the deceased[8] are varied or the benefit is disclaimed by an instrument in writing[9] made by any of the persons who benefit (or would have done so) under those dispositions, then for IHT purposes, the variation or disclaimer shall not be a transfer of value, but shall be treated as if the variation had been effected by the deceased or (as the case may be) as if the disclaimed benefit had never been conferred (IHTA 1984, s.142: reproduced in Appendix 3).[10] To achieve such result the instrument must contain a statement by the parties declaring such is their intention.[11] However such a re-writing of a testamentary disposition for fiscal purposes can be carried out only once.[12]

Section 142 of the IHTA 1984 is applicable whether or not the administration of the estate is complete, and whether or not the property concerned has been distributed in accordance with the original dispositions; in relation to a disclaimer, it must be borne in mind that under the general law, entitlement cannot be disclaimed after any benefit has been accepted, nor can an entitlement be disclaimed in part. The section does not apply if the variation or disclaimer is made for any consideration, other than variation or disclaimer within the section.

Correspondingly, a statement of intention may be included for CGT purposes, under TCGA 1992, s.62 (as amended) (reproduced in Appendix 3). The inclusion (or otherwise) of this statement of intention serves principally to determine what is the acquisition cost of assets to the beneficiary.

It will depend upon the particular circumstances whether or not it is advantageous for the written instrument to contain such a statement for the purposes of either CGT or IHT, or both. The written statements can be given independently of one another.

In a case where the deceased has failed to make a will,[13] or where a will has not been regularly reviewed, these provisions will enable the beneficiaries in effect to substitute a will in terms which the deceased might have been advised to make[14] in the light of circumstances as they were at the time of his death; or perhaps in terms which seem preferable to the beneficiaries, quite independently of any supposed wishes of the deceased.

However, it must be borne in mind that these provisions have effect only for purposes of IHT and CGT. They have no counterpart for purposes of IT. The consequences of this may be adverse, to a greater or lesser extent.

For IT purposes a variation has no retrospective effect as regards any liability to tax on income which has already arisen. The provisions of ICTA 1988, ss.695–701 (as amended) are applied accordingly. Further, a person making a variation may thereby become a settlor for purposes of ICTA 1988, Part XV and so may incur unexpected liabilities (in particular) under the provisions of ICTA 1988, s.660B relating to settlements on children. It is generally believed that these consequences would not arise in the case of a disclaimer, but this is not certain, nor is a disclaimer always practicable. It is certain they would not have arisen at all if the disposition had actually been made by will.

For stamp duty purposes, even though it contains an element of voluntary disposition, a variation does not normally attract a claim to duty. Tax considerations apart, difficulty may arise in relation to a variation, if the desired rearrangement requires the agreement of some person who is not willing to co-operate. Difficulty may also arise if some person is unable to consent because of minority or other disability, or if those prospectively interested may include persons yet unborn. In these cases, it will be necessary to apply to the court under the Variation of Trusts Act 1958 (VTA 1958). While no doubt an order would be obtained in a proper case, this may prove costly in terms of the provision which the court may be expected to require to be made in favour of those on whose behalf consent is given.

Discretionary powers of variation conferred by will

The above provisions are widely used to rearrange beneficial entitlements where this is thought desirable, whether for purely personal reasons, or in the wider interests of good estate planning. Nevertheless, in view of the difficulties referred to above, the result may still be less favourable to beneficiaries in some cases, than if the preferred disposition had been contained in the will itself. It is possible for most of these difficulties to be circumvented by including in the will provisions enabling the trustees to override the dispositions of the will as they stand, by means of what is in effect a special power of appointment, exercisable within the same two-year time limit as applies to variations and disclaimers, in terms of IHTA 1984, s.144 (reproduced in Appendix 3).

Section 144 provides that where property comprised in a person's estate immediately before his death is settled by his will, within two years after his death, and before any interest in possession has subsisted in the property, an event occurs on which IHT would otherwise be chargeable[15] under the provisions relating to settlements without an interest in possession (ICTA 1984, Chapter III, Part III), the property is exempted from any such charge and is treated as if the will had provided that on the testator's death the property should be held as it is held after the event. To summarise, the effect of exercising this kind of power to rearrange beneficial entitlements is fully retrospective for IHT purposes. There is however no corresponding provision for CGT purposes.

It is suggested that advantage might be taken of this important provision more generally than is, perhaps, the case. There has been some reluctance among professional advisers to do so, no doubt because a testator who confers such a power on his trustees necessarily places a very high degree of reliance upon them; in doing so, he surrenders to some the power of disposing of his own estate. Certainly some testators will be deterred by these considerations, though they should be aware that even if no such power is given to their trustees, beneficiaries can enter into variations, which will equally override the testator's intentions. The kind of power under discussion is of course discretionary, and trustees may be expected to exercise it cautiously, with the best interests of the testator's family in view.

A suggested clause intended to take advantage of this provision appears in Precedent clause G1.1, which is accompanied by some further notes. The inclusion of such provision in the will is recommended in any case where the burden of IHT is likely to be such that action to mitigate it may be a possibility. However, because they would constitute 'related settlements' within the meaning of IHTA 1984, s.62, Precedent clause G1.1 should not normally be included in a will which also includes Precedent clause E4.1.

Other cases

Further related provisions in IHTA 1984 deal with special cases. Section 143 protects transfers in pursuance of a so-called 'precatory trust'. This provision is shortly discussed in the note to Precedent clause D4.1.

Sections 145 and 93 of IHTA 1984 deal respectively with the right of election by a surviving spouse (AEA 1925, s.47A) to redeem a life interest on intestacy, and with disclaimer of an interest in settled property. These provisions call for no special comment.

CHAPTER NOTES

1   The conflicting decisions in *Re Benham's Will Trusts, Lockhart* v. *Harker, Read and the Royal National Lifeboat Institution* (1995) STC 210 and *Re Ratcliffe, Holmes* v. *McMullan* (1999) STC 262 indicate the difficulty faced by the draftsman. The will should make it clear whether a chargeable part of residue is to bear its own tax (no grossing) or if it is not (when it will need to be grossed).

2   Specifically, on 'relevant property' within the meaning of IHTA 1984, s.58. It will be in view that these tax charges have not been in any way mitigated in the transition from capital transfer tax to IHT, and in particular the favourable treatment of potentially exempt transfers has no application to discretionary trusts.

3   Paragraph (iii) of Precedent clause H7.1 will effect this: should TA 1925, s.31 be excluded altogether, the entitlement to income should be preserved.

4   As was already the view of the Inland Revenue; see [1975] BTR 437.

5   Whether or not a resettlement has this result depends upon the particular circumstances: see *(inter alia) Roome* v. *Edwards* [1982] AC 279 (HL); and Inland Revenue Statement of Practice SP7/84, which replaced a 1981 Statement, the Revenue wishing to add a mention of the decision in *Bond* v. *Pickford* [1983] STC 517. In that case the Court of Appeal explained that the nature of the powers which the trustees purported to exercise must be examined, for these may not authorise the removal of assets from the original settlement, and in general, that the parties' intention has to be determined objectively.

6   Finance Act 1986, s.102(5): hence, for example, a purchase by one spouse followed by conveyance to both spouses as tenants in common is officially considered not to be a gift with a reservation; albeit the death of the donor might give rise to a claim to tax on other grounds.

7   For the special treatment for IHT purposes of a specific gift of business or agricultural property within a partly exempt estate, under FA 1986, s.105 see para.4.5.

8   For this purpose including a reversionary interest (or other excluded property) but not including settled property in which the deceased had an interest in possession, nor property chargeable as a gift with reservation: IHTA 1984, s.142(5) (as amended).

9   For the Revenue's requirements about the contents of this instrument, see the note in [1985] *Gazette*, 22 May, 1454.

10   Different provision applied before 11 April 1978.

11   Personal representatives must join if additional tax becomes payable, but cannot refuse to do so unless they hold insufficient funds to discharge any additional tax. Previous provisions requiring an election by the parties to the instrument were replaced with effect from 31 July 2002 by FA 2002, s.120.

12   See *Russell v IRC* [1988] 2 All ER 405, per Knox J, affirming the official view; but rectification of deed may be possible, *Lake* v. *Lake & Ors* (1989) Ch D.

13   Or, perhaps, a new will; as where there has been a divorce or second marriage (see Chapter 2).

14   Having regard *(inter alia)* to the same estate planning considerations as are discussed in this book: see this chapter, *passim,* and specific points noted in the context of Precedent clauses.

15   See *Frankland* v. *IRC* [1996] STC 735 where an event within three months of death was not 'otherwise chargeable' so denying spouse exemption under the will.

5

Administration of
Justice Act 1982

5.1 Introduction

Because this is a drafting handbook and not a textbook, it has never contained any general discussion of the law of wills as such, but only some comments bearing on practical aspects of the drafting process. The practitioner is already well served by standard works of reference which are available if required.

However, the changes introduced by the Administration of Justice Act 1982 (AJA 1982) are of such major importance that they cannot be allowed to pass unnoticed. The text of the more important of the relevant provisions of the 1982 Act (as amended) has been reproduced in this book, and may be found in Appendix 6. The succeeding paragraphs of this chapter are intended to provide a brief introduction, directed mainly at considering how (if at all) those provisions may affect existing practice.

With two exceptions these amendments in the law have effect in relation to *deaths* on or after 1 January 1983, irrespective of the date of the will; however, subsequent amendments to AJA 1982, s.18A by the LR(S)A 1995 in relation to dissolution or annulment of marriage (see para.5.2) have effect in relation to deaths on or after 1 January 1996. The main exception to this, s.18(1) is concerned with the revocation of wills by marriage and with wills in contemplation of marriage (see para.5.2) and has effect only in relation to *wills executed* on or after 1 January 1983.

The other exception concerns two groups of provisions in ss.23–26 and ss.27–28, which are yet to come into force on a day or days to be appointed. These are briefly referred to in para.5.4 below, but are not reproduced in Appendix 6.

5.2 Amendments to the Wills Act 1837

Sections 17–19 of AJA 1982 replace the former provisions in ss.9, 18 and 33 of WA 1837 (and other related enactments, including in particular s.177 of LPA 1925). The 1982 Act substituted into WA 1837, new ss.9, 18 and 33 and introduced an additional s.18A (see below for details).

Section 9 (substituted)

The purpose of this provision is indicated in the side-heading: 'Relaxation of formal requirements for making wills'. Two changes are made. First in place of the former requirement that the testator should sign at the 'foot or end' of the will (with its attendant difficulties of construction), the requirement as now expressed is that 'it appears that the testator intended by his signature to give effect to the will'. Clearly, this requirement will be satisfied on the face of a professionally drawn will, as was the former requirement in any case where the execution of the will was properly supervised. No change in normal practice is called for.

Second, it becomes permissible for a witness either to sign or else to acknowledge a previous signature, in the presence of the testator and of second witness (in effect reversing *Re Colling* [1972] 1 WLR 1440). This provision will save a few wills which might previously have been invalidated in unusual circumstances, where a witness was called away before the formalities of execution were completed and witnesses did not sign afresh. Such cases need not have occurred if the witnesses had subscribed only in the presence of each other as well as the testator. While signature by witnesses in one another's presence has never been and still is not a legal requirement, it has always been the practice in the profession that they should do so and this practice is reflected in all common form attestation clauses. Although intended to guard against dangers which now seem to have been removed, this practice will no doubt continue to be followed, not only because it is so familiar, but also to obviate any risk of inconsistency between the terms of the attestation clause, and what is actually done. Precedent clause I1.1 therefore remains as it was.

Section 18 (substituted)

In essence, this section preserves the former law that marriage revokes a will,[1] unless the will was made in contemplation of marriage.[2] However it has been redrawn in significantly different terms, with the intention of preventing failure in those cases[3] where the contemplation of marriage did not extend to the will as a whole. Protection now extends not only to cases where it appears that the testator 'intended that the will should not be revoked by the marriage', but also to cases where such an intention appears in relation to any individual disposition (s.18(4)) in the will. In the latter case, if there are other dispositions, these also take effect notwithstanding the marriage, unless it appears that the testator intended them to be revoked.

As mentioned above, this section applies only to wills made on or after 1 January 1983. The former law still applies in relation to any earlier will. If it was made with professional assistance, the validity of a will made in contemplation of marriage, before 1983, ought not to be in doubt. Nevertheless such a will ought sensibly to have been replaced by a new will, once the marriage had taken place, or, equally, if it did not. Should such a will be made now, on the basis of previously accepted precedent forms, there should equally be little room for doubt that this would show the requisite intention (in terms of the substituted WA 1837,

s.18) that it should not be revoked by the marriage which the testator was 'expecting'. But in view of the more flexible terms in which the substituted s.18 is
framed, and of the different statutory language now adopted, a new Precedent
clause A2.1 was introduced into this book, in terms which were intended to
reflect the altered statutory provisions directly. The notes to that form draw attention to difficulties of a more practical nature which have always required consideration in relation to a will of this kind, and which still do so.

Section 18A (inserted)

This section extends the former law as to the effect of marriage upon a will, by
providing for the possibility of divorce. Although in that event an existing will is
not revoked, it takes effect as if any appointment of a former spouse as executor
or trustee were omitted, and any devise or bequest to a former spouse lapses,[4]
unless in either case a contrary intention appears by the will. If the former spouse
was given a life interest, interests in remainder are accelerated. If an interest given
to some other person in remainder was contingent upon surviving the former
spouse it ceases to be subject to that contingency.

As mentioned earlier, AJA 1982, s.18A took effect in relation to deaths on or
after 1 January 1983. Section 18A(1) has itself been substituted (in part) by provisions in LR(S)A 1995, s.3 in relation to deaths on or after 1 January 1996. The
original substitution, as interpreted in *Re Sinclair* [1985] Ch 446 (CA), continues
to apply to wills where the death occurred before 1 January 1996.

For the practitioner, the real significance of this provision lies in the fact that a
client who is a party to divorce proceedings should always be advised to make a
new will (preferably at an early stage) in order to avoid the possibility of a total
or partial intestacy, and, where appropriate, to fill a vacancy in the executorship.
No doubt similar advice would formerly have been given although not for quite
the same reason.

Section 18A: Re Sinclair

The consequences of lapse of a devise or bequest by the operation of WA 1837,
s.18A were considered in *Re Sinclair*, where a bequest to the testator's wife was followed by a direction that in the event of his wife predeceasing him or failing to
survive him for a period of one month, the estate was to pass to charity. It was
held by the Court of Appeal (affirming the decision at first instance) that on the
true construction of s.18A, if a devise or bequest to a spouse 'lapsed' by reason of
divorce, it failed without qualification and irrespective of the consequences. In
particular, the devise or bequest was not deemed to have failed (as might perhaps
have been supposed) with the same consequences as if the former spouse had
predeceased the testator. If in the event the former spouse happened to survive
the testator, gifts in the will contingent on the former spouse having predeceased
the testator must fail to take effect.

There are many precedent forms published before the decision in *Re Sinclair*, in which gifts over to children or others are in fact expressed as taking effect in the event that the spouse should predecease the testator, or fail to survive the testator's death by some further period. Where a will has been drawn in this way, the interest of the alternate beneficiary must clearly be at risk in the event of dissolution, annulment or avoidance of the testator's marriage, unless it so happens that in the event of partial intestacy, precisely similar beneficial entitlement would arise anyway, or unless the terms of the will have been reconsidered. Quite apart from the fact that the testator's probable intentions will have been frustrated, the draftsman might in such circumstances also find himself in breach of a duty of care owed to the disappointed beneficiary: see Chapter 7.

In relation to any gift over intended to take effect when a primary gift to or for the benefit of a spouse fails, it is necessary to express the terms of the contingency with care. If the gift to the spouse is to be absolute in the event of survival, this may usually be done quite simply (as in Precedent clauses F5.1 to F8.1, and Will 1 in Appendix 8) by stipulating that the gift over is to have effect if the spouse 'fails to attain a vested interest'; an expression which must be apt to cover contingencies of any kind, including statutory 'lapse'. If the spouse is given a limited interest, it will usually be sufficient (as in Precedent clauses F9.1 to F11.1, and Will 3 in Appendix 8) to express interests in remainder as being 'subject thereto'.

Section 18A: death on or after 1 January 1996

Statutory 'lapse' and the associated problems of construction addressed by the Court of Appeal in *Re Sinclair* cease to be of concern to the draftsman in view of the provision inserted into WA 1837, s.18A by LR(S)A 1995, s.3. It is provided that 'any property devised or bequeathed to a former spouse shall pass as if a former spouse had died on that date', i.e., the date of the divorce or annulment.

As a consequence, it is no longer essential for the draftsman to include the words 'fails to attain a vested interest' (see above); such wording, necessary to overcome the particular problem revealed by *Re Sinclair*, can be omitted with safety. A return to precedents in use before *Re Sinclair* providing gifts over to children (or others) in the event the spouse should predecease, or fail to survive the testator by a stated period, will be appropriate. However as the words 'fails to attain a vested interest' are adequate to cover the majority of contingencies, their continued use should not cause difficulty; in some instances they might even be preferred to the more familiar 'gift over'.

Section 18A: spouse as executor

Apart from the effect on beneficial entitlement, WA 1837, s.18A also denies the spouse who is divorced his or her appointment as executor or trustee. While the provision substituted by the AJA 1982 has caused no particular problems it too has been replaced by LR(S)A 1995, s.3. Any appointment of the former spouse as executor or trustee 'shall take effect as if the former spouse had died on the date on which the marriage is dissolved or annulled'. If this were to happen, an administrator with the will could of course be appointed, and it seems unlikely that any serious inconvenience would result. However the careful draftsman will wish to cover the possibility. This may be done most simply by appointing a second executor and trustee, jointly with the spouse, intending that if the entitlement of the spouse takes effect, he or she should prove alone; whereas if it does not, the surviving or continuing executor can prove as such. Precedent clause B1.1 is drawn in this way, although for more general reasons. Otherwise, the will can embody an alternate appointment, an example of which may be found in Precedent clause B1.2. Another form of alternate appointment, again with a more general purpose, is embodied in Will 1 in Appendix 8.

Section 33 (substituted)

Formerly, where a gift to a child or issue of the testator who predeceased was saved from lapse by the survival of issue of the original beneficiary, the gift was treated as an accretion to the original beneficiary's estate and devolved accordingly upon those entitled under the original beneficiary's will or intestacy (as in *Re Basioli* [1953] Ch 367, which is, in effect, reversed). Under the substituted WA 1837, s.33, it devolves instead upon the surviving issue themselves, on a stirpital basis. It does so whether the original beneficiary would have been entitled as an individual or (contrary to the former provision) as a member of a class.

Although the substituted WA 1837, s.33 effects a substantial alteration of the law, it will be unlikely to affect existing practice, since the inclusion in a will of an express substitutional gift in favour of the children of a deceased child is virtually common form. Such provisions were already included, at least optionally, in all the forms in this book under which children of the testator are intended to benefit. This is also done in the knowledge that, for IHT purposes, such a substitution will not infringe the conditions for an accumulation and maintenance settlement, discussed in para.4.7.

It has been suggested[5] that the new WA 1837, s.33 obviates the need for any express substitutional provision. However, reliance on the statutory provision may result in failure to give effect to a testator's probable intention.

In particular:

1. Subtitutional provisions are usually made in relation to a class gift. Although presumably intended to do so, it is not clear that the statutory provision applies to the normal form of such a gift to children (or grandchildren) 'living at my death'. Section 33(2)(b) depends on the predecease of 'a member of the class', but it is not natural in this context to refer in those terms to someone who could never have become a member of the class. Beneficial entitlements should depend upon the express intention of the testator, and not upon niceties of construction.

2. If the primary entitlements under a class gift are contingent, the statutory substitution will presumably take effect subject to the same contingency. Under an express substitutional gift it is not uncommon for a lower age of vesting to be stipulated, than as required in relation to the primary

entitlement. The age at which different entitlements vest ought to be considered, and not assumed.

3.   The statutory substitution can occur only where a primary beneficiary fails to survive the testator. Where beneficial interests are contingent, it is equally important to provide for substitution where a beneficiary survives the testator but thereafter dies without having attained a vested interest.

4.   The statutory substitution precludes any possibility of benefit to a widow or widower of a deceased beneficiary; as might have arisen under the former law, on his intestacy. While it is certainly unusual for such a benefit to be conferred by express provision, this ought to be considered by the testator even though in particular circumstances it may not be thought appropriate. It is perhaps significant that this possibility is envisaged by the conditions for an accumulation and maintenance settlement which expressly allow the substitution of 'children, widows or widowers' (see IHTA 1984, s.71(2)(b)(ii)).

The better view must be that express provision should be made in all cases, in terms appropriate to the circumstances, and on the basis of express instructions.

5.3   Rectification and interpretation of wills

Section 20 of AJA 1982 confers jurisdiction to rectify a will where the court is satisfied that this is so expressed that it fails to carry out the testator's intentions, in consequence either of a clerical error[6] or of a failure to understand his instructions. As a general proposition it appears that any remedy available to a complainant should be pursued and exhausted before an action in negligence is commenced.[7] This provision adds to the burdens of personal representatives in that (as also in relation to possible family provision applications) they cannot distribute within six months from the grant except at their own risk.

Section 21 allows evidence of the testator's intention[8] (as well as other extrinsic evidence) to be admitted in cases where any part of a will is 'meaningless', and also where there is an ambiguity; even if the ambiguity is patent and not (as formerly) only if it were latent.

These provisions will not directly affect the practitioner in his capacity as draftsman and are therefore not further discussed in this chapter. However as a practical point, since the draftsman will usually be in possession of the best evidence as to what was in fact intended by his client, it is perhaps more important now that he should make and preserve careful notes of his instructions, in case of some future dispute.

Section 22 adds a rule of construction to cover those cases where a gift to a spouse is made in terms which in themselves would indicate an absolute interest, but where the will also purports to give an interest to issue. Unless a contrary intention is shown, the spouse takes an absolute interest. Most practitioners will have faced, at some time, the need to clarify the instructions of a client who has some such mixed intention. This section is clearly framed with a view mainly to cases where the testator has not had the benefit of legal advice.

5.4   Registration of wills and international wills

It is necessary only to mention the existence of ss.23–26 of AJA 1982 containing provisions relating to the deposit and registration of the wills of living persons (the existing facilities for which are notoriously very little used) and of ss.27–28, giving effect to the 1973 Washington Convention providing Uniform Law on the Form of International Wills, which is likely to be of importance only to a small (if increasing) minority of clients.

CHAPTER NOTES

1   But now, as to a disposition exercising a power of appointment, only if in default of appointment the property appointed would pass to the deceased's personal representatives. This alters the former law, and has the effect of preserving not only appointments under special powers, but also some appointments under general powers.
2   Wills Act 1837, (original) s.18, in conjunction with LPA 1925, s.177.
3   Such as *Re Coleman* [1976] Ch 1, which is, in effect, reversed.
4   Though expressly without prejudice to any right of the former spouse to apply for financial provision: as to which see Chapter 3, text and endnote 3.
5   See Abbas Mithani: 'Reform of Section 33 of the Wills Act 1837' [1979] *Law Society's Gazette*, 1113.
6   An error in the process of recording the intended words of the testator, *Wordingham* v. *Royal Exchange Trust Co Ltd* [1992] Ch 412.
7   *Walker* v. *Geo H Medlicott & Son* [1999] 1 All ER 685 and *Horsfall* v. *Haywards (a firm)* [1999] 1 FLR 1182 (negligence claims brought against solicitors).
8   See Michael Sladen: 'Evidence of Testator's Intentions' [1986] *Gazette*, 15 January, 97–8) discussing *Re William (otherwise Cook), decd; Wiles v Madgin* [1985] 1 WLR 905, apparently the first reported case under s.21.

6

Family Law Reform Act 1987

6.1 Introduction

The general purpose of the Family Law Reform Act 1987 (FLRA 1987) is to remove legal disadvantages to children flowing from the consequences of birth outside marriage. The provisions of FLRA 1987 referred to below came into force on 4 April 1988.

6.2 Provisions reproduced in this book

The purpose of the provisions reproduced in Appendix 7 is as follows:

Section 1 – Rules of construction as to certain statutory provisions referring to relationships and birth. By virtue of FLRA 1987, ss.18 and 19 (below), these rules are further applied on intestacy and in relation to wills and codicils made on or after the commencement date.

Section 18 – Presumptions and rules of construction relating to intestacy.

Section 19 – Rules of construction and other provisions relating to dispositions of property, *inter vivos* or by will or codicil.

Section 20 – Removal of protection previously afforded to trustees and personal representatives by the Family Law Reform Act 1969, s.17.

Section 21 – Presumptions affecting entitlement to grants of probate and administration.

7

The draftsman's responsibilities

Clients look to their solicitor to make sure not only that their wills give clear and correct expression to their wishes, but also that they are effective. In other words, that they are duly executed and attested,[1] and in particular that they are not witnessed by any person who is a beneficiary or spouse of a beneficiary under the will; their general concern is that the intended benefit takes effect (WA 1837, s.15).

Where the will is executed in the office or with the solicitor in attendance, there will be no difficulty in ensuring that the necessary formalities of execution are strictly complied with. These are well known and straightforward, but in the note to Precedent clause I1.1 a simple procedure is outlined, compliance with which should serve to make any error virtually impossible.

If for some exceptional reason the will has to be executed elsewhere, special care is needed[2] to ensure that the client understands what is required. The risk of error will be much reduced if the chosen witnesses are people such as bank employees who are wholly independent and who know the formalities. In all such cases however it is essential that the original will is *always* returned afterwards to the solicitor to be checked and to enable him to make up his draft with the date and particulars of execution. This is probably still better practice than taking a photographic copy.

As well as the formalities of execution, the identity of the witnesses should be checked. Apart from the possibility that the testator's intentions may be frustrated if the will is witnessed by a beneficiary or spouse of a beneficiary, the solicitor may be held personally liable to a disappointed beneficiary if the client was not fully advised.

Although it was previously understood that the liability of a will draftsman was to his client alone (as in *Hall* v. *Meyrick* [1957] 2 QB 455), it is now clear that in carrying out any kind of transaction including a will to confer a benefit on an identified third party the solicitor may be held liable to that third party for failure to use proper care in carrying out his client's instructions.(*Ross* v. *Caunters* [1980] Ch 297; and see also *White* v. *Jones* [1995] 1 All ER 691 (HL); *Carr-Glynn* v. *Frearson* [1998] 4 All ER; *Corbett* v. *Bond Pearce* [2001] WTLR 419 (CA)). Further, the draftsman's duty is to prepare a will to reflect his client's instructions 'with proper expedition and care'; whether a solicitor has been negligent in terms of delay following receipt of his client's initial instructions will depend on the facts of each case.[3]

Liability in negligence may also result where instructions are received in relation to a gift by will of property but are ineffectively implemented owing to the testator's interest in that property being an (unsevered) interest as beneficial joint tenant (*Kecskemeti* v. *Rubens Rabin & Co, The Times*, 31 December 1992; *Glynn* v. *Frearsons* (a firm) [1999] Ch 326). However, any such duty must have its limits. Thus where a solicitor was instructed to prepare a will including a specific devise of certain property, but was later instructed to carry out a conflicting instruction in relation to the same property *inter vivos*, no duty arose in favour of the prospective devisee, for the duty of the solicitor was to carry out his client's instructions (see *Clarke* v. *Bruce Lance & Co* [1988] 1 All ER 364 (CA)).

When the will has been executed, it is good practice for the previous will to be destroyed in the presence of the client and by his direction. Destruction is not necessary to revoke the previous will. Assuming the new will contains a revocation clause (as in Precedent clause A1.1), the execution of the new will of itself revokes all others. It is simply a matter of convenience, to avoid possible future uncertainty or mistake if revoked wills are allowed to remain in existence.

In his own interests, the client should be encouraged to leave the original will for safe custody in the office or else at his bank. He should certainly be discouraged from keeping it at home. A copy should be supplied for his reference. If the will is not left in the office, a note of its whereabouts should be endorsed on the draft.

It will be most helpful to keep a comprehensive register of all wills made in the office, whether originals are held or not. Among other uses, this will serve as a reminder system to identify wills which may be due for review. This sort of reminder is an important part of the solicitor's service to his clients. How soon may a will need to be reviewed? This will depend on the individual client's circumstances, but as a generalisation it may be suggested that five years might be too soon, but that after seven years most wills begin to look distinctly out of date. Changes in the law or in the client's personal circumstances may, of course, call for special consideration.

CHAPTER NOTES

1 In accordance with WA 1837, s.9 (as substituted by AJA 1982, s.17, reproduced in Appendix 6 and discussed in Preliminary Note 5.2).
2 Notwithstanding relaxation of the formal requirements for execution in terms of WA 1837, s.9, above.
3 *X* v. *Woollcombe Yonge* [2001] WTLR 301 (seven-day period to prepare a will not negligent, in the absence of special circumstances); see also *Smith* v. *Claremont Haynes, The Times*, 3 September 1991, *Hooper* v. *Fynmores (a firm)* [2001] WTLR 1019.

PART II

Precedent Clauses

Commencement

A1 Introductory words, including revocation

The more traditional opening, 'This is the last Will and Testament of me . . . of . . . etc' introduces an acceptable though unnecessary element of solemnity into the process of will making. If the draftsman adopts it, he must also incorporate the words of revocation or preferably embody these in a separate clause.

Care should be taken to set out the full baptismal names and surname of the testator, since many people do not habitually use their full name. If it transpires that the testator does not, it may avoid difficulty later to enquire further as to whether any property or investments may have been conveyed or transferred to the testator without the use of his or her full name. If so, it will be convenient to add after the true name, '(sometimes known as . . .)' which will facilitate the inclusion of the relevant alias in the grant of probate.

The inclusion of the testator's address and occupation or description serves no purpose other than as an aid to correct identification. However, it is usual and correct practice.

Clause A1.1

I *[full name, address and occupation or description]* HEREBY REVOKE all former wills and testamentary dispositions made by me AND DECLARE this to be my last will.

A2 Contemplation of marriage (or re-marriage)

This clause is intended to provide for the situation in which what was formerly known as a 'will in contemplation of marriage' would have been made, in reliance on LPA 1925, s.177. That section having been replaced by provisions inserted into WA 1837, s.18 by AJA 1982, s.18 (see Preliminary Note 5.2 and Appendix 6), it is advisable to frame such a will in conformity with the new statutory language. Paragraph (1) of the following clause seeks to do this.

It is relatively unusual for such a will to be made before marriage, unless as a purely interim measure, pending execution of another will in a more permanent form once the marriage has taken place, which is to be strongly advised. Unless that is the intention, or where an intended second marriage is in view, special care is needed. Quite apart from the application of s.18, the requirements of which are easily satisfied, it is necessary to consider in such cases not only what is to happen if the marriage is prevented by the testator's death (the possibility against which such a will is presumably intended mainly to provide), but also what is to happen if the marriage does not take place for any other reason.

If the engagement were broken, the testator would be likely to make a new will, and should clearly do so. Nevertheless, it may be advisable to express the present will as ceasing to have effect if the marriage should not take place within whatever may be thought to be a reasonable time. This in turn makes it necessary to consider what is to happen at the end of that time. If a possible intestacy is to be avoided it may be desired that as a stop-gap (pending the execution of a new will) the testator's previous will should be revived.

All these eventualities make for difficult and complex drafting, and, as suggested above, it will be much better if the substantive will is made after marriage, with any will made in anticipation of the marriage regarded as purely temporary and framed in the simplest terms possible. However as the consequences of possible failure to make a further will must necessarily be kept in view, paragraphs (2) and (3) of the following clause are included. While these paragraphs can offer no more than an outline for a draft, since circumstances are various, it is hoped that they will serve as a reminder of the difficulties and a framework for their solution.

Clause A2.1

(1)   At the time of making this will I expect to be married to [   ] and intend that this my will (other than paragraphs (2) and (3) of this Clause) shall not be revoked by my marriage to the said [   ]

(2)   If I die within the period of [   ] months from the date hereof without having been married to the said [   ] [the following provisions of] [this my will] [shall nevertheless take effect without alteration] [shall take effect subject to the following alterations that is to say   ] [shall become void to all intents and purposes] [and in that event (*continue as in (3) below*)]

(3)   If in any circumstances my said intended marriage shall not have been solemnised within the period of [   ] months from the date hereof then at the end of that period this my will shall become void to all intents and purposes [and in that event any testamentary dispositions made by me before the date of this my will and which are revoked hereby shall then revive and have effect] [as if the same had been re-executed at the date hereof] [as if this present will had never been made]

B

Executor and trustees

B1   Appointment of individuals; solicitors; bank

For the purposes of the normal family will, under which in all probability the whole estate or at least the whole of residue will pass to the spouse, an appointment of the spouse as executor will usually be dictated by convenience and represent the wish of the testator. However, as such a will normally includes alternate beneficial dispositions in case the spouse should fail to survive, it will normally include some form of alternate appointment of one or more executors and trustees. The following clause is intended to embody such an appointment in the simplest possible way, by providing for a joint appointment of the spouse and some other person. It is envisaged that if the spouse takes, the other appointee would not need to prove the will, whereas if the spouse does not take, the other appointee will prove as surviving executor and may later appoint an additional trustee, should this appear desirable.

Dissolution or annulment of marriage

As to the effect of the Wills Act 1837, s.18A (as added by AJA 1982), the decision in *Re Sinclair* [1985] Ch 446 (CA) and the LR(S)A 1995 see para.5.2. Should the testator's marriage later be dissolved or annulled, a joint appointment of executors and trustees as in Clause B1.1 will have covered the deemed omission of any appointment of the former spouse by virtue of the amended s.18A; as will an alternate appointment in Clause B1.2, should this be preferred.

Clause B1.1

I APPOINT   of   and   of
(hereinafter called 'my Trustees' [which expression where the context admits includes any trustee hereof for the time being]) to be the executors and trustee of this my will [and I bequeath to each of those above-named who shall prove this will [and accept the trusteeship] the sum of £   for his or her own use and benefit absolutely] [and I declare that any of my Trustees being a Solicitor or being engaged in any other profession or business shall be entitled to charge and be paid all usual professional or other charges for business done services rendered or time spent by him or his firm on any

matter connected with the administration of my estate or the trusts of this will including anything which a trustee who was not engaged in any profession or business could have done personally]

Clause B1.2

I APPOINT my [said] [wife] [husband] [   ] to be the sole [executrix] [executor] of this my will but if [she] [he] is unwilling or unable to prove my will before the expiration of [   ] [weeks] [months] after my death then I APPOINT [of] to be [the sole] [jointly] [executor][s] and [trustee][s] of my will in [her] [his] place

Appointment of professionals

Where the testator wishes to appoint a professional executor, he will usually wish to appoint his solicitor or his accountant (or both), personally, by name. In doing so, he will probably envisage that the work of the executorship and of any trust arising will be done by the firm of which the appointee is a member. If so, this should obviate any difficulty in the event of the appointee having retired from practice during the testator's lifetime. Where there is no particular personal reason for appointing an individual, the testator may wish to appoint the firm as such. It should thereby be made clear that the appointment is of the partners at the date of death, as it would otherwise take effect as an appointment of the partners at the date of the will. It is also desirable to provide (if this is in fact acceptable to the testator) that the appointment should extend to any firm which at the date of death may be carrying on the practice of the firm named, though in the event of a change involving anything more than a reconstruction or amalgamation, the testator ought clearly to be invited to reconsider the position. Where a firm is appointed, it will be for the partners to decide how many and which of them should prove the will and the testator must be willing to leave this in their discretion. The only alternative is to appoint one or more individuals by name.

For convenience, the usual power to charge professional and similar fees is included in the form of appointment. If preferred, it can be included in the clause dealing with trustees' powers (see Clause H13.1), though as the matter of remuneration is an essential aspect of the appointment, it seems preferable to deal with both together. Neither the appointee nor any present partner should witness the will. As to the default provisions for remuneration for services provided and expenses incurred by a personal representative or trustee acting in a professional capacity see TA 2000, ss.28 and 31 (reproduced in Appendix 4).

Clause B1.3

I APPOINT the partners at the time of my death in the firm of
Solicitors of   (or in any other firm by which at the time its practice is then carried on) (hereinafter called 'my Trustees' [which expression where the context admits includes any trustee hereof for the time being]) to be the executors [and trustees] of this my will [and so that a sole principal or one only of such partners may act alone in the administration of my estate and of the trusts of this will] AND I DECLARE that my Trustees

[other than any new trustee who is not engaged in any profession or business] shall be entitled to charge and be paid all usual professional or other charges in connection with the administration of my estate and the trusts of this will in all respects as if they were acting professionally therein for lay executors or trustees

Appointment of a bank or other trust corporation should always be made in the particular corporation's own published form to ensure that the appointment will be acceptable. This clause will always incorporate by reference the terms and conditions on which the appointment will be accepted by the corporation. It is necessary that these should be understood by and acceptable to the testator.

Clause B1.4

I APPOINT   Bank plc [or as the case may be] (hereinafter called 'the Bank') to be the sole executor and trustee hereof . . . [*continue in terms of the published forms of the particular bank or trust company relating to terms and conditions, remuneration and powers, according to circumstances*]

Testamentary guardians

C1   Appointment of an individual

Part I of the Children Act 1989 (CA 1989) (reproduced as amended in Appendix 7) introduced changes in the law of guardianship. It was brought into force with effect from 14 October 1991, but is not confined to appointments of testamentary guardians in wills made on or after that date. If such an appointment is not yet effective (the death of a testator not having occurred) it will on that event be subject to CA 1989, s.5 and Sched.14, paras.12, 13).

Under CA 1989, s.5 a parent may appoint a testamentary guardian if he or she has parental responsibility for the child, i.e. 'all the rights, duties, power, responsibilities and authority which by law a parent of a child has in relation to the child and his property' (CA 1989, s.3). Both the mother and father of the child have parental responsibility if they were married to one another when the child was born; if not the mother alone has parental responsibility unless the father acquires it (see CA 1989, s.4 (as amended)). Once the appointment takes effect, the guardian has parental responsibility and the power to appoint his or her successor (CA 1989, s.5(4)).

If the other parent with parental responsibility survives, any appointment by the will of the deceased parent will normally not take effect until the surviving parent dies or loses parental responsibility under CA 1989, s.4 (as amended). In exceptional circumstances, the appointment may take effect on the first death so that the guardian and surviving parent will both have parental responsibility: CA 1989, Sched.14, paras. 8 and 13. If the other parent with parental responsibility has predeceased, the appointment by the surviving parent will take immediate effect on his or her death (as in Clause C1.1).

Although an appointment of a testamentary guardian will normally only take effect on the death of the surviving parent, it seems there is a choice open to the draftsman when framing the appointment to insert it in the will of each parent. Each will could make an appointment but in such a way that only the appointment in the will of the survivor is to be effective (as in Clause C.2 – if used, the will of each spouse should contain similar provision). Instead, either will alone could contain the appointment, but in terms that it takes effect only after the death of both parents (as in Clause C.3). As the first possibility will always leave the survivor free to change the appointment by a later will, this may be the preferred method because of its greater flexibility. Depending on the order of deaths, the second possibility may mean the survivor is unable to alter the appointment.

If there are young children, the joint appointment of a married couple (if practicable) would clearly be desirable. If a trust arises in favour of the children it might be convenient to appoint the guardian(s) to act also as trustee(s), unless the trusteeship seems likely to call for special expertise.

Clause C1.1

I APPOINT   [and   jointly] to be the guardian[s] of any of my children who have not attained the age of 18 at the time of my death

Clause C1.2

I APPOINT   [and   jointly] to be the guardian[s] of any of my children who have not attained the age of 18 at the time of my death if my [said] [wife] [husband] has died in my lifetime

Clause C1.3

I APPOINT   [and   jointly] to be the guardian[s] of any of my children who have not attained the age of 18 at the death of the survivor of myself and my [said] [wife] [husband]

Specific gifts

PERSONAL CHATTELS

D1   Chattels generally, by statutory or alternative definitions

Absolute gift

In all cases where the whole estate is not certain to pass absolutely to a single beneficiary, it is most desirable that the testator's personal chattels should be disposed of specifically. Great inconvenience may result if the terms of the will are such that these may be sold, or may become subject to any kind of trust (compare with the proviso to AEA 1925, s.33(1), under which personal chattels are normally excepted from the statutory trust for sale on intestacy).

Definition

Although enacted for a different purpose, it is usual to adopt the definition in the AEA 1925, s.55(1)(x), illustrated in Clause D1.1. It is however important that the draftsman should consider whether this definition is in fact appropriate to the circumstances, particularly as to what is excluded. The terms of the statutory definition are contained in Appendix 1. Anything not self-evidently included in that definition (for example, gold coins, or a boat and tackle) which are intended to pass with personal chattels should be added expressly to the gift. Anything which might be within the definition but which is not intended to pass with personal chattels should be otherwise expressly disposed of. Express instructions should always be taken as to the testator's wishes with regard to any items of substantial value.

   Clause D1.2 offers a simplified alternative definition in more general terms which should include everything which the normal testator would think of as part of his personal effects. Such a formula is perhaps more in keeping with modern conditions and does not require reference to anything outside the will for explanation to the testator.

Shared gifts

A gift of personal chattels will usually be made to a surviving spouse. Where this is not the case, and the gift is to be shared between two or more beneficiaries, some provision should be made as to the basis of division in order to avoid disputes and an undesirable sale. For a simple and adaptable formula, see Clause D2.2.

Tax

If the gift is to a surviving spouse, it is exempt from IHT. In other cases, a gift of personal chattels, like any other specific gift of personalty, is in effect free from IHT which, as a testamentary expense, is normally payable primarily out of the general personal estate. Accordingly, it is not the practice of draftsmen to express specific gifts of personalty as being 'free of tax'.

Clause D1.1

I GIVE to [my] [said] [wife   ] [   ] absolutely [all] [such of] my personal chattels as defined by section 55(1)(x) of the Administration of Estates Act 1925 [as are not hereby or by any codicil hereto otherwise specifically disposed of] [and also any motor car belonging to me even though used wholly or partly for business purposes] [and also my   ] [but not my   ]

Clause D1.2

I GIVE to   absolutely [all] [such of] my chattels and effects of personal domestic or household use or ornament [as are not hereby or by any codicil hereto otherwise specifically disposed of] [excepting money and securities for money] [and excepting any chattels and effects used solely for business purposes] [but including any chattels or effects of personal use which may also be used partly for the purposes of any business or employment] [and also my   ] [but not my   ]

D2   Particular chattels: jewellery, household effects, legatee's choice

Identification

The description of anything given specifically should not only be full enough to distinguish it from all other things of the same kind but also not so full as to risk failure of identification because of some error of detail. Descriptions of jewellery, in particular, may present difficulties of this kind: reference to the description in an insurance valuation may be of assistance.

Substitutions

As to descriptions of property, a will speaks from death (WA 1837, s.24), and is therefore construed, prima facie, by reference to the testator's possessions at the time of death. However, in relation to a specific legacy, in which the testator intended to give a particular designated thing, the gift can take effect only if the estate of the testator included that thing at the time of death; otherwise, the gift is adeemed. Even if, having parted with the thing given, the testator should later have acquired a similar thing, the substitute cannot pass under the original gift (as to application of WA 1837, s.24, see *Williams on Wills* (8th ed.), pp.573 and 617) unless the terms of the gift are wide enough to include such a substitute. Whether a gift is specific is a matter of construction: as a generalisation, any gift of a particular thing prefaced by the word 'my' is likely to be so held and gifts of particular chattels are therefore usually so framed. In the case of chattels, it will not usually be necessary or practicable to make provision for possible substitutions. By way of comparison and contrast, see the suggested provisions in relation to specific gifts of shareholdings and houses in Clauses D6.1 and D7.1.

Shared gifts: basis of division

Clause D2.2 adopts what is thought to be the most straightforward basis for division *in specie* between beneficiaries, whereby recourse to the executors is required only in so far as the beneficiaries may be unable to agree.

Right of selection

Sometimes it is desired to give to one beneficiary the first choice of the testator's effects, or of some particular category. Clause D2.3 seeks to do this as simply as possible. It can be further simplified where the property not chosen passes to the beneficiary entitled to those personal chattels not specifically disposed of. A time limit for the selection should be imposed for practical reasons.

Expenses

Since the expenses of putting a legatee into possession of his legacy (including the cost of insurance) falls on the legatee (*Re Leach* [1923] 1 Ch 161), in the absence of provision to the contrary it will usually be desired to transfer this burden to the general estate. Clause D2.2 does so. Where chattels are to be selected, the title of the beneficiary derives from the selection, and expenses *up to that time* do fall on the estate (*Re Collins' Will Trusts* [1971] WLR 37).

Tax

See note to Clauses D1.1 and D1.2.

Clause D2.1

I GIVE the following specific legacies absolutely:

(i)   To [my] [God-daughter] [   ] my two-stone diamond ring

(ii)   To [my] [daughter] [   ] and to [   ] [the wife of
        my son   ] [in equal shares] all the [jewellery] [and furs] which belonged to
        my late wife

Clause D2.2

I GIVE absolutely and in equal shares to my [grand]children living at my death all my
household furniture furnishings and effects to be divided among them as they shall agree
but so that in default of such agreement the division shall be made by my Trustees in their
absolute discretion [and without any obligation upon my Trustees to obtain any professional valuation] [save at the joint expense of my said [grand]children] and shall be final
and binding upon all my said [grand]children [AND I DIRECT that all costs and expenses
of packing carriage and insurance incurred for the purpose of giving effect to this gift shall
be paid out of the residue of my estate]

Clause D2.3

I GIVE to [   ] absolutely such of my [   ] as [he] [she]
may select [within three months after my death] [and subject thereto I give the same to
[   ] absolutely]

D3   Incorporation of memorandum or list

Where a testator wishes to give a number of legacies (usually small specific legacies) it is not uncommon for these to be set out in a separate memorandum or list
which it is proposed to incorporate into the will by reference, instead of repeat-
ing the contents verbatim in the will.

Although such a list may be validly incorporated in this way, and in due course
admitted to probate as part of the will (provided all the requirements described in
the note to Clause F14.1 can be shown to have been fully satisfied), this practice
involves risks; the use of Clause D3.1 is therefore *not* recommended except in
case of urgency or in other special circumstances.

If this clause is used, care should be taken to ensure that the list is clearly iden-
tifiable and properly signed and dated. This is to assist in its identification, to
avoid separation of the list from the will, as a precaution against accidental loss,
and to avoid any possibility that, in ignorance of the law, the testator might later
attempt to substitute a different list.

Clause D3.1

I GIVE to such as are living at my death of the several people named in a list [dated
20   ] [bearing even date with but] prepared and signed by me [before executing
this my will] such items of [my personal chattels] [my household furniture furnishings and

effects] [my jewellery furs and articles of personal use and ornament] as are respectively
described therein opposite to their respective names

D4   Precatory trust

Testators sometimes wish to delegate or defer decisions as to who is to benefit
under a gift, by making the gift to a particular legatee, coupled with the expression of a wish or hope that the legatee will apply the gift either to some particular purpose or at his or her own discretion.

If the terms of a gift of this kind are such as to show an intention to create a
trust, then it may take effect in equity as a half-secret trust. However the present
note is not concerned with such trusts because no testator would be well advised
to create such a trust intentionally, in any but very exceptional circumstances.

It is usual and necessary to provide expressly when making a gift of the kind
under consideration, that this is not intended to create any trust or obligation, in
order to avoid any possibility of doing so by inadvertence. The term 'precatory
trust', commonly used to describe such a gift, is therefore misleading. It is the
essence of such a gift that it takes effect as an absolute gift to the legatee who has
an absolute discretion as to how, if at all, it should be applied. Naturally such a
gift should be inserted in the will only where there are explicit instructions that
this is the result intended.

Because any subsequent application by the legatee in accordance with the testator's wish would otherwise be liable to attract IHT, it is specifically enacted that
where a testator expresses a wish that property bequeathed by his will should be
transferred by the legatee to other persons and the legatee transfers any of the
property in accordance with that wish within two years after the death, that transfer is not a transfer of value, and tax is chargeable (or not) as if the property transferred had been bequeathed by will to the transferee (see IHTA 1984, s.143
(reproduced in Appendix 3)).

This clause is intended for use (being adapted as may be appropriate) where
the testator wishes to give to some person (probably his or her spouse) the opportunity to re-dispose of some part of the estate within this provision, if this may
result in a saving of tax. It will generally do so only if a transfer by the legatee
would attract a higher rate of tax than is payable on death.

Clause D4.1

(1)   I GIVE to [   ] [my Trustees] absolutely such and so many of [my
personal chattels] [my stocks and shares] [the assets comprising my personal estate] as
within the period of   months after my death [he] [she] [they] may select

(2)   WITHOUT PREJUDICE to the generality of the preceding paragraph of this Clause
and without imposing any trust or obligation whatsoever on [the said   ] [my
Trustees] and without conferring any legal equitable or other interest whatsoever on any
other person I express the wish (within the meaning of section 143 of the Inheritance Tax
Act 1984 or any enactment for the time being amending or replacing that section) that
[the said] [my Trustees] should select such only of [my personal chattels] [my stocks and

shares] [the assets comprising my personal estate] as may be described in any memorandum left by me which shall come to [his] [her] [their] knowledge within the said period of months after my death expressing my wishes as to the disposal or distribution thereof respectively and that [the said   ] [my Trustees] should make such transfer or transfers as may be necessary for the purpose of giving effect to such my wishes PROVIDED ALWAYS that no such memorandum or expression of my wishes shall have or be deemed to have any testamentary effect nor shall create nor be deemed to create any trust right liability or obligation whatsoever nor shall [the said] [my Trustees] be in any way answerable or accountable to any person whomsoever in relation to anything done omitted or suffered by [him] [her] [them] in relation to anything whatsoever contained in or implied or alleged to be implied by either of the paragraphs of this Clause or any part or parts thereof respectively

D5   Choses in action: words of bequest; life policy; bank account; building society account; local authority bond

In wills disposing of the smaller estates, it is sometimes desirable to include what is in essence a pecuniary legacy, but is in form a specific legacy, in as much as the amount is to be the balance at the time of death in a particular bank or savings account or the proceeds of a life policy. Clauses D5.1 and D5.2 and what follows give effect to a variety of gifts of this kind and may readily be adapted.

The testator should, however, consider whether a pecuniary legacy of a stated amount might not be more satisfactory, in the interests of certainty. There is also the danger that a specific gift might be adeemed if the particular account is closed in the testator's lifetime or that the amount of the eventual benefit to the legatee might be substantially less or more than the testator expected at the time of making the will.

Although not really of direct concern to the draftsman, it is perhaps as well to bear in mind the statutory provisions by which investors in national savings investments (except National Savings Certificates), and trustee savings banks, friendly societies and industrial and provident societies may direct payment to be made, in the event of death, by way of nomination, to a named person (National Savings Bank Act 1971, s.8; Trustee Savings Bank Act 1981, s.27; Friendly Societies Act 1974, ss.66, 67; Industrial and Provident Societies Act 1965, ss.23, 24; Credit Unions Act 1979, s.4, Sched.1, para.12; and various regulations thereunder). Nominations are not testamentary documents, and are not revoked by a later will and there is some danger that they may be overlooked. In the case of Post Office investments, there is no limit to the amount which may be nominated: in other cases, the maximum amount is £5,000 (Administration of Estates (Small Payments) (Increase of Limit) Order 1984 (SI 1984/539)).

Clause D5.1

I BEQUEATH to   absolutely

Clause D5.2

the full benefit of a Policy of Assurance [   ][the Company] dated the
            19   and effected by me on my own life with the Company and all
moneys (including any bonus) to become payable thereunder [but free from liability for
any charge or other incumbrance thereon which (if there be any such at the time of my
death) shall be discharged from my residuary estate]

Clause D5.3

the balance (including accrued and current interest if any) standing at the time of my
death to my credit on [my] [any] [current] or [deposit] account with [the
Branch of] [   ] Bank plc [to which I may be solely and beneficially entitled]

Clause D5.4

all money [including accrued] [and current] [interest] standing to my credit at the time of
my death on [Share Account number   ] [any share deposit or other investment
account] with the   Building Society [or any other Building Society to
which its engagements may hereafter be transferred]

Clause D5.5

all moneys for the time being secured by a Bond dated the   19
and numbered   effected by me with the
[County] [District] Council or by any Bond of the said Council for the time being subsisting whether directly or indirectly by way of renewal or replacement thereof PROVIDED
ALWAYS that if the said Council shall be unwilling to transfer the said Bond then its nominal value [as at the time of my death] shall be paid out of my residuary estate in satisfaction of this gift.

D6   Stocks and shares

It is comparatively unusual for a testator to make a specific gift of a particular
holding of quoted shares or stock to an individual legatee. Such a gift is more
likely to be envisaged where the testator is disposing of shares in a family or other
unquoted company, probably in favour of some person already associated with
the business of the company who may not necessarily be entitled to the residue
of the estate.

In either case, it must be appreciated that if a particular holding is specifically
disposed of by will or if the testator's holding(s) for the time being in a particular
company are so disposed of, and at the time of death the testator does not possess such a holding, the gift will be adeemed. If so, the legatee will not be entitled
to any substitute holding, unless the terms of the gift are wide enough to include
it. Such a substitution may commonly occur in the case of equity shares, where

there is any kind of takeover or amalgamation or even where there is merely reconstruction. In the case of fixed interest securities redemption may occur with or without conversion into other securities or equity shares.

Even where the testator still possesses the particular holding at the time of death, difficulty may arise if this has been specified too exactly because a gift of a particular number of shares or amount of stock will be strictly construed and will pass only that number of shares or amount of stock, even though the holding so described in the will may subsequently have been enlarged (whether by any bonus (for a particularly hard case see *Re Tetsall* [1961] 1 WLR 938) or rights issue, or equally by gift, inheritance or purchase).

There are so many ways in which the composition of such an investment may change that it is not easy to cover all eventualities. Clause D6.1 should be found sufficiently wide to safeguard the legatee in most foreseeable circumstances but it should be used with some caution, and should be adapted as may be appropriate.

It is particularly important, in relation to a gift of this kind (assuming it be of substantial value), that the will should be kept under regular review and the testator should be so warned.

Clause D6.1

I GIVE absolutely to   all [shares] [stocks] [debentures] [debenture stock] [loan stock] [and other interests or rights (if any)] to which at the time of my death I may be beneficially entitled in the capital of   plc/Limited [or in the capital or assets of corporation any other company or in the public funds to which at the time of my death I may have become beneficially entitled whether directly or indirectly (except by purchase in the open market) either in right of or by way of substitution for any previous beneficial interest in the capital of the said   plc/Limited]

INTERESTS IN LAND

D7   Private residence: absolute

The following clause provides for an absolute gift of the matrimonial home (or of the testator's interest where the parties are tenants in common), which it is sometimes desirable to make if the residue is left in trust, or for any other reason does not pass absolutely to the surviving spouse.

Where such a gift is made, it may be desired that this should be contingent upon the spouse surviving for a minimum period (see note to Clause F5.1 on 'Vesting'). It will usually be advisable to impose such a condition in any case where this would have been advisable in relation to an absolute gift of residue, in as much as the matrimonial home will commonly be the most important and possibly the most valuable single asset in the estate.

Like any other specific gift, this gift carries the risk of possible ademption in the event of the testator moving house after the date of the will. Should this happen, the safest course (in view of the particular importance of this gift) would

be to make a codicil, substituting the new house. However, as this may be overlooked, it seems most desirable that the original gift should be framed in terms
wide enough to extend to whatever is the matrimonial home at the date of death.
In this respect, the only difficulties are purely drafting difficulties. First, the
phrase 'house or flat' may be too narrow, in as much as people sometimes live in
accommodation which is neither. If this seems a possibility in the particular case,
the cautious draftsman may prefer the expression 'dwelling house', though it is
difficult to be sure that even this expression would extend to a houseboat or a car-
avan. Second, in case the testator may have more than one residence, it is necessary to establish which is meant. To facilitate this, the expression 'only or main
residence' is borrowed from the legislation relating to CGT. It is considered that
the meaning should be clear without further definition. For an alternative form
of words see Clause F3.1.

It will usually be considered right (see note to Clause D10.1) to provide
expressly that the gift is to be free of any mortgage or charge which may be subsisting at the time of death, thereby displacing AEA 1925, s.35. The effect of such
provision on the value of residue should be carefully estimated if, as has been
presupposed, the beneficial interests are different.

Clause D7.1

I GIVE absolutely to my [said] [wife] [husband] [if [and only if] [she] [he] survives me by
twenty-eight clear days] [my freehold] [leasehold] [dwelling house] [house] [flat] known
as   [all my share and interest of and in the [freehold] [leasehold]
[dwelling house] [flat] known as   ] and the proceeds of sale thereof
[or such other [dwelling house] house or flat (if any) as may be the only or main residence
of myself and my said [wife] [husband] at the time of my death] [free from any mortgage
or charge affecting the same at the time of my death which shall be discharged from the
residue of my estate]

D8   Private residence: in trust

Where, because of the value of the estate or some other special reason, the testator wishes to leave residue in trust for a surviving spouse for life only, it is for consideration whether the family home (if the testator is sole owner) or the testator's
share in it (if the parties are tenants in common) should be dealt with as part of
the residuary trust fund, or dealt with specifically.

In many such cases, it will be thought better not to restrict the spouse to a limited interest in the house but to leave this to the spouse absolutely as in Clause
D7.1. This frees the spouse from any dependence on the trustees which, even
though mitigated by provisions such as those in Clauses F3.1 and H5.1, is
contrary to what many testators would wish.

If the above is unacceptable (and a settlement on the spouse as tenant for life
under the SLA 1925 no longer being an option (TOLATA 1996, s.2(1)), it may be
desired to declare trusts in respect of the house separate from those of residue
whereby the spouse is given a life interest but (as in Clauses F3.1 and H5.1,

referred to above) protected by provisions requiring consent to any sale, allowing a right of occupation pending sale and permitting a purchase elsewhere from the proceeds of any sale. Clause D8.1 embodies such provision. See generally the notes to Clause F3.1 and Preliminary Note 4.8, where the IHT and CGT implications of various possible arrangements as to occupation are discussed.

Whether to use the mechanism of the trust for sale, as Clause D8.1 does, is a matter for consideration by the testator and one on which the draftsman will need clear instructions. Following TOLATA 1996 there is no longer any need for a trust for sale, although it remains a possibility, except in those cases where the testator may (perhaps uncommonly) wish the duty to sell to override. If instead the gift of the house is simply 'on trust' (for which purpose Clause D8.1 can readily be modified) the trustees will have power to sell but must be unanimous as to their decision before selling. Clause D8.1 is offered for use where the testator decides upon a trust for sale; in the absence of an express power to postpone sale TOLATA 1996 implies power for the trustees to do so. Continued use of a trust for sale of land carries an implied power to postpone sale (TOLATA 1996, s.4(1)).

Apart from optional variations of detail, the effect of Clause D8.1 is similar to the effect of Clauses F3.1 and H5.1 (read in conjunction with Clause F2.1) (see notes to these clauses). The advantage of dealing with the house separately from the rest of the estate is simply that, as a matter of drafting, all provisions relating to the house are incorporated into one clause. This may also be of assistance in directing attention to the matters which, in the interest of the spouse, ought to receive careful consideration.

Although Clause D8.1 can be adapted to include the contents of the house in the trust, this is not normally recommended.

Clause D8.1

(1) I GIVE to my Trustees my [freehold] [leasehold] [dwelling house] [house] [flat] known as   [or such other [dwelling house] house or flat as may be the only or main residence of myself and my [said] [wife] [husband] at the time of my death] [and all furniture furnishings and effects of household use or ornament therein not otherwise specifically disposed of by this my will or any codicil hereto] UPON TRUST [with consent of my said [wife] [husband] during [her] [his] life to sell the same (but with full power to postpone sale without being liable for any loss) and to hold the net rents and profits (if any) until sale and the net income from the proceeds of sale in trust for my said [wife] [husband] during [her] [his] life and after [her] [his] death my Trustees shall hold the said [dwelling house] [house] [flat] or other [dwelling house] house or flat for the time being held by them UPON the TRUSTS of this gift or the net proceeds of sale or the investments for the time being representing the same [and the said furniture furnishings and effects] UPON the TRUSTS [and with and subject to the powers and provisions] hereinafter declared concerning my residuary estate.

(2) Pending sale of the said [dwelling house] [house] [flat] and if the same be sold then pending sale of any other such [dwelling house] house or flat for the time being held by my Trustees upon the trusts of this gift they shall allow my said [wife] [husband] to occupy

the same [and to use the said furniture furnishings and effects] for so long as [she] [he] shall wish to do so UPON such terms and conditions as in their absolute discretion my Trustees shall from time to time think fit to require as to the payment of [rent] taxes and other outgoings in respect thereof and as to the insurance and repair thereof AND so that in the like discretion if my Trustees shall from time to time think fit to do so they shall have power (but shall not be under any obligation) to discharge any of the last mentioned liabilities or any part thereof out of the income or capital (or partly out of the income and partly out of the capital) of my residuary estate in priority over any beneficial interest therein

(3) My Trustees shall have power at the request of my said [wife] [husband] to apply the whole or any part of the proceeds of any sale under the trusts of this gift in or towards the purchase of another [dwelling-house] house or flat [PROVIDED that such purchase can be recommended to my Trustees by a professionally qualified surveyor and valuer] [if in their absolute discretion my Trustees shall think fit to do so] and thereupon the same shall be held upon the trusts of this gift and with all the powers applicable thereto [AND I DIRECT that if in their absolute discretion my Trustees shall think fit to do so they shall have power (but shall not be under any obligation) to apply any part of the capital of my residuary estate [not exceeding £   )] towards the cost of any such purchase as an advance by way of loan from my residuary estate upon such terms and conditions as in the like discretion my Trustees shall from time to time think fit to require]

D9   Private residence: previously settled under SLA 1925

Although new strict settlements (with certain exceptions) are prohibited after the commencement of TOLATA 1996 (1 January 1997), existing settlements will continue (s.2(1)).

Where such provision exists in the will of a testator who died before 1 January 1997 the spouse, as tenant for life, will continue to enjoy all the powers of trustees for sale. In the event of a sale, he or she would be entitled as of right (SLA 1925, s.75(2), in conjunction with s.73(1)(xi)) to direct the application of the proceeds to the purchase of another house while the original or any substitute house would still remain an asset of the estate.

The notes which follow, and Clause D9.1, may be of assistance in those cases where a will contains a strict settlement governed by SLA 1925. Clause D9.1 should *no longer* be used as a precedent.

'to my . . . wife . . . for life'

The duty of the executors is to vest the house in the wife as tenant for life, by vesting assent. This is the only formality that is required.

'she paying all taxes and other outgoings'

This is usually considered to be a reasonable requirement. The wife, presumably, will be in receipt of the income of residue.

'and keeping the same in good repair'

If the estate is substantial enough to warrant a settlement, it may also be thought reasonable that the tenant for life should bear the cost of repairs out of income. Unless the trust instrument expressly so requires, the tenant for life is not generally under any duty to keep the trust property in repair (*Re Cartwright* (1889) 41 Ch D 532).

'[fair wear and tear excepted]'

This suggested limitation may be considered, as an alternative to keeping in good repair, though it may lead to undesirable difficulties between the tenant for life and the trustees, i.e., as to the extent of the tenant for life's obligation, which such a limitation does not necessarily discharge altogether (see *Brown* v. *Davies* [1958] 1 QB 117, a landlord and tenant case).

Clause D9.1

[Not for use in wills executed on or after 1 January 1997]

(1)   I GIVE my freehold property [dwelling house] known as   unto my [said] wife for her life she paying all taxes and other outgoings and keeping the same in good repair [fair wear and tear excepted] and insured against loss or damage by fire to the full value thereof as my Trustees shall approve And from and after the death of my said wife I GIVE the same unto   absolutely

(2)   I APPOINT my Trustees to be trustees for the purposes of the Settled Land Act 1925 of the settlement hereby made

(3)   I DIRECT that capital money arising under the said Act may be invested or applied (in addition to the other modes of investment or application authorised by law) [with the consent of my Trustees] in any manner authorised by this my will in relation to moneys forming part of my residuary estate [but so that nothing herein contained shall be taken to exclude the application of section 73(2) of the said Act]

D10   Investment property

Although it is somewhat unusual, the testator may wish to make a specific devise of realty, other than his or her own home, in favour of some person other than the residuary legatee. Clause D10.1 should be readily adapted to the circumstances of the case.

It is not strictly necessary to make the gift expressly subject to leases, tenancies, etc. A gift by reference simply to the description of the property will undoubtedly pass whatever estate or interest the testator may have,[1] and will take effect subject to all rights of third parties subsisting at the date of death. The words in the relative square brackets may therefore be omitted.

In case the property is subject (or at the time of death might have become subject) to any mortgage or charge, the testator should consider whether the gift is to take effect subject thereto (as, by virtue of AEA 1925, s.35, it would in the absence of a contrary intention), or whether any such incumbrance is to be discharged out of residue. It is strongly recommended that whichever is the intention, this should be *expressed* in the will as AEA 1925, s.35 allows a contrary intention expressed by 'will deed or other document', the *absence* of which may be difficult or impossible to establish.

It is also strongly recommended that the testator should consider whether the gift is to take effect subject to, or free from, IHT. As explained in Preliminary Note 4.4, IHT on a specific gift of realty in the UK is a testamentary expense, and as such is normally payable out of residue, unless the will directs otherwise. If the specific beneficiary is to bear the tax (as also in the case of leaseholds, and undivided shares in land held on trust for sale), the gift must be made expressly subject to tax. However as the incidence of tax between beneficiaries is a matter which must receive the testator's direct consideration, the will ought (as in relation to a possible mortgage) to *express* the testator's considered intention. Further, as to the incidence of IHT, any will made before the decision in *Re Dougal* [1981] STC 514 (and see Preliminary Note 4.3) which does not expressly declare such an intention should by now have been reconsidered. This important matter should be considered against the background of the statutory rules as to the incidence of tax, and as to the liability of personal representatives, discussed in Preliminary Note 4.4.

It is also most important to guard against the possibility of ademption, especially in relation to any agreement for sale or compulsory acquisition. Assuming that the testator would wish the devisee to receive the consideration or compensation money in either event, para (ii) of Clause D10.1 so provides. It would otherwise usually pass to the residuary legatee.

Clause D10.1

[(i)]   I GIVE to   of.   absolutely my [freehold] [leasehold] property known as   [and comprised in Title number
at HM Land Registry] [SUBJECT to and with the benefit of all leases tenancies and contractual or other rights and obligations for the time being affecting the said property or any part or parts thereof and all covenants agreements and conditions for the time being subsisting in relation thereto] [AND SUBJECT to] [but FREED AND DISCHARGED from] [any legal mortgage or equitable charge for the time being affecting the said property or any part or parts thereof] [which I DIRECT shall be discharged out of my residuary estate in exoneration of the said property] [AND SUBJECT to the due payment by the said
          [from] [all liability in respect of Inheritance Tax attributable by reason of my death to the said property or to this gift thereof] [which I DIRECT shall be discharged out of my residuary estate in exoneration of the said property]

[(ii)   I DIRECT that if at the time of my death any local or public authority or any tenant or any other person whosoever shall have acquired or shall be entitled or prospectively entitled to acquire the said property or any part or parts thereof or any interest therein (whether under power conferred by or deriving from any statute or by way of private treaty) then the said   shall be entitled to receive absolutely all if any compensation or consideration money or other payment whatsoever which at the time of my death may have become receivable or which may thereafter become receivable by reason or in consequence of any such acquisition or entitlement or prospective entitlement as aforesaid]

CHAPTER NOTE

1   Care is still needed, because the court cannot re-write the will of a testator who is under a misapprehension as to what he owns: see, for example, *Re Lewis's Will Trusts* [1985] 1 WLR 102; applying *Re Tetsall*, cited at p.67.

E

Pecuniary legacies

GENERAL (ABSOLUTE)

E1   Individuals; grandchildren; nephews and nieces

These clauses are concerned only with legacies to individuals. For legacies to charities, see Clause E2.1. Clauses E1.1 and E1.3 envisage that the gift is immediate. Clause E1.2 provides for the more unusual requirement that the legacy should be payable only after the death of a life tenant.

Tax

It may be thought as a matter of construction that the simple gift of a sum of money, with no reference to tax, would necessarily take effect as the gift of a clear tax-free sum. As in the case of the specific legacy, this will usually be the position because any tax in respect of amounts given by way of pecuniary legacy has always been a testamentary expense in so far as the legacy is payable out of the general personal estate. However the long-standing practice of draftsmen is to provide expressly that pecuniary legacies should be 'free of tax' because, if payable from the proceeds of a mixed fund of realty and personalty, they will be liable to bear a proportion of the tax on realty, see *Re Spencer Cooper* [1908] 1 Ch 130 and *Re Owers* [1941] Ch 17. For IHT purposes a pecuniary legacy cannot now bear any tax unless expressly so directed by the will (see Preliminary Note 4.4). The practice of expressing legacies to be 'free of tax' will no doubt continue. It still cannot be wrong to show the intention expressly, though if the legacy were very substantial, the incidence of tax ought to receive special consideration. Another possible reason for providing expressly that pecuniary legacies should be free of tax is that the estate may otherwise be exempt from tax because it passed to a surviving spouse. By IHTA 1984, Part II, Chapter III, where the only non-exempt gifts in an otherwise exempt estate are tax-free legacies, the nil rate band is available and, if this is not exceeded by the amount of the non-exempt legacies when added to the cumulative total of any chargeable lifetime transfers by the testator, no tax at all will be payable on the estate. Thus in most normal circumstances, the gift of normal pecuniary legacies will not give rise to any tax liability.

Minors

Where any legatee may be a minor at the time of death, it will be an advantage to that legatee and simplify the administration of the estate if the executors are empowered to make payment to a parent or guardian, or to make some appropriate investment in the name of the minor legatee. National Savings investments are envisaged as the most suitable if the legacy is of a comparatively modest amount.

Without such a provision, the executors would be obliged in most cases to retain the legacy in trust until the legatee attains majority, because in the absence of an express provision to the contrary, a minor cannot give a good receipt, either for capital or for income. It is open to the executors, alternatively, to appoint separate trustees of a legacy to a minor who is absolutely entitled, under AEA 1925, s.42, but this power is thought not to be widely used. For the provisions of that section, see Appendix 1.

Clause E1.3 includes alternative provisions which should be readily adapted to the requirements of the particular testator, and should also be appropriate to any other form of gift to beneficiaries who may possibly include one or more minors. It should perhaps be borne in mind that such a power may place the executor in a difficult position if, in the particular circumstances, he does not think fit to exercise it. It is envisaged that, in any such case, the gift will be absolute and will not be subject to a condition as to attaining majority or in any other way contingent. If the testator wishes to attach any such condition to the gift, the kind of provision under discussion will clearly be inappropriate. For a more general provision, see Clause H10.1.

Clause E1.1

I GIVE the following pecuniary legacies absolutely [and free of all taxes]:

(i)　　To　　　　　　of　　　　　　　　the sum of £

(ii)　　To　　　　　　of　　　　　　　　or if [he] [she] does not survive me [by twenty-eight clear days] then to [his] [her] [wife] [husband] [　　　　] if [she] [he] survives me [by twenty-eight clear days] the sum of £

Clause E1.2

I GIVE to each of my living grandchildren at the death of the survivor of myself and my [said] wife absolutely [and free of all taxes] the sum of £　　　　to be paid within six months after the death of such survivor [and if not so paid to carry interest thereafter until payment at the rate of　　　　per centum per annum]

Clause E1.3

I GIVE to each of my nephews and nieces [and the nephews and nieces of my late wife] living at my death the sum of £   absolutely and free of all taxes [AND I DIRECT] that if at the time when his or her legacy is payable any individual legatee has not attained the age of eighteen years [my Trustees may pay the same to his or her parent or guardian whose receipt shall be a full discharge to my Trustees] [my Trustees may in their absolute discretion] [open an account in the name of the legatee with the National Savings Bank and pay into that account the said sum of £   ] [or may] [apply the said sum of £   in the purchase of National Savings Certificates in the name of the legatee] [and may in the like discretion accept the receipt of the parent or guardian of the legatee for the [Bank Book] [Certificates] as a full discharge for that legacy]

E2   Charitable

'charitable legacies'

As such, these legacies are free of IHT (see IHTA 1984, s.23). This exemption may also reduce the rate of tax on the rest of the estate. It is the duty of the draftsman to verify the existence and name of the charity (see *Re Recher's Will Trusts* [1972] Ch 526, at 544 per Brightman J).

'general charitable purposes'

Unless the testator has a particular application of his legacy in view (in which case it should be set out) these general words serve at once to ensure the application of the legacy to the charitable objects of the legatee, and to ensure that the exemption from IHT arises.

'full power to expend capital'

A simple pecuniary legacy for charitable purposes would normally be construed as enabling the charity to expend the whole amount and not as requiring that the legacy be invested as a capital fund, the income of which might alone be expendable. However, if the amount of the legacy is substantial, it may be desirable to consult the testator's wishes, and to make them explicit.

'my Trustees shall not be concerned'

Though sometimes included *ex abundanti cautela,* it is thought that these words are only declaratory and therefore serve no real purpose.

'the receipt of the person appearing'

These words ensure that the trustees are not put upon any enquiry as to the authority of any person giving a receipt on behalf of the charity.

Clause E2.1

I GIVE the following charitable legacies absolutely:

(1) To   of   the sum of £   [etc]

[in each case for the general charitable purposes of the legatee] [and with full power to expend capital as well as income for such purposes] [and so that my Trustees shall not be concerned to see to the application thereof] [AND DIRECT that the receipt of the person appearing to my Trustees to be the Treasurer or other proper officer for the time being of each of the above named legatees shall be a full discharge to my Trustees for the legacy given to that legatee]

TAX SAVING (ABSOLUTE OR SETTLED)

E3   Immediate gift in trust for children (or grandchildren) within nil rate band of IHT

This clause may be used where it is considered possible and desirable to divide the estate with a view to mitigating IHT (as discussed in Preliminary Note 4.2), by setting aside for the immediate benefit of the children an appropriate amount up to the current nil rate band for IHT, so as to utilise this as fully as possible and to reduce the taxable estate of the spouse at his or her death.

The same result could be achieved by dividing residue into shares (for associated partial exemption implications, see Preliminary Note 4.5), but it seems desirable that the children's fund should comprise a definite amount and this is most conveniently done by means of a legacy in trust.

The trustees are given the same extended powers as are applicable to residue. It is envisaged that the spouse would normally be a trustee. Residue itself will be given to the spouse either absolutely or in trust, according to circumstances, with gift over or remainder to the children. Where a substitutional gift is intended, in case a child should die prematurely and leave a surviving child or children, this should preferably be made by express provision as here, and not left to the operation of s.33 (as substituted) of WA 1837: see Preliminary Note 5.2.

To ensure compliance with the requirements for an accumulation and maintenance settlement (as to which see Preliminary Note 4.7), the substitution should be limited to children of the deceased child and should not extend to issue, though the widow or widower of a deceased child may likewise benefit. See also Clause E4.1.

Clause E3.1

(1) I GIVE to my Trustees [the sum of   thousand pounds] [such a sum as can be transferred on my death without being chargeable to Inheritance Tax (disregarding any exemption or relief) at any rate above the nil rate of tax] [or one equal part of my residuary estate (hereinafter defined) whichever is the less] UPON TRUST for such of my children living at my death as shall attain the age of [eighteen] [ ] years [or marry under that age] and if more than one in equal shares absolutely PROVIDED ALWAYS that if any child of mine shall die in my lifetime leaving a child or children living at my death who shall attain the age of [eighteen] [ ] years [or marry under that age] such last-mentioned child or children shall take by substitution and if more than one in equal shares the share of this gift which such deceased child of mine would have taken if he or she had survived to attain a vested interest

(2) In relation to the trusts of this gift my Trustees shall have all such and the like powers and discretions hereinafter conferred upon them or otherwise applicable in relation to my residuary estate as are for the time being capable of being exercised in relation to this gift

E4 Discretionary trust, within nil rate band of IHT for spouse, children and others; and subject thereto, on the trusts of residue

The following clause may be considered as an alternative to Clause E3.1. Its purpose is likewise to save IHT (where the estate is large enough) by making a non-exempt gift which will take up the testator's nil rate band of IHT (or balance of it) and also reduce the chargeable estate and the effective rate of IHT when the spouse dies.

Clause E3.1 does this simply by making a direct gift to the children. However, the spouse can have no access to the income or capital of the amount so given. If when the testator dies it is found that the residue of the estate is insufficient for the needs of the spouse, a difficult position may arise. If the children are of age and consent, the will can be varied in favour of the spouse. If they are not, there can be no certainty that the court would consent to a variation (under VTA 1958, s.1) which must in law be seen as being to some extent against their interest. The only alternative might be a family provision application (see Chapter 3 and Appendix 2). It is easy to say that the will ought not to include such a gift unless the estate is amply sufficient to support it, but the unexpected may sometimes happen. If the gift to children can thereby be made in such a way as not to deprive the spouse of recourse to the funds given, should this be necessary, this will not only provide a valuable insurance against changes in circumstances in marginal cases, but will also extend the opportunities for obtaining the IHT saving in relation to estates which would not otherwise be thought large enough to divide.

One possibility might be to couple a gift in terms of Clause E3.1 with a discretionary power, based perhaps on one or other part of Clause H8.1, for the trustees to pay capital to the spouse. The latter clause would need to be made applicable not to residue, or not only to residue, but also to the children's legacy fund. This may suffice to meet the possible needs of the spouse for capital, but not income.

It seems preferable to take the idea a stage further, giving the trustees a full discretion as to capital and income alike. By establishing such a discretionary trust, as under this clause, the testator can make a gift to the children utilising his nil rate band for IHT while at the same time effectively postponing their enjoyment until the death of the spouse, without thereby rendering the fund chargeable to IHT at the death of the spouse as part of the spouse's estate. During the lifetime of the spouse the trustees can appoint as much or as little of the income or capital of the fund to the spouse as they think fit. It will normally be in contemplation that the spouse will in fact receive all or most of the income, but probably not any of the capital unless this is needed for some special purpose. As always where wide discretions are conferred, it will be advisable for the testator to assist the trustees by leaving with the will a letter explaining his intentions in these or other appropriate terms.

The trust fund is, of course, settled property for IHT purposes; and as there is no interest in possession (IHTA 1984, ss.49, 50) (with the result that the fund does not form part of the estate of the spouse, save in so far as capital is actually appointed to the spouse[1]), and as the conditions for an accumulation and maintenance settlement are not satisfied, the fund is 'relevant property' for the purposes of IHTA 1984, Part III, Chapter III. However, if the value of the trust fund is such that no tax above the nil rate is attracted, the fund may be held without liability to IHT throughout the life of the trust and until final distribution. The reason is that although the normal charges to tax on a settlement with no interest in possession are not avoided, no actual liability to tax is incurred while the amount of any particular chargeable transfer remains within the nil rate band.

As long as the amount of the testator's nil rate band is not exceeded, IHT will not be payable at his death provided that the balance of the estate is left (as it should be) either to the spouse, or possibly within some other relevant exemption, and provided also that no other interest in possession settlement is created by the will, because of the possible effect of the anti-avoidance rules concerning 'related property'.

Subsequently, IHT will not become payable under the ten-yearly charge or at the time of final distribution, provided that the value of the trust fund at a relevant date is still not such as to attract any liability to tax above the nil rate at the time.

Should values increase over and above the rate of inflation (in real terms), charges to IHT would arise at any ten-yearly anniversary[2] (if the trust continues so long), and on a proportional basis (IHTA 1984, s.65) when the trust comes to an end or if meanwhile capital is appointed out to any of the beneficiaries.[3] Even if the above were to happen (and it could do so only if there were an increase in real values), the amount of any such liabilities to tax may be expected to be less than the liability which would have been incurred if the same property had been left to pass through the estate of the spouse at death. It may however be seen as a disadvantage that charges to CGT are likely to be incurred whenever absolute entitlements to capital arise (TCGA 1992, s.71); that is to say, whenever capital assets are appointed out of settlement to beneficiaries (if they are), and more significantly, when the trust comes to an end. At that time, the amount of unrealised gains within the fund may be considerable. Once again however the effect of the CGT indexation allowance and (since April 1998) taper relief will be that only real gains are in fact vulnerable, and the build-up of such gains may well have been reduced during the life of the trust by disposals within the trustees' annual exemption. In so far as gains are chargeable at the time of distribution, the liability may be postponed by election (TCGA 1992, s.260) with their concurrence to hold over such gains to the beneficiaries.

If the estate will not include enough invested capital to set up a settled legacy fund, in terms of the following clause it may still be possible and advantageous for that fund to comprise or include the matrimonial home, or the testator's interest in the matrimonial home, up to the value of the nil rate band for IHT. In a larger estate, it may likewise be beneficial to settle the matrimonial home, or the testator's interest in it, so as to free invested capital which would then pass as residue, absolutely to the surviving spouse. It may be better for the spouse to hold realisable investments than a house which in reality it will not usually be wished to realise. For these purposes, suggested additional sub-clauses are given in Clause E5.1 and further explained in the note to that clause.

It will be advisable to confer the power to appoint new trustees (as in Clause H14.1) on the spouse.

As a drafting point, where a substitutional gift is intended in relation to the ultimate trusts, in case a child should die prematurely and leave a surviving child or children, this should here be made by express provision. Reliance upon s.33 (as substituted) of WA 1837 would be inappropriate: see Preliminary Note 5.2.

Because they would constitute 'related settlements' within the meaning of IHTA 1984 s.62, Clause E4.1 should not be included in a will which also includes Clause G1.1.

Clause E4.1

(1)   I GIVE to my Trustees [free of all taxes] [the sum of [   ] thousand pounds] [such a sum as can be transferred on my death without being chargeable to Inheritance Tax (disregarding any exemption or relief) at any rate above the nil rate of tax] (which said sum and all investments and property for the time being representing the same is hereinafter referred to as 'the Settled Legacy') UPON the TRUSTS and with and subject to the powers discretions and provisions contained in the succeeding paragraphs of this Clause

(2)   For so long during the period of [eighty years from my death] [twenty-one years from the death of my said [wife] [husband]] (the perpetuity period applicable hereto) as any of the persons hereinafter mentioned is living my Trustees shall have power at any time and from time to time if and whenever they shall in their absolute discretion think fit to pay or apply the whole or any part or parts of the income or of the capital or of the income and the capital of the Settled Legacy to or for the benefit of all or any one or more exclusively of the others or other of the following persons that is to say my [said] [wife]

[husband] and any of my children and any [widow widower or] child (born during the life-time of the survivor of myself and my [said] [wife] [husband]) of any child of mine who may predecease such survivor and with power during the period of twenty-one years after my death to accumulate any income of the Settled Legacy not so paid or applied and to add any such accumulations to the capital thereof

(3)   As trustees of the Settled Legacy my Trustees in addition to the powers and dis-cretions otherwise conferred upon them by law shall have all such and the like powers and discretions hereinafter conferred upon them or otherwise applicable in relation to my residuary estate as are for the time being capable of being exercised in relation to the Settled Legacy

(4)   If any of my Trustees is or may become personally interested as a beneficiary in the exercise of (or omission to exercise) any or all of the powers and discretions hereby con-ferred upon my Trustees generally he may from time to time join in exercising that power or any such discretion as if he were not so interested and may nevertheless retain for his own use any benefit which in good faith he may derive in consequence thereof as if he were not a trustee

(5)   Subject to the foregoing provisions of this Clause and to any and every exercise of the powers and discretions hereinbefore conferred upon them my Trustees shall hold the Settled Legacy UPON TRUST for such of my children living at [the expiration of twenty-eight clear days after] the death of the survivor of myself and my said [wife] [husband] as shall attain the age of [eighteen] [   ] years [or marry under that age] and if more than one in equal shares absolutely PROVIDED ALWAYS that if any child of mine shall fail to survive the survivor of myself and my said [wife] [husband] [by twenty-eight clear days] but shall leave a child or children who shall so survive such survivor as afore-said and shall attain the age of [eighteen] [   ] years [or marry under that age] then such last mentioned child or children shall take by substitution and if more than one in equal shares the share of the Settled Legacy which such deceased child of mine would have taken if he or she had not so failed to survive as aforesaid

[OR]

(5)   Subject to the foregoing provisions of this Clause and to any and every exercise of the powers and discretions hereinbefore conferred upon or otherwise exercisable by them my Trustees shall hold the Settled Legacy UPON such and subject to the like TRUSTS and with such and subject to the like powers discretions and provisions as are hereinafter declared concerning or otherwise applicable to my residuary estate and are for the time being subsisting and capable of taking effect

E5   The same: supplemental provisions as to matrimonial home

This clause embodies additional sub-clauses for use with Clause E4.1, to autho-rise appropriation of the matrimonial home as an asset of the settled legacy, in the circumstances mentioned at the end of the note to that clause. It also allows appropriation of the testator's interest, in case the parties already own the property beneficially as tenants in common; or of part of that interest, in case the value might exceed whatever is at the time the amount of the nil rate band of IHT. This amount should not be exceeded without careful consideration: see generally note to Clause E4.1.

Because an appropriation of *part* of the testator's interest might not otherwise fall within the provisions of s.41 of AEA 1925 (reproduced in Appendix 1), it is further provided that such an appropriation is an authorised 'investment', and requires no consent (see AEA 1925, s.41(1), proviso, para.v, and note to Clause H2.1).

The purpose of authorising such an appropriation is to keep the matrimonial home or a part interest in it out of the estate of the testator's spouse, but without detriment to the spouse. This seems to involve a departure from the principle which has been advocated elsewhere in this book, that the matrimonial home should not normally be made an instrument of tax planning. It is a matter of judgment in relation to the particular circumstances whether such a departure is justified.

It is in general the case that a surviving spouse will enjoy full security in the matrimonial home (or any substitute) only if she (or he) is absolute owner, or else has a legal right of occupation in conjunction with a life interest: where the whole beneficial interest in the matrimonial home *is* included in the estate of the spouse for IHT purposes. If beneficial ownership is in any way divided between the surviving spouse and other members of the family, the security of the spouse is necessarily placed at risk to some extent. It is therefore, in principle, undesirable from the point of view of the spouse to reduce the spouse's estate by creating beneficial entitlements in the matrimonial home in favour of the children. It may however seem to be undesirable from the point of view of the children to incur maximum IHT at the death of the spouse just because much of the value of the estate is represented by the matrimonial home and cannot be divided.

Against this background, a discretionary trust such as is under discussion here may be seen as offering an acceptable compromise. Whatever interest in the matrimonial home is appropriated to such a trust is kept out of the estate of the spouse. At the same time, there should be no doubt that the spouse will enjoy de facto security. Although this lies in the discretion of the trustees, they will clearly understand the intention of the testator to be that, as between the spouse and the children, the need of the spouse will in all normal circumstances be regarded as paramount. Although these priorities may seem almost to go without saying, the testator will no doubt place them informally on record, in a letter to the trustees, to accompany the will. It will also be advisable to provide in the will that the spouse is to have the power of appointing new trustees, as in Clause H14.1.

In terms of IHT and CGT, the general position after an appropriation will be as summarised in the note to Clause E4.1. In that note, it was pointed out that liability to CGT must usually be expected to arise when the discretionary trust comes to an end, though this should be greatly exceeded by the IHT saving. However, where an interest in the matrimonial home is comprised in the trust, the question arises whether the CGT relief on disposal of a private residence (TCGA 1992, ss.222–224) may be available to the trustees (TCGA 1992, s.104). It would be so if the spouse were 'entitled to occupy under the terms of the settlement'. It has been held that a sufficient entitlement for this purpose does arise where occupation is permitted by the trustees of a discretionary trust, in exercise of a power expressly conferred upon them for that purpose (*Sansom v. Peay* [1976] 1 WLR 1073). As against this, the exercise of such a power by trustees is officially considered to give rise for IHT purposes to an interest in possession (see para.4.8 and Inland Revenue Statement of Practice SP10/79 on the power for trustees to allow a beneficiary to occupy a dwelling house).

This clause has been drawn on the basis that no express power to permit beneficial occupation is to be given to the trustees, and that if such a power is given elsewhere in the will in relation to residue (as in Clause H5.1), it should be excluded in relation to the settled legacy. However, in as much as permissive occupation by the spouse necessarily rests upon the exercise by the trustees of *some* power or discretion to allow it, this might still be regarded by the Inland Revenue as giving rise to an interest in possession. In the face of that possibility the clause includes an optional power for the trustees to grant a lease or tenancy, which should not have that result. If at an undervalue, a liability to IHT would be incurred but any liability is unlikely to be considerable.

Although this clause undoubtedly achieves its purpose, it does so (as just discussed) at the risk of giving rise to an interest in possession unless a power to grant a lease or tenancy is exercised. Where there are sufficient assets in the estate another, and more secure, method of achieving the tax planning objective using the interest in the home is available, provided the personal representatives have adequate powers. It involves the personal representatives distributing outright the matrimonial home to surviving spouse as beneficiary of the residuary gift in the will (thereby giving full security of the home to that spouse) but on terms whereby this would be charged with the payment of an amount sufficient to constitute the settled legacy. The loan (or debt) created is retained as an asset of the estate and appropriated by the personal representatives as funds (or part of the funds) attributed to the settled legacy. No interest in possession in the loan (as an asset of the settled legacy) arises even if the spouse is a discretionary object of the settled legacy. On the death of the surviving spouse, although the value of the entire home will attract IHT as an asset of her estate, the amount of the loan will reduce the value of the home, and thus, her own estate for IHT purposes. In circumstances where a will does not contain a legacy (settled or otherwise) as just described, the same result can be achieved through use of a post-death variation whereby such a legacy is first retrospectively introduced into the will.

Clause E5.1

[For optional inclusion as part of Clause E4.1]

(6)(i)   Without prejudice to the generality of their other powers my Trustees shall have power to appropriate in or towards satisfaction of the Settled Legacy the whole or any part (being either a part or share having a specific monetary value or else an aliquot part or share of the whole) of any beneficial interest to which at the time of my death I may be entitled in respect of whatever dwelling house is at that time the only or main residence of myself and my said [wife] [husband] and for the avoidance of doubt I DECLARE that any such interest or part thereof so appropriated shall be deemed to be an investment authorised for the investment of money subject to the trusts of the Settled Legacy and further that no consent shall be required to such appropriation

(ii)   If my Trustees make such an appropriation as aforesaid then in relation thereto and to the Settled Legacy generally the powers conferred by [paragraph   of] [Clause   ] hereof[4] shall not apply but my Trustees shall have the following powers (without prejudice as aforesaid) in relation to the Settled Legacy (exercisable as if my trustees were an absolute beneficial owner of the money and property subject to the trusts of the Settled Legacy) that is to say:

  (a)   power to apply money subject to the trusts of the Settled Legacy in or toward the purchase or in the improvement of any freehold or leasehold dwelling house [within the United Kingdom]

  [(b)   power to contribute to the purchase of any such dwelling house in common with any one or more of the persons referred to in paragraph (2) of this Clause upon such terms and conditions as my Trustees think fit]

  [(c)   power from time to time to borrow and to give security for the payment of money [(and to join with any of the before-mentioned persons in so doing)] for the purposes of any such purchase [(or contributory purchase)] as aforesaid]

  [(d)   power (to the extent of their interest) to grant and determine leases tenancies and licences to occupy in relation to any dwelling house for the time being wholly or partly subject to the trusts of the Settled Legacy with or without rent and upon and subject to such terms and conditions as my Trustees think fit]

CHAPTER NOTES

1   With a view to keeping capital advances out of the estate of the spouse, the will may include a power for the trustees to make loans as under Clause H8.2. An interest-free loan out of settled property should not give rise to an interest in possession for IHT purposes.

2   IHTA 1984, s.64 see also Inland Revenue Statement of Practice SP8/86 concerning the treatment of accumulated income of discretionary trusts.

3   See endnote 1.

4   Clause H5.1, or equivalent.

F

Dispositions of residue

F1 General clause

This clause is for use where no life interest is created. The corresponding clause where residue is held for persons in succession is Clause F2.1. An alternative short clause, suitable for general use, is Clause F4.1. The traditional use of a trust for sale to precede a disposition of residue is now generally redundant for wills made on or after 1 January 1997 (see Preliminary Note 4.8 and Clause D8.1).

The clause is used to precede either an alternate gift to children in case of non-survival of a spouse otherwise absolutely entitled, or beneficial trusts for spouse and issue where the spouse is given only a limited interest.

'my debts and funeral and testamentary expenses'

It is usual and good practice to include an express declaration as to the incidence of debts and liabilities in every will as a matter of course, even though the direction simply reflects the effect in the particular circumstances of the statutory rules as to the order of application of assets in discharge of liabilities which have effect subject to the provision of the will (AEA 1925, s.34(3) and Sched.1, Pt II). Commonly, the general estate is the only possible fund for payment, but in any case where the incidence of liabilities might affect the entitlement of one beneficiary as against that of another, the position should be carefully considered.

Should a debt have been incurred without full consideration or in other circumstances such that it is disallowable as a deduction from the estate for IHT purposes (FA 1986, s.103), it will be viewed for administration purposes that the debt may nevertheless still take effect as a liability of the estate.

Clause F1.1

I DEVISE AND BEQUEATH all [the remainder of] my real and [the remainder of my] personal property whatsoever and wheresoever not hereby or by any codicil hereto otherwise specifically disposed of unto my Trustees UPON TRUST to pay thereout my debts and funeral and testamentary expenses and all legacies bequeathed hereby or by any codicil hereto and to hold the balance (hereinafter called 'my residuary estate') UPON the

TRUSTS and with and subject to the powers and provisions hereinafter declared and contained

F2   Limited interest

See Clauses F1.1 and F4.1. Clause F1.1 is intended for use where no life interest arises, but where residue may be held in trust for minors.

Clause F2.1 is intended for use where a life interest is created and is extended (by the provisions in square brackets) to deal with certain matters affecting the possibly divergent interests of the life tenant – interested in income, and of the remainderman – interested prospectively in capital.

In general, where these have not been declared expressly, certain intentions are imputed in equity to the testator with a view to holding a fair balance between the rights of those interested in income and capital respectively. (The comments in this note are much simplified. The standard works on equity should be consulted for further detail.) These presumptions may be displaced by contrary provision and it is the almost invariable practice of draftsmen to make such provision. The traditional clause of such a provision is included in the square brackets in paragraph (1) of Clause F2.1 as an illustration: a short, much simpler and preferable alternative is given in Clause H9.1.

The equitable presumptions so displaced derive from the following principal authorities:

(a) *Howe v. Dartmouth* (1802) 7 Ves 137 whereby if a high income is derived from the retention of unauthorised investments, part is capitalised to compensate the remaindermen for the implicit risk of capital loss;
(b) *Re Earl of Chesterfield's Trusts* (1883) 24 Ch D 643 whereby, conversely, part of the eventual capital proceeds of an investment which was not itself income producing, is apportioned retrospectively to income; and
(c) *Allhusen v. Whittell* (1867) LR 4 Eq 295 whereby payments in discharge of liabilities, before residue can be ascertained, are taken to have been made partly from capital and partly from the income deriving from such capital.

In modern conditions, the possible advantage in terms of greater fairness as between beneficiaries is usually considered not to justify the trouble and expense of making what may be difficult or at least complex calculations.

Apart from the equitable rules for apportionment as between capital and income, it may be proposed also to exclude the effect of the Apportionment Act 1870; this too being on the basis of the time and expense involved in making the appropriate calculations. Under this Act income current at the date of the testator's death is apportionable on a time basis by reference to the period to which it relates, the proportion so applicable to the period after the death being alone regarded as income of the life tenant and the balance being capitalised. This clause does not exclude the Act (but see Clause H9.1 which does, see also the related notes for the income tax effects of exclusion of these provisions).

Clause F2.1

(1) I DEVISE AND BEQUEATH all [the remainder of] my real and [the remainder of my] personal property whatsoever and wheresoever unto my Trustees UPON the following TRUSTS [and so that income of my [real leasehold and personal] [property however constituted or invested] [(including the income of property required for the payment of debts and other payments made in due course of administration in payment whereof the proceeds of such sale calling in and conversion are hereinafter directed to be applied)] shall as from my death be treated as income] [and that a reversionary or future interest shall not be sold prior to falling into possession unless my Trustees shall see special reason for such earlier sale] [and so that the net rents and profits of my real and leasehold property for the time being unsold after payment thereout of all outgoings which my Trustees shall consider payable out of income shall go and be applied as if the same were income of authorised investments made of the proceeds of an actual sale thereof] [and so that no property not actually producing income shall be treated as producing income]

[(2) (*Here take in Clause F3.1, if desired*)]

[(3) or (2)]

(a)   Upon trust to pay thereout all my just debts and funeral and testamentary expenses [and legacies]

(b)   Upon trust to invest the residue after such payment in any investment hereinafter authorised (with full power to vary and transpose investments from time to time) and to hold the same (hereinafter called 'my residuary estate'). Upon the trusts and with and subject to the powers and provisions hereinafter contained

F3   No sale of residence without consent

See notes to Clause D8.1. Clause F3.1 is intended for use in cases where the surviving spouse has only a limited interest in residue and where residue includes the family home. However unlikely it may seem that this would be sold against the wishes of the spouse, the inclusion of an express declaration that it should not be so sold may be thought to provide the minimum of security to which the spouse should normally be entitled. It may also serve to protect the trustees who, in order to hold a fair balance between the life tenant and remaindermen, might in some circumstances otherwise feel obliged to sell where they were offered the inducement of a very high price. The court nevertheless has jurisdiction under LPA 1925, s.30 on the application of any person interested, to direct a sale by trustees for sale where a necessary consent has been refused (*Re Beale's Settlement Trusts* [1932] 2 Ch 15). As to the nature of the court's discretion see *Re Holliday (A Bankrupt)* [1981] Ch 405 (CA).

Similarly, the inclusion of an express declaration that the spouse may occupy the house seems desirable, even though such a right is probably implicit in the gift of a life interest. It should certainly be made explicit where the testator does not wish the spouse to bear any of the burden of repairs.

To carry the protection of the spouse a stage further, it will usually be desirable to cover the contingency that the spouse may wish to move house, perhaps for the sake of economy, by giving an express power to the trustees to purchase else-where. This may conveniently be done by separate provision (see Clause H5.1 and notes thereto).

Clause F3.1

[For incorporation, if desired, as part of Clause F2.1]

(2)   I DECLARE that no sale of my residence known as   (or other my [only or main] residence at the time of my death) shall be made during the lifetime of my [said] [wife][husband] without [her] [his] consent [and that pending sale thereof my Trustees shall permit my said [wife] [husband] to occupy the same for so long as [she] [he] may so wish] [and without any liability on] [her] [his] [part for the repair or maintenance thereof]

F4   Short alternative clause

This clause incorporates provision for payment of IHT, extending to joint prop-erty and/or *inter vivos* gifts. See also Clauses F1.1 and F2.1.

Paragraphs (1) and (3) of this clause are suggested as an alternative to the much fuller traditional clause exemplified in Clause F2.1. Apart from the omis-sion of the provisions as to exclusion of the equitable rules on apportionments (a short alternative clause for which appears in Clause H9.1) it is not thought that the effect of these paragraphs is significantly different from that of the corre-sponding paragraphs of Clause F2.1, and they may be thought to be more readily intelligible to the testator, as well as being more economical.

Paragraph (2) deals with the discharge of liabilities of the estate and is option-ally extended to include provision which in certain cases the testator may wish to make for IHT.

First, as to any non-exempt gifts in the will which by their express terms or by operation of law exonerate the legatee or devisee from any liability to pay tax on their value, it is expressly provided that such tax is to be paid out of the general estate before residue is ascertained (see notes to Clauses D10.1 and E1.1 and Pre-liminary Notes 4.3 and 4.4). This provision is merely declaratory but does serve to draw attention to the possible effect on the value of residue.

Second, in case the testator wishes the estate to bear any tax payable (by rea-son of the death) by third parties (for example, in respect of property owned jointly with some person other than a spouse or, more commonly, an *inter vivos* gift within seven years before death (IHTA 1984, s.199 as amended) payment can likewise be conveniently directed to be made out of the general estate. This is despite the fact that, strictly speaking, such tax is not primarily a liability of the estate and consequently the direction for payment may really amount to a bene-ficial gift of the amount of the tax. As such, this may itself be taxable and in case of deficiency of assets may be liable to abatement.

The general words 'any transfer of value made by me during my lifetime' appearing (optionally) in paragraph (2) should be adapted as necessary to suit the circumstances. As they stand, they serve as a reminder that a liability to IHT may arise, not only in relation to any potentially exempt transfer made within seven years before the testator's death, but also in relation to gifts made at any time 'with reservation' in terms of FA 1986, s.10. The statutory rules as to the incidence of tax, and as to the liability of personal representatives, are discussed in Preliminary Note 4.4.

Clause F4.1

(1)   I GIVE to my Trustees all my real and personal property not otherwise specifically disposed of UPON the following TRUSTS

(2)   My Trustees shall pay and discharge therefrom all my debts [(including any debt which is a charge on any property in which at the time of my death I have a beneficial interest)] and funeral and testamentary expenses and all tax payable by reason of my death [(including tax attributable to [any devise or bequest given free of tax] [and any property to which at the time of my death I may be beneficially entitled jointly with any other person] [and any tax payable by any person in respect of any transfer of value made by me during my lifetime])] and all legacies given by this my will or any codicil

(3)   My Trustees shall hold the balance of my said real and personal property remaining after such payments (hereinafter called 'my residuary estate') UPON the beneficial TRUSTS and with and subject to the powers and provisions hereinafter declared and contained

F5   Absolute gift to surviving spouse

Vesting

Although an absolute gift of residue to a surviving spouse necessarily places the subsequent destination of the testator's estate in the hands of the spouse and beyond the testator's own control, most testators making such a gift would consider the interests of their children or others who would take in the event of the spouse's failure to survive, to be sufficiently protected by arranging for the spouse to make an appropriate will, accepting whatever risk there may be that such a will might later be altered or revoked. They would also normally accept whatever risk there may be that the spouse's enjoyment might be only comparatively short-lived.

If the deaths of husband and wife should occur to all appearances simultaneously (for example, as the result of an accident) then for the purposes of succession of property, the younger is normally deemed to succeed the elder (see LPA 1925, s.184 and *Hickman v. Peacey* [1945] AC 304). However, for IHT purposes they are deemed to have died at the same instant so that the estate of the one never becomes part of the estate of the other (see IHTA 1984, ss.4(2) and 54(4)).

It is however very common practice to guard against the contingency of an accident as a result of which the spouse might actually survive only for a nominal period, by stipulating that the gift is conditional upon the spouse surviving for some specified period, usually 28 days. This ensures that in the event of near-simultaneous deaths, the devolution of the testator's estate will be governed by his own will and that it will be administered by his own executors, and not as part of the estate of the spouse. See Preliminary Note 4.6.

'all my . . . property . . . not . . . otherwise . . . disposed of'

It is very common practice to include these words in square brackets, with a view to facilitating later alterations by codicil but it is not at all necessary to do so. The other dispositions contemplated are specific devises and bequests. Pecuniary and other general legacies are normally payable out of the general estate, before residue is ascertained, and this should be expressly directed as below.

'subject to . . . debts and . . . legacies'

It is usual to direct in this way that the liabilities of the estate and the pecuniary legacies (if any) given by the will, or by any later codicil, are all to be discharged out of the general estate before residue is ascertained (as to debts which may be disallowed as a deduction for IHT purposes see the notes to Clause F1.1). This is so even where they could not in fact have been dealt with in any other way.

The tax payable on the testator's free personal estate is included in this direction, being a testamentary expense. For references to other tax liabilities, see Clause F4.1. These will not normally be relevant in relation to the will here under consideration.

'the succeeding provisions . . . shall take effect'

If Clause F5.1 is used, it will be followed by Clause F1.1 and Clause F2.1 (alternate beneficial trusts for children or issue). Separating the primary gifts to the spouse from the alternate gift (which is not very likely to take effect), this sequence is preferred by some draftsmen as reflecting as explicitly as possible what the testator actually contemplates.

It is however more usual to declare a trust in any event as in Clause F1.1, following this by a composite declaration of the beneficial trusts (in favour of the spouse if surviving and otherwise in favour of children and issue, as in Clause F7.1).

Considered purely as a matter of drafting, it is immaterial which approach is adopted, but if Clause F5.1 is used, care should be taken to ensure that as the 'succeeding provisions' referred to in paragraph (2) become operative only in the event that the spouse fails to survive, these should not include any which may be required in any event (for example, a charging clause).

'if [and only if] she survives me by twenty-eight clear days'

The words in square brackets are not commonly found in survivorship clauses. Their purpose is to make it clear that the gift to the spouse is intended to be contingent upon the spouse surviving the specified period, and is not to be construed[1] as a vested gift subject to divesting should the spouse fail to survive that period or, in other words, that the survivorship condition is a condition precedent and not a condition subsequent. Although it seems quite clear that under a condition of either kind the effective disposition for IHT purposes[2] is that which in the event takes effect, it has been doubted whether a condition subsequent is apt to secure that if the spouse does survive, the spouse exemption (IHTA 1984, s.18) will apply.[3] It seems most unlikely that the exemption would be denied in such a case[4] but, in view of its importance, the draftsman may wish to avoid the possibility.

'fails to attain a vested interest hereunder . . .'

See Preliminary Note 5.2, as to the position in the event of divorce and the continued use of such words following the amendments made to WA 1837, s.18A by LR(S)A 1995.

Clause F5.1

(1)   I DEVISE AND BEQUEATH all my real and personal property whatsoever and wheresoever [not hereby or by any codicil hereto otherwise specifically disposed of] [SUBJECT to the payment of my debts and funeral and testamentary expenses] [and all legacies given hereby or by any codicil hereto] unto my [said] wife [ ] [if [and only if] she survives me by twenty-eight clear days] absolutely

(2)   If my said wife fails to attain a vested interest hereunder (but not otherwise) the succeeding provisions of this my will shall take effect

[*Here follow provisions as in Clause F6.1 or F7.1 (or as may be appropriate to the circumstances); and such as may be appropriate of the provisions in section H; and Clause I1.1*]

F6   Gift over to children

This is intended for use where the primary gift in favour of a surviving spouse is made as a direct gift, as in Clause F5.1, and where a trust is imposed only in the event of the failure of the spouse to survive. In that event, the gift over to children (with substitution of grandchildren) follows and takes effect under the trust.

'living . . . twenty-eight . . . days after my death'

Normally, the testator will intend that if the gift over takes effect, residue will be shared between such of his children as may be living at his death, who attain majority or a stipulated age. However, where the interest of the spouse is made contingent on surviving for a period after the testator's death, some draftsmen think it a sensible precaution to prevent the parent's estate from passing through that of a deceased child by imposing a survivorship condition on the gift to the child. If so, a further gift over should perhaps be added to avoid possible intestacy.

It is thought better not to frame the gift (as in some precedents) in favour of children living at the death of the survivor of the spouses, in case this might give rise to difficulty in the event of divorce.

'attain the age of . . . years [or marry under that age]'

The age of vesting is entirely a matter for decision by the testator. It should however be borne in mind that the longer vesting is postponed, the more important it is that the trustees should be carefully chosen and that they should be given greatest possible freedom to advance capital. The age of vesting should not normally be more than 25 to avoid incurring unnecessary IHT liabilities (IHTA 1984, s.71). For the position as to CGT, see Preliminary Note 4.7.

'provided always . . .'

Where a substitutional gift is intended, in case a child should die prematurely and leave a surviving child or children, this should preferably be made by express provision, as here, and not left to the operation of s.33 (as substituted) of WA 1837: see Preliminary Note 5.2.

To ensure compliance with the requirements for an accumulation and maintenance settlement (as to which see Preliminary Note 4.7), the substitution should be limited to children of the deceased child and should not extend to issue, though the widow or widower of a deceased child may likewise benefit.

Clause F6.1

MY TRUSTEES shall hold my residuary estate UPON TRUST for such of my children as shall be living at [the expiration of the period of twenty-eight clear days after] my death and shall attain the age of [eighteen] [   ] years [or marry under that age] and if more than one in equal shares absolutely PROVIDED ALWAYS that if any child of mine shall have died during my lifetime or having survived me shall die without having attained a vested interest hereunder leaving a child or children living at my death then any such child or children (meaning in either case a grandchild or grandchildren of mine) as shall attain the age of [eighteen] [   ] years [or marry under that age] shall take by substitution and in equal shares if more than one *per stirpes* the share of my residuary estate which such deceased child of mine would have taken had he or she survived and attained a vested interest

F7   Spouse and children

This clause is intended for use where a trust is imposed in any event; the primary gift in favour of a surviving spouse and the gift over in favour of children, both taking effect under that trust. Clause F5.1 will not then be appropriate, but see note thereto as to vesting of the gift in the spouse. See also notes to Clause F6.1.

Clause F7.1

MY TRUSTEES shall hold my residuary estate upon the following trusts:

(1)   UPON TRUST for my said [wife] [husband] if [and only if] [she] [he] survives me [by twenty-eight clear days] absolutely but

(2)   If my said [wife] [husband] fails to attain a vested interest then UPON TRUST for such of my children . . .

[continue as in Clause F6.1]

F8   Gift over to issue (based on the statutory trusts)

The use of this clause is suggested as offering a means of incorporating with the greatest possible brevity provisions to the same general effect as those of Clauses F1.1, F5.1 and F6.1. This is done by reference to the statutory provisions applicable in relation to intestacy. It is not however suggested for use otherwise than in cases of great urgency because it is generally (and rightly) considered by draftsmen to be undesirable to incorporate any substantive provision by reference. Testators equally (and understandably) prefer documents which are complete in themselves.

For convenience of reference, the terms of the statutory provisions referred to are set out in Appendix 1.

Clause F8.1

(1)   If [and only if] my said [wife] [husband] [   ] survives me [by twenty-eight clear days] I DEVISE AND BEQUEATH all my real and personal property whatsoever and wheresoever unto my said [wife] [husband] absolutely

(2)   If my said [wife] [husband] fails to attain a vested interest I DEVISE AND BEQUEATH all my said property as aforesaid unto my Trustees upon such and subject to the like trusts as are declared by section 33 of the Administration of Estates Act 1925 as if I had died intestate and my Trustees shall hold my residuary estate (within the meaning of that section) upon the statutory trusts for my issue contained in section 47 of that Act but with the additional powers hereinafter contained

F9   Limited interest, with remainders

This clause is intended for use in conjunction with Clauses F2.1, F3.1 and F4.1 and declares beneficial trusts in favour of the spouse for life, with remainder to surviving children, including the children of any child of the testator who may not have survived. Clause F10.1 embodies alternative provisions to the same effect.

'during [her] [his] life'

Some of the older published precedents include an alternative provision determining the interest of a surviving spouse on remarriage. On purely personal grounds few testators wish to impose a limitation in modern times. If this were done, and the surviving spouse did remarry, the life interest ends and the life tenant makes a PET (IHTA 1984, s.52(1)). Thus IHT will be charged on the value of the trust fund when the interest ended if the life tenant dies within seven years. Moreover, the exemption from CGT on the death of a life tenant (TCGA 1992, s.73) would not be available, though the exemption based on the life tenant's occupation of a house comprised in the trust (TCGA 1992, s.225) should not be affected, assuming this to be then sold.

'living at [my death] [the death of the survivor]'

This clause may be compared with Clause F6.1 which makes immediate provision for children where a spouse fails to take an absolute interest. As in that clause, the entitlement of children is here made contingent upon their attainment of a specified age, or (if desired) marriage under that age.

However, the present clause is concerned with a different situation in that where there is a life interest, whatever their expectations may be, no child can become *absolutely entitled* until both parents have died, that is, normally until after the life tenant's death. The question for consideration is, what should be the nature of their entitlement (if any) in the meantime? Should a child who is living at the testator's death, and who has already attained or subsequently attains the stipulated age (or marries) be entitled to a *vested* reversionary interest, expectant on the death of the life tenant, or should the interests of all children of any age be made contingent upon surviving *both* parents? This clause provides in the alternative for either possibility.

Because a child who is living at the testator's death might predecease the life tenant, many practitioners think it desirable that no child should have a vested interest during the life tenant's lifetime, for fear that if a child should predecease, that child's share might otherwise devolve (as a reversionary interest) under the child's will or intestacy, and not under the testator's own will. Instead, it is quite usual to give merely contingent interests adding a provision (as in this clause) by which the share of a deceased child passes by substitution to his children (if any) (i.e. the testator's grandchildren) contingently upon their attaining likewise a specified age (or marrying). Some clauses extend the substitution to issue of any degree, but this may not be desirable (see Clause F10.1 and notes thereto).

Such a substitutional gift must be made by express provision, and not left to the operation of s.33 (as substituted) of WA 1837: see Preliminary Note 5.2.

To ensure compliance with the requirements for an accumulation and maintenance settlement (as to which see Preliminary Note 4.7), the substitution should be limited to children of the deceased child and should not extend to issue, though the widow or widower of a deceased child could also benefit.

The testator should be invited to consider whether it is really in the interests of his children to make their entitlements contingent upon surviving the life tenant. It is suggested that there will normally be no serious disadvantage in giving a child an interest contingent only upon attaining an appropriate age, even if that child should die during the lifetime of a surviving spouse. On the contrary, inconvenience and sometimes real hardship may result if he is *not* allowed to have a vested interest during the lifetime of the life tenant. The uncertainty as to his entitlement may make it difficult for him to make proper provision for his own family and may prevent him from obtaining finance for some necessary purpose, for which there may perhaps be no spare capital for the trustees to advance.

As to the possibility that a child whose interest in capital is contingent might be given a vested interest in income, see Preliminary Note 4.7. Whether the interests of children are capable of vesting on the first or only on the second death, IHT will be payable on the death of the surviving spouse, as on a notional transfer by the spouse (IHTA 1984, s.49(1)). It will similarly be payable if the interest of the spouse comes to an end within the seven years before his or her death (IHTA 1984, s.52(1) and s.3A(6)). Not all the exemptions for individuals are available (IHTA 1984, s.19(5), in conjunction with s.57).

If a child with a vested interest dies while this is still a reversionary interest, it is excluded property (IHTA 1984, s.48(1)) and no IHT is payable on it.

If on the determination of the life tenant's interest in possession the interest of any of the children is still contingent, no IHT will be payable on the vesting of that child's interest (or at any intermediate time) so long as the conditions for an 'accumulation and maintenance settlement' (IHTA 1984, s.71 and see Preliminary Note 4.7) are established, as declared in this clause.

If the interests of the children are *not* vested at the testator's death, even if the children are then of age, difficulty may be experienced in making a variation (should this be desired) of the testator's dispositions, for IHT or CGT purposes: see Preliminary Note 4.10. Because of the possibility of minority and/or unborn interests arising, an application to the court (VTA 1958, s.1) will be unavoidable, and although consent may be given, expensive provision for those interests may be required. This difficulty might, however, be avoided, if a discretion to vary is given to the trustees, as under Clause G1.1.

No CGT will be payable when the life tenant dies (TCGA 1992, s.73) but the assets will be revalued as at that time for purposes of any future disposal (TCGA 1992, s.72).

If any child (or grandchild) is still under age at that time, there will be a disposal for CGT purposes when that child becomes absolutely entitled (TCGA, s.71), unless the interest of that child was a vested interest at the outset (see Preliminary Note 4.7): under this clause, it is not.

Clause F9.1

MY TRUSTEES shall hold my residuary estate UPON the following TRUSTS:

(1)   UPON TRUST to pay the income thereof to my [said] [wife] [husband] [   ] during [her] [his] life and subject thereto

(2)   UPON TRUST for [all or any of] [such of] my children or child [who] [as] shall be living at [the expiration of twenty-eight clear days after] my death and who shall have attained or shall attain the age of [eighteen] [   ] years [or marry under that age] and if more than one in equal shares absolutely PROVIDED ALWAYS that if any child of mine

[has already died] [or shall die in my lifetime] [or shall die after my death without having attained a vested interest in my residuary estate] but shall leave a child or children living at [the expiration of twenty-eight clear days after] my death who shall attain the age of [eighteen] [ ] years [or marry under that age] such last-mentioned child or children shall take by substitution and if more than one in equal shares the share of my residuary estate which his her or their parent would have taken if he or she had survived to attain a vested interest

F10   The same (alternative clause)

See notes to Clause F9.1, to which this clause is an alternative.

'and for all or any of the issue'

In this clause, which is based closely on the 'statutory trusts' embodied in AEA 1925, s.47(1)(i) (applicable to intestacy), the provision as to substitution in case of the death of any of the testator's children during the lifetime of a surviving spouse is extended to include any of the issue of the deceased child and is not confined to the deceased child's own children unlike the provision Clause F9.1. The statutory provisions are reproduced in Appendix 1.

Such an extension appears to envisage what may be thought a very unlikely possibility, that the only descendants of the deceased child living at the distribution date (normally, the death of the surviving spouse) might be that child's grandchildren or (further straining credulity) more remote descendants. Thus, although many published clauses of precedents provide in this way for the substitution of issue of a deceased child, this seems very unlikely to serve any real purpose. Moreover, the substitution of issue appears to go beyond what is contemplated for the purposes of the exemption from IHT in respect of the vesting of an interest under any trust which is an 'accumulation and maintenance settlement'. In relation to substitutional entitlements, the exemption extends only to a widow, widower or child of the deceased beneficiary; though in the case of others, it does appear to be still available if the substitutional interest vests within 25 years of the death of the testator (IHTA 1984, s.71(2)(b) as reproduced in Appendix 5).

As under the statutory trusts (compare note to Clause F9.1), the beneficial interests are given to those who are living at the death of the testator, and to the issue then living of any who have predeceased, and who themselves attain the stipulated age or marry under that age.

Such a substitutional gift should preferably be made, as here, by express provision; and not left to the operation of s.33 (as substituted) of WA 1837: see Preliminary Note 5.2.

Clause F10.1

MY TRUSTEES shall hold my residuary estate UPON the following TRUSTS:

(1)   UPON TRUST to pay the income thereof to my [said] [wife] [husband] [   ] during [her] [his] life and subject thereto

(2)   UPON TRUST in equal shares if more than one for all or any of my children living at [the expiration of twenty-eight clear days after] my death [who attain the age of [eighteen] [   ] years] [or marry under that age] and for all or any of the issue living at my death [who attain the age of [eighteen] [   ] years] [or marry under that age] of any child of mine who shall have predeceased me such issue to take through all degrees according to their stocks in equal shares if more than one the share which their parent would have taken if living at my death and so that no issue shall take whose parent is living at my death and so capable of taking

F11   Limited interest, with special power of appointment, and gift over in remainder

This clause differs from Clauses F9.1 and F10.1 in that, after the life interest in favour of a surviving spouse, residue devolves on the children as the surviving spouse may appoint, or on the children equally in default of appointment, as under those clauses.

Such a power of appointment may be useful where the children may be too young at the time of making the will for the testator to be able to judge how they may develop, or what their needs may be. It may also be useful where there is any reason to think that the needs of the children may turn out to be different and where the testator is prepared for the ultimate division to be made on the basis of needs, rather than of strict equality.

In all such cases, the purpose of conferring a power of appointment on the spouse is to preserve the greatest possible flexibility and freedom of action. By postponing any decision as to the ultimate distribution of residue, the needs of the children can be more exactly evaluated in the light of the financial situation existing at the time.

As an alternative, the testator could provide for these possibilities more simply by vesting the children's interests (as under Clause F9.1) at a relatively later age (anything up to 30 might be appropriate), at the same time giving the trustees extended powers to advance capital in the meantime, so leaving the trustees as judges of what is in the best interests of the children. Such a course implies that the testator has the fullest confidence in the trustees, but there is no reason why the surviving spouse should not be one. Clause H6.1 and H7.1 should then be used to extend the relevant provisions of TA 1925, ss.31 and 32 respectively. If the trustees have this element of discretion, it can be exercised after the death of the surviving spouse; a power of appointment cannot.

For the reasons explained in Preliminary Note 4.7, it is important to ensure that powers of appointment are not possibly exercisable outside the requirements for an accumulation and maintenance settlement for IHT purposes. It is therefore recommended that this clause should be used only in conjunction with Clause H15.1, which is intended to avoid that possibility.

Where a substitutional gift is intended, in relation to the gift in default of appointment, this should preferably be made by express provision as here and not left to the operation of s.33 (as substituted) of WA 1837: see Preliminary Note 5.2.

Clause F11.1

MY TRUSTEES shall hold my residuary estate UPON the following TRUSTS:

(1)   UPON TRUST to pay the income thereof to my [said] [wife] [husband] during [her] [his] life and subject thereto

(2)   UPON TRUST for all such one or more exclusively of the others or other of my children [and any widow widower or child born during my lifetime] [of any child of mine who may predecease me] at such ages or times and if more than one in such shares and for such limited or absolute interests and with such provisions for their respective maintenance education advancement and benefit generally as my said [wife] [husband] shall by any deed or deeds revocable or irrevocable or by will or codicil appoint AND in default of and subject to any and every such appointment and so far as no such appointment shall extend UPON TRUST for all or any of my children or child living at my death [who being male] attain the age of [eighteen] [   ] years [being female] [attain that age] [or marry under that age] and if more than one in equal shares absolutely [PROVIDED ALWAYS that no person who shall take any share of or interest in my residuary estate under an appointment by virtue of the power hereinbefore contained shall [in default of appointment to the contrary] be entitled to any share of the unappointed part without bringing into account the share or interest appointed to him or her]

F12   Absolute gift to grandchildren (immediate or deferred)

This clause envisages the possible situation that the children of the testator have been provided for during his or her lifetime or are in no need of a beneficial interest in the residue of the testator's estate, so that it is possible (and if substantial tax liabilities on the children's own deaths are in prospect, it may be desirable) for the testator's estate to be left directly to grandchildren.

If there is a spouse for whom a prior life interest is to be provided, this will be done by paragraph (1). If there is none, or if the spouse has been otherwise sufficiently provided for paragraph (2) will stand alone, as an immediate gift. It will be appreciated that if there is a spouse for whom it is necessary to make provision, such a disposition in favour of grandchildren is possible only if the spouse will be sufficiently provided for by a life interest and that it will be desirable if not essential in the interests of the spouse to give to the trustees a wide power to 'advance' capital to the spouse (see Clause H8.1).

Even so, the possible saving of tax by 'skipping' a generation in this way may be obtained only at the expense of equality of distribution. If, as in this clause, the gift is to grandchildren 'living at my death', any grandchildren who might be born subsequently would be excluded from benefit. If all possible grandchildren were to share, it would be necessary to postpone distribution until the death of the last child of whom a child might possibly be born. This is plainly unrealistic, as is any intermediate provision which might be proposed. The advantage of a gift in these terms may therefore be much less than appears at first sight, unless it is confined to the children of an individual who has already died, or unless the birth of further grandchildren is so unlikely as not to be a practical possibility.

In a gift to the testator's own children, it is common to include a substitutional gift to the children of any child of the testator who may predecease, or otherwise fail to attain a vested interest. Where the gift is to grandchildren, the intention may be to benefit only such grandchildren as are living at the relevant date, and not to substitute the issue of any who may have died. If so, it would be necessary to displace WA 1837, s.33 (as substituted by s.19 of AJA 1982; see Preliminary Note 5.2) by expressing a contrary intention. The optional Declaration at the end of this clause does so. If a substitutional gift is desired, this should preferably be made by express provision and not by reliance upon the statute (see the same para.5.2), in which case the proviso clause in Clause F9.1 may be incorporated, *mutatis mutandis*. This is advisedly limited to children of a deceased grandchild, and not extended to issue, thereby avoiding a possible breach of the requirements for an accumulation and maintenance settlement; see Preliminary Note 4.7

Clause F12.1

MY TRUSTEES shall hold my residuary estate
[(1) UPON TRUST to pay the income thereof to my [said] [wife] [husband] [   ] during [her] [his] life and subject thereto]
[(2) UPON TRUST in equal shares absolutely for all my grandchildren living at my death [who attain the age of [eighteen] [   ] years] [or marry under that age] [AND I DECLARE that the provisions of section 33 of the Wills Act 1837 (as substituted therein) shall have no application to this gift]

F13   Absolute gift to nephews and nieces (immediate)

This clause envisages the possible situation that the testator has no immediate family for whom to provide and that after whatever individual legacies may be appropriate, he or she wishes residue to be shared between the children of his or her brothers and sisters. It will usually be preferred to benefit the children, rather than the brothers and sisters themselves but, if not, the clause is readily adapted.

As a matter of construction, the expression 'nephews and nieces' includes only the testator's own nephews and nieces, and not those of the testator's (late) spouse. If the latter are to be included, this should be made clear.

As this clause stands, the basis of division is equality between individuals. If a stirpital division is required (i.e., on the basis of equality between families the share of each family being subdivided between individuals), which would be unusual, the gift may be expressed as 'in equal shares *per stirpes* absolutely'.

Clause F13.1

I GIVE all my estate both real and personal whatsoever and wheresoever [not hereby or by any codicil hereto otherwise specifically disposed of] to my Trustees UPON TRUST to pay my debts and funeral and testamentary expenses [and any legacies bequeathed hereby or by any codicil hereto] [and all taxes on any gift made free of tax] and to hold the residue after all such payments UPON TRUST for such of my nephews and nieces [and also such of the nephews and nieces of my] [late] [wife] [husband] as are living at my death [and attain the age of eighteen years] equally between them if more than one absolutely

F14   Gift upon trusts of an existing settlement

It may sometimes happen that the intended destination of some part of the estate (or more probably of residue) is similar to that of the property comprised in some subsisting settlement or other trust fund. While it is usually better practice to set out on the face of a will the beneficial interest and powers taking effect under the will so that it is complete and self contained, the will may in some cases be simplified by the device of incorporating the existing trusts by reference, as in this clause. If this is done, the instrument referred to becomes part of the will, and a copy of it will form part of the grant of probate.

It is however only an existing document which can be incorporated in this way and then only in so far as its provisions are definitive and incapable of variation. More specifically, it is clear on the authorities (see *inter alia*, *Re Keen, Evershed* v. *Griffiths* [1937] Ch 236, and *University College of North Wales* v. *Taylor* [1908] P 140) that in order to form part of a will, such a document must be clearly identified in the will, must actually exist at the date of the will and must be referred to in the will as being in existence at that date. If it cannot be found at the date of death, the provision for its incorporation is ineffective (*Re Barton, Barton* v. *Bourne* (1932) 48 TLR 205). If the trusts of that document include a power of appointment, those trusts can be incorporated only in so far as they could take effect in default of appointment (*Re Edwards' Will Trusts* [1948] Ch 440).

Clause F14.1

I GIVE to my Trustees [   ] UPON such and the like TRUSTS and with and subject to such and the like powers and provisions (if and so far as at the time of my death such trusts powers and provisions or any of them are capable of taking effect) as are declared by [Clause   of] [a Settlement dated the   day of   20 who died on the   day of   20   ] [in relation to [the residue of] [his] [her] estate]

F15   Limited interest of spouse, extended rights: redemption of life interest; appropriation of interest in dwelling house

These clauses are intended for use in case it may be desired to give to a surviving spouse who has only a life interest in residue the same absolute rights as arise in favour of the spouse where that spouse is entitled to a life interest in part of the residue of the estate of an intestate: see Chapter 2.

Clause F15.1 incorporates by reference the provisions of AEA 1925, s.47A as to redemption of a life interest. Subsection 7, which is excluded, deals with notices to the Family Division of the High Court. Section 47A of AEA 1925 is reproduced in Appendix 1.

Clause F15.2 incorporates by reference the provisions of IEA 1952, s.5 and Sched.2 as to appropriation of the deceased's interest in a dwelling house in which the surviving spouse was resident at the time of death, in or towards satisfaction of any absolute interest of the spouse in the estate. If it is desired to use this clause, with the object of giving the matrimonial home to the spouse without real loss to the estate, this should be done in conjunction with Clause F15.1 in order that the spouse may acquire an absolute interest against which the appropriation may be made.

The excluded paragraphs in IEA 1952, Sched.2 deal with applications to the court which may be required in certain circumstances, under an intestacy. This Schedule is reproduced in Appendix 1.

Clause F15.1

The provisions of section 47A of the Administration of Estates Act 1925 (other than subsection (7) thereof) shall apply to the life interest in my residuary estate given by this my will to my said [wife] [husband] in all respects as if that interest were a life interest in part of the residuary estate arising on my intestacy

Clause F15.2

The provisions of section 5 of the Intestates' Estates Act 1952 and of the Second Schedule to that Act (other than paragraph 2 and subparagraphs (2)[5] and (3) of paragraph 3 of that Schedule) shall apply to the administration of my estate under this my will as if I had died intestate

CHAPTER NOTES

1   Under the rule of construction known as the rule in *Phipps* v. *Ackers* (1842) 9 Cl. & Fin. 583 (HL) as applied and extended in *Re Heath* [1936] Ch 259 and *Re Kilpatrick's Policies Trusts* [1966] Ch 730 and explained by Ungoed-Thomas in *Re Penton's Settlements* [1968] 1 WLR 248; and see also *Brotherton* v. *RC* [1978] 1 WLR 610 (CA).
2   IHTA 1984, s.92 applies 'where . . . property is held for any person *on condition that he survives another* for a specified period of not more than six months'.
3   Ibid, s.18(3) whereby the exemption is in general denied 'if the . . . disposition . . . takes effect on the termination after the transfer of value of any interest or period'; but not

'by reason only that the property is given to a spouse *only if* he survives the other spouse for a specified period'.

4   Having particular regard to the retrospective operation of ibid, s.92.

5   Subparagraph (2) makes a written notification to the personal representative irrevocable. As this seems somewhat arbitrary, and could cause difficulty in relation to a possible future variation, the suggestion is made that it should be inapplicable.

Overriding discretionary trusts

G1 Special power of appointment, to facilitate variation of will

Since it is impossible for a testator to foresee exactly what will be the circumstances of his family or the value of his estate at the time of his death, the dispositions made by the most carefully considered will may turn out not to have been the most suitable, either from the point of view of individual beneficiaries or (with regard to the incidence of IHT) in the interests of the estate as a whole.

This may happen if a will has not been kept under regular review. It may happen if the testator's wife (or husband) should unexpectedly have died first; or if the estate of whoever is the first to die turns out to have a value substantially more or less than was anticipated; or in the event of a change in the law, by which some new tax charge is imposed; or else some exemption or relief is withdrawn, or is so framed as to be unavailable in the particular circumstances; with the result that the testator (or those advising him) may not have appreciated the existence or extent of a tax liability.

It may happen, in short, whenever any of the assumptions on the basis of which the will was planned should turn out to have been falsified by events.

As discussed in Preliminary Note 4.10, it is open to the beneficiaries to disclaim a beneficial interest, or to vary any of the dispositions of the will. For all purposes, including IHT and CGT, a disclaimer within two years after the death is treated as though the disclaimed benefit had not been conferred. If so declared within the instrument, a variation within two years after the death is treated for IHT and/or CGT purposes as if it had been effected by the deceased. Without such declaration, however, the variation will generally amount to a potentially exempt transfer for IHT purposes and/or as a disposal for CGT purposes, as in any case it would have been, but for these provisions.

These are valuable options, but they have their limitations. A disclaimer (by its nature) cannot be made once any benefit has been accepted. If made, it serves simply to accelerate the interests of those who would have been entitled if the person making it were dead. This may not be the desired result. A variation may be made even where a benefit has been accepted, and indeed even where the administration of the estate has been completed. It may however be precluded if it depends on the agreement of some person who is not prepared to co-operate, or it may require the sanction of the court on behalf of any person who is unable to consent because of minority or other disability, or if those prospectively interested may include persons yet unborn.

With a view to avoiding this inconvenience it is sometimes suggested that the trustees should be given express powers to consent to a variation on behalf of possible minor or unborn beneficiaries. No clause is given in this book for such a provision because it is thought that this might entail legal and practical difficulties, and moreover there is statutory warrant for conferring a wider and more flexible power, as the present clause seeks to do.

By virtue of IHT 1984, s.144 (reproduced in Appendix 3 and discussed in para.4.10), a discretionary power can be conferred on the trustee to vary any of the testator's dispositions, within two years after the death, by what is in effect an overriding power of appointment. This power is given to the trustees, so it has been doubted whether it may be exercised before the administration of the estate is complete when (but not before) the trusts are complete. In view of this an express provision permitting exercise of this power during the administration period may be inserted. For IHT purposes the exercise of such a power is treated as though the will had provided that the property concerned should be so applied or held on the testator's death. However, because of the effect of IHTA 1984, s.144(1)(a) in conjunction with s.65(4), the power ought not to be exercised within three months of the death (see *Frankland* v. *IRC* (1987) STC 1450 and para.4.10).

Such a power cannot be considered for inclusion in the will unless the testator has the fullest confidence in his trustees and is prepared to leave it entirely in their hands to act or not as they think best for the beneficiaries. There seems to be no reason, however, why the surviving spouse should not be one of the trustees. The position of the spouse can (and should) be further safeguarded by nominating the spouse (TA 1925, s.36) as the person to appoint new and additional trustees, under Clause H14.1.

Always bear in mind that (as is clearly implicit in the preamble to the present clause) the remaining provisions of the will are intended to take effect unless, in their discretion, the trustees see compelling reasons to override them. It will be most desirable to leave with the will a letter to the trustees making this absolutely clear (though without in any way derogating from the terms of the will itself), and that the powers of variation and disclaimer are intended to be exercised only in such a way as to prevent any detriment to the interests of the beneficiaries named in the rest of the will in case of any unforeseen change of circumstances occurring (whether or not in the testator's lifetime) after the will was made. Seen in this way, such a provision can give a most useful safeguard against the possibility of a will ever becoming altogether out of date.

In his letter to the trustees it might be as well for the testator to emphasise that it will normally be in the interests of the beneficiaries for the necessary decisions to be taken with the least possible delay. This will also be desirable for IHT and CGT reasons as mentioned below. Indeed, with or without such a power executors and trustees should always make it one of their first duties to review the terms of the will in relation to the current circumstances.

It is the purpose of this note to suggest that the inclusion of provisions on the lines of this clause in a will may be very beneficial. In particular:

1. If a discretion is given to the trustees, they will be bound to consider whether or not to exercise it, and therefore if some exercise of their powers would be in the best interests of the beneficiaries, this is unlikely to go by default. In the absence of such powers, beneficiaries will usually be advised to make an appropriate variation, but may not necessarily have the benefit of such advice.

2. An appointment by trustees in favour of a child will not involve a parent in liability as settlor for IT purposes. A variation by the parent might have done so, though a disclaimer would probably not. In other cases, where an original beneficiary would continue to be assessable to IT on estate income despite a variation, trustees can make an appointment to compensate for this.

3. In relation to an appointment by trustees, no application to the court will be necessary in a case where any beneficiary is a minor or otherwise under disability, nor where there are possible unborn interests, under the substantive provisions of a will. A variation might involve such an application.

4. An appointment by trustees which is seen by them to be desirable cannot be obstructed by any person whose concurrence in a variation might have been required.

These are considerable advantages. On the other hand, there are certain possible disadvantages which may attach to the exercise by trustees of a power of appointment, as compared with a variation by beneficiaries. In particular:

1. However much of the estate passes in the end to surviving spouse, the IHT exemption does not arise unless and until it does so; however, an appointment (after three months from death, see *Frankland* v. *IRC* (1997) STC 1450 and Preliminary Note 4.10) of property to the surviving spouse, attracting the IHT exemption, will enable the executors to obtain a grant, paying IHT on only so much of the estate passing other than to the spouse. Any cash flow disadvantage of paying IHT in full, followed by a reclaim of the amount attributable to property passing to the spouse, can be avoided with advantage.

2. For IHT purposes an appointment under the power is necessarily treated as if effected at the death (IHTA 1984, s.144(2)). No requirement for a declaration arises (IHTA 1984, s.142), and so there is no right *not* to make such declaration. In some cases the effective rate of IHT in the estate of the deceased might exceed the effective rate in the estate of an individual making a similar variation, particularly since the potentially exempt transfer may never become chargeable where no declaration is made within the instrument of variation.

3. No requirement for a declaration arises for CGT purposes either as an appointment under the power is not an 'instrument . . . made by the persons or any of the persons who benefit' (TCGA 1992, s.62(6)–(9) as amended by FA 2002, s.52), nor does the appointee appear to be a 'legatee' (TCGA 1992,

s.64(2)). On the contrary, property subject to this power is clearly 'settled property' (TCGA 1992, s.68) and a charge to CGT may arise wherever property is appointed to a beneficiary absolutely (TCGA 1992, s.71), or if there is an appointment on new trusts (see Preliminary Note 4.7). However, if action is taken promptly any chargeable gain may be eliminated or at least reduced by virtue of the annual exempt amount available to executors and trustees respectively (TCGA 1992, s.3(7) and (8)) it would seem that it may otherwise not be held over (by election) to the beneficiary.

It has also been suggested that the benefit of a declaration for CGT might be secured, if it were provided that any exercise of the trustees' powers and discretions should be made subject to the consent of the beneficiaries, or at any rate of the surviving spouse. Such a requirement may have much to commend it on personal grounds, and is provided for as an optional variation in the preamble to Clause G1.1.

For CGT purposes, it seems to be arguable that an appointment with such consent (at least if the appointment and the consent were embodied in the same 'instrument') would be a variation made, as is required 'by the persons or any of the persons who benefit or would benefit under the dispositions' (TCGA 1992, s.62(6)–(9) as amended by FA 2002, s.52(1)). However, if the prospective liability to CGT is significant it might be safer for the trustees to allow the relevant dispositions of the will to stand, by releasing or partly releasing their powers, so enabling the beneficiary or beneficiaries concerned to vary those dispositions of their own motion.

4. Should the power not have been exercised before the end of the administration period (which seems unlikely) income arising after that period and before exercise or expiry of the power would be liable to tax at the rate applicable to trusts in the hands of the trustees, although it would carry a correspondingly enlarged tax credit on distribution (see Preliminary Note 4.7).

5. An appointment is necessarily restricted to objects of the power. A variation may be made in favour of anyone.

While these disadvantages must be kept in view, it is of course the case that the existence of a power of appointment in no way precludes a variation by beneficiaries if this would be preferable in the circumstances. In usual cases the existence of the power might perhaps serve to restrain a possibly irresponsible variation, and in such circumstances might recommend itself to the testator on this ground alone.

Since the powers and discretions conferred by this clause will, if exercised, override some or all of the other provisions of the will, these other provisions should be adapted appropriately. The clause disposing of residue or defining the beneficial interests in residue should be introduced by the words 'Subject to the provisions of Clause . . .' (meaning this clause). Should the will include any substantial legacy (as under Clause E3.1) which there is also to be power to override, that clause should be modified similarly. If there were any provision which is not to be overriden, the preamble to this clause should be modified in such a way as to show which of the 'foregoing provisions' are 'subject to the overriding powers and discretions'. However, if this clause is to be used at all, it seems better that it should apply generally and not selectively.

For the reasons explained in Preliminary Note 4.7, it is important to ensure that powers of this kind are not exercisable outside the requirements for an accumulation and maintenance settlement for IHT purposes. It is therefore recommended that this clause should be used only in conjunction with Clause H15.1, which is intended to avoid that possibility. It will be desirable to also include Clause H10.1, as to the sufficiency of receipt for payments by the trustees, and also (as suggested above) Clause H14.1, as to the power of appointment of new trustees.

Clause G1.1 should not be included in a will which also includes Clause E4.1, because they would constitute 'related settlements' within the meaning of IHTA 1984, s.62.

Clause G1.1

I DECLARE that the foregoing provisions of my will are made and the dispositions of my estate herein contained shall have effect only (if at all) subject to the overriding powers and discretions which I hereby confer upon my Trustees but so that all such powers and discretions shall be exercisable only (if at all) with the consent of my [said] [wife] [husband] [and all or any of my children who shall then have attained the age of [eighteen] [   ] years] that is to say:

(1)   During the period of twenty-three months following my death (or so much of that period during which any part of my estate continues to be subject to the trusts and powers of my will) my Trustees shall accumulate the income of my residuary estate (or so much thereof as is not from time to time applied for the maintenance education or benefit of any person pursuant to the provisions of paragraph (2) of this Clause) and shall hold such accumulations by way of addition to the capital of my residuary estate

(2)   During the period aforesaid my Trustees shall have power at any time and from time to time if and whenever they may in their absolute and uncontrolled discretion think fit to pay or apply the whole or any part or parts of the income or of the capital or of the income and the capital of my residuary estate to or for the benefit of all or any one or more exclusively of the others or other of the following persons that is to say my [said] [wife] [husband] and any of my children and any [widow] [widower or] child born during the lifetime of the survivor of myself and my [said] [wife] [husband] of any child of mine who may predecease such survivor

(3)   If any of my Trustees is or may become personally interested as a beneficiary in the exercise of (or omission to exercise) any or all of the powers and discretions hereby conferred upon my Trustees generally he may from time to time join in exercising that power or any such discretion as if he were not so interested and may nevertheless retain for his own use any benefit which in good faith he may derive in consequence thereof as if he were not a trustee

(4)   My Trustees may exercise any or all of the powers and discretions hereby conferred upon them at any time after my death and in particular whether or not probate of my

will has been granted and whether or not the administration of my estate has (subject to any exercise of any of the said powers and discretions) been completed

(5)   Notwithstanding the fiduciary nature of the powers and discretions hereby conferred on my Trustees I further DECLARE that my Trustees may at any time wholly or in part release the same but without prejudice to any payment or application of capital or income previously made by them thereunder

Trustees: powers;
extended and additional powers

Technical drafting

The will draftsman is called upon to accept considerable responsibility for framing the draft in such terms as are best suited to the circumstances. While it goes without saying that the draft must meet with the client's full approval in all respects, there are many aspects of the will-making process as to which the client will depend almost entirely on his professional adviser, and as to which it is therefore essentially the task of the professional adviser to take the initiative.

For the most part the matters in question will be concerned with the way in which the beneficial entitlements are framed, having regard to both personal considerations and also relevant tax considerations. Many such matters are discussed elsewhere in this book, generally in Chapters 1–7, and more specifically in the notes to the various clauses.

Beyond this there are important concerns as to the administrative (and sometimes dispositive) powers which ought in the particular circumstances to be available to the trustees in the interests of good administration of the trusts; there is the related question whether relevant statutory powers may need to be modified or excluded.

The following notes list 15 clause sections which are concerned with the important administrative powers. The notes to these clauses deal with a number of specific points in their context.

Powers of executors and trustees

It is usually considered advisable, except in the very simplest case where the estate is to pass absolutely to a very few individuals, to confer various express powers on the executors and trustees by way of modification of, or addition to, their powers under the general law (see notes to Clause H1.1). The purpose of these express powers is in all cases to facilitate the efficient administration of the estate and any trust which may arise under the will. It is very much the function of the draftsman to suggest their inclusion, and advise as to their effect. The inclusion of these, as of any provision, requires the testator's express approval.

The clauses include provisions for the matters most commonly dealt with in this way, as well as some of less common application. The purpose and effect of each clause is shortly explained in the accompanying notes.

The subject matter of these clauses is as follows:

H1   General words
H2   Power to appropriate without consents
H3   Power to insure without restriction
H4   Power to invest at discretion
H5   Power to acquire and/or improve a residence
H6   Power to advance capital at discretion
H7   Power to apply income for maintenance and to accumulate surplus income during minority
H8   Power to make payments, advances and loans out of capital
H9   Power to disregard statutory and equitable rules as to apportionment of income
H10 Power to accept receipts for payments to or on behalf of minors
H11 Power in relation to companies
H12 Power to act although personally interested; power to purchase trust property
H13 Power to charge for professional services
H14 Power of appointing new or additional trustees
H15 Power of trustees to be exercisable only within requirements for an accumulation and maintenance settlement

H1   General words

'their powers under the general law'

Discussion of the statutory powers of trustees is outside the scope of this book. The principal statutory provisions, to which reference may be made, are the following:

1.   TA 1925, ss.12–19, 20, 22, 24–28, 31–33: general powers of trustees and personal representatives, additional to the powers conferred by the instrument creating the trust, and applicable if a contrary intention is not expressed in and subject to the terms of that instrument (s.69(2)). Sections 19, 31 and 32 are reproduced in Appendix 4.

2.   TA 2000: (with effect from 1 February 2001) intended to remedy various deficiencies in powers otherwise available to trustees (and personal representatives) in earlier legislation. A statutory duty of care is introduced as are provisions dealing with (*inter alia*) powers of investment, delegation, remuneration and insurance. Sections 1–11, 28–33 and 35 are reproduced in Appendix 4.

3.   TOLATA 1996: whereby creation of most new strict settlements under SLA 1925 are prohibited from 1 January 1997, and a non-excludable power to

postpone sale is implied into any express trust for sale of land (TOLATA 1996, s.4(1)). Sections 2, 4, 10–13, 18 and 19 are reproduced in Appendix 4.

Powers derived from these statutes are referred to as necessary in context.

Clause H1.1

My Trustees shall have the following powers in addition to their powers under the general law:

H2   Power to appropriate without consents

The terms of the statutory power of appropriation extended by this clause are found in AEA 1925, s.41, which is reproduced in Appendix 1.

'without . . . any such consents as are referred to in that section'

It is usual to dispense with any consent to the exercise of the statutory power. Originally this was to avoid incurring any liability to *ad valorem* stamp duty, as on a conveyance on sale (in view of *Jopling* v. *IRC* [1940] 2 KB 282). However, conveyance on sale duty has ceased to be chargeable and, providing no consideration is given in return, an appropriation in or towards satisfaction of a general legacy of money is exempt from Stamp Duty Land Tax.

The personal representatives must clearly still have regard to the interests of the beneficiaries, both on general principles and also by virtue of the terms of AEA 1925, s.41(5).

'and even though . . . beneficially interested'

These words are intended to remove any doubt which might possibly arise as to whether an appropriation by a trustee in his own favour might be open to objection (even though made in good faith) as amounting to the purchase of trust property.

Clause H2.1

Power to make any such appropriation as is authorised by section 41 of the Administration of Estates Act 1925 but without being required to obtain any such consents as are referred to in that section [and even though one or more of my Trustees may be beneficially interested in the appropriation]

H3   Power to insure without restriction

The terms of the statutory power to insure, which this clause extends, are found in TA 1925, s.19 (substituted by TA 2000, s.34) which is reproduced in Appendix 4.

'fire or . . . any other insurable risk'

It is considered that trustees should in all cases be enabled to insure on the normal comprehensive terms.

'to any amount'

It is likewise considered that trustees should in all cases be enabled to insure up to the full insurable value, whatever this may be.

Clause H3.1

Power to insure against loss or damage by fire or from any other insurable risk any property for the time being comprised in my residuary estate to any amount and to pay all premiums for any such insurance at their discretion out of the income or capital of my residuary estate and so that any money received under any such insurance shall be applicable at their discretion either in or towards making good the loss or damage in respect of which it was received or otherwise as if it were proceeds of sale of the property insured

H4   Power to invest at discretion

In the absence of express power, trustees have a 'general power of investment' conferred by TA 2000, s.3 which permits them to make investments of any kind, other than in land, as if absolutely entitled to the trust assets (for investments in land see notes to H5.1). In exercising this power trustees are subject to the duty of care introduced by TA 2000, ss.1 and 2, and must exercise it having regard to the general investment criteria (TA 2000, s.4) and the duty to take advice (TA 2000, s.5). TA 2000 does not define 'investment'. Hitherto it has frequently been construed to exclude non-income producing assets (see *Re Wragg* [1919] 2 Ch 5). To permit the purchase of assets such as works of art or non-income producing bonds, trustees are often given additional powers to invest as an absolute owner whether the 'asset is income producing or not'.

An unrestricted power of investment as in this clause is generally thought to authorise the retention of any of the testator's existing investments so long as the trustees act honestly and with ordinary prudence.

It would seem that even this power may not authorise the retention of the testator's assets in a business which the trustees have no power to carry on (*Re Peczenik's Settlement Trusts* [1964] 1 WLR 720), neither would it authorise a loan on merely personal credit (*Re Berry* [1962] Ch 97). In exercising either of the above powers (or any other power of investment not within TA 2000) the trustees remain under the duty under the general law to act honestly and with ordinary prudence. Loans on personal credit are sometimes expressly authorised, envisaging the possibility of loans to beneficiaries. If appropriate to the will under consideration, the power of the trustees to advance capital under Clause H6.1 will suffice. An express power to make loans is incorporated in Clause H8.3 for use in other circumstances.

The power to invest is also commonly further extended to enable the purchase or improvement of a residence (not an investment as such); as in Clause H5.1.

Clause H4.1

Power to invest trust money and to vary and transpose investments from time to time with the same full and unrestricted freedom in their choice of investments [and whether producing income or not] as if my Trustees were a sole absolute beneficial owner

H5   Power to acquire and/or improve a residence

See also Clause D8.1 and notes thereto.

This clause is intended for use where residue is to be held in trust, during the lifetime of a surviving spouse (or perhaps during the minority of children) and complements Clause F3.1, paragraph (2) which provides that an existing house should not be sold without the consent of the spouse, and that the spouse should have the right of occupation pending sale. The following clause enables the trustee to apply capital in buying and improving a replacement. It does not require them to do so.

It is not sufficient to rely on Clause H4.1 (extension of trustees' powers of investment), because the purchase of a house for occupation is not an investment and so it is not thereby authorised.

Normally, this clause will be applicable where the family home belongs absolutely to the testator or where the testator and spouse are beneficial tenants in common. Its use should be considered even where the house will pass to the spouse as survivor under a beneficial joint tenancy as circumstances may change, and the testator may not wish the spouse to be necessarily obliged to repurchase only from her or his own funds. By empowering the trustees to purchase, the testator is in effect enabling them to make additional capital available to the spouse, by freeing capital already in the hands of the spouse for other purposes.

In the absence of express powers of this nature, trustees are authorised to acquire UK freehold or leasehold land as an investment, for occupation by a beneficiary or for any other reason. When exercising such power the trustee is given all the powers of an absolute owner in relation to the land (TA 2000, s.8) thus (unless the will provides otherwise) enabling them to carry out repairs or improvements to it, mortgage or lease it. In exercising the power the trustees are subject to the statutory duty of care (TA 2000, Sched.1, para.2).

Clause H5.1

Power to apply trust money at any time and from time to time in the purchase or in the improvement of any freehold or leasehold dwelling house [within the United Kingdom] [in any part of the world] and to permit any such dwelling house to be used as [her] [his] residence by my [said] [wife] [husband] [and any of my said children] upon such terms and conditions as in their absolute discretion my Trustees may from time to time think fit to require

H6   Power to advance capital at discretion

The terms of the statutory power of advancement which this clause varies are found in the TA 1925, s.32, reproduced in Appendix 4. It may be excluded or modified by virtue of TA 1925, s.69(2).

It will be seen that this clause does not greatly extend the statutory power but it should be sufficient for the purposes of most wills. For wider powers which may be considered for adoption in special circumstances, see Clause H8.1.

It is for consideration whether the power in Clause H6.1 should be limited to one half of the beneficiary's entitlement, as under the statutory power, or whether the amount of any advances should be left wholly within the discretion of the trustees, as is more usual.

It is also for consideration whether the beneficiary advanced should be required to bring the advance into account on final distribution, as is usually stipulated.

For the reasons explained in Preliminary Note 4.7, it is important to ensure that powers of this kind are not exercisable outside the requirement for an accumulation and maintenance settlement for IHT purposes. It is therefore recommended that this clause should be used only in conjunction with Clause H15.1, which is intended to avoid that possibility.

It must of course be accepted that this may preclude an advancement by way of resettlement, unless effected within those requirements. If it should be desired to retain the freedom to exercise the power more widely, accepting the IHT implications (which may adversely affect the entire fund, and not just the property advanced), Clause H15.1 would have to be omitted.

It should also be appreciated that if assets are advanced *in specie* or are realised to provide cash for an advance of cash, this will be a disposal for CGT purposes and any consequential liability to tax will fall on the fund as a whole (though without leading to inequality on final distribution).

Clause H6.1

Power at any time or times to pay or apply any capital money from my residuary estate for the advancement or benefit in such manner as my Trustees may in their absolute discretion think fit of any person or persons presumptively entitled to any share of or interest in the capital of my residuary estate PROVIDED THAT the money so paid or applied for the advancement or benefit of any person shall not exceed altogether in amount [one half of] the presumptive or vested share or interest of that person in my residuary estate AND PROVIDED THAT if that person is or becomes absolutely and indefeasibly entitled to a share in my residuary estate [I leave it within the discretion of my Trustees whether and if so to what extent] the money so paid or applied shall be brought into account as part of such share

H7 Power to apply income for maintenance and to accumulate surplus income during minority

It is usually considered sufficient to rely on the statutory power of maintenance during a minority, conferred on executors and trustees (unless the will shows a contrary intention) by TA 1925, s.31 (reproduced in Appendix 4). This power applies where property is held in trust for a minor for any interest, either vested or contingent but, in the case of a contingent interest, only if the disposition carries the intermediate income of the property. It may be excluded or modified by virtue of s.69(2).

The statutory power is therefore available where minor children become contingently entitled on failure of the spouse to take an absolute interest. It is not available (nor is it required) during the lifetime of a spouse who has a life interest in residue but it would become available on the death of that spouse if any child were then still a minor.

It will be seen that this power is subject to certain qualifications, some or all of which it may sometimes be thought desirable to modify.

This clause provides for any or all of the following modifications to be made:

(a) conferring an absolute discretion on the trustees as to the amount of income applicable;
(b) removing the restriction as to the amount of income applicable, where other funds are available; and
(c) substituting a different age for purposes of TA 1925, s.31(1)(ii).

As to receipts for trustees' payments, see Clause H10.1 and notes thereto.

Clause H7.1

The provisions of section 31 of the Trustee Act 1925 shall apply to this my will and shall be exercisable by my Trustees with the following modifications that is to say as if
[(i) the words 'as my trustees shall in their absolute discretion think fit' were substituted for the words 'as may in all the circumstances be reasonable' in paragraph (i) of subsection (1) thereof] [and]
[(ii) the proviso to subsection (1) thereof had been omitted therefrom] [and]
[(iii) references to attainment of the age of [   ] years were substituted for references to attainment of the age of eighteen years wherever they occur (references to 'infancy' being likewise construed accordingly)]

H8 Power to make payments, advances and loans out of capital

The statutory power of advancement (considered above in relation to Clause H6.1) is necessarily confined to beneficiaries who are or will be entitled, either absolutely or contingently, to a share in the capital of the trust fund, since an advance is in fact an anticipation of that entitlement.

Where the testator's spouse is given an absolute interest, the power of advancement becomes relevant only if the spouse fails to survive and if any of the children who then become entitled should be a minor. If however the spouse is given only a life or other limited interest with no access to any of the capital of the estate, it will often be essential and always prudent for the testator to provide means whereby capital may be made available to the spouse in case of need. This can be done only by conferring a discretion on the trustees. If the testator finds it repugnant that the spouse should be dependent on the trustees in this way, this may be in itself a sufficient reason for giving an absolute and not limited interest.

If a discretion is to be given, it is suggested that this should be framed in wide terms. The following clauses should be readily adaptable.

A discretion in such terms really amounts, in effect, to a power of appointment. It is not however thought that this derogates from the existence of an interest in possession for IHT purposes.

If the power is exercised in favour of the spouse no IHT will be payable because for tax purposes the trust fund is treated as part of the estate of the spouse. If the power is exercised in favour of another beneficiary, there will be a notional transfer of value by the spouse which will be a potentially exempt transfer provided the conditions of IHTA 1984, s.3A are met (in conjunction with s.3(4)). If the power were exercised in favour of the spouse with a view to enabling the spouse to make transfers attracting use of their own lifetime exemptions, this object might not be achieved: if there were any kind of agreement or arrangement, the transactions could be attacked as 'associated operations' (IHTA 1984, s.268).

If payments are actually made to a beneficiary to supplement income, or otherwise with any degree of regularity, such as to become 'annual payments' for purposes of income tax, these will be grossed up and included in the total income of the beneficiary for the purposes of excess liability, even though the payment was actually made out of the capital of the trust (see *Stevenson v. Wishart and others* [1987] 2 All ER 428).

This danger may be avoided if the amounts made available to the spouse or other beneficiary are treated as loans, repayable on death or as may be desired. It should not however be thought that this arrangement saves any IHT, since tax payable on the death of the spouse is computed by reference to (*inter alia*) the combined values of the trust fund and the free estate of the spouse.

As to receipts for trustees' payments, see Clause H10.1 and notes thereto.

For the reasons explained in Preliminary Note 4.7, it is important to ensure that powers of this kind are not exercisable outside the requirements for an accumulation and maintenance settlement for IHT purposes. It is therefore recommended that this clause should be used only in conjunction with Clause H15.1, which is intended to avoid that possibility.

It must be accepted that this may preclude an advancement by way of resettlement, unless effected within those requirements. If it should be desired to retain the freedom to exercise the power more widely, accepting the IHT implications (which may adversely affect the entire fund, and not just the property advanced), Clause H15.1 would have to be omitted.

Clause H8.1

Power at any time and from time to time to pay or apply capital money from my residuary estate [to any extent] [up to a maximum of   ] to my [said] [husband] [wife] or for [his] [her] benefit as my Trustees [other than my said [husband] [wife]] in their absolute discretion may think fit

Clause H8.2

Power at any time and from time to time to advance capital money from my residuary estate to my [said] [husband] [wife] by way of loan [to any extent] [up to a maximum of   ] upon such terms and conditions as my Trustees [other than my said [husband] [wife]] in their absolute discretion may think fit [but so that my Trustees shall not be required [to charge interest to] [nor] [to take any security for repayment from] [nor] [to call for any repayment by] my said [husband] [wife] during [his] [her] lifetime]

Clause H8.3

Power at any time and from time to time [so long as my Trustees are at least two in number or a trust corporation] to raise and apply capital money from my residuary estate [to any extent] [up to a maximum of   ] as my Trustees in their absolute discretion may think fit [for the following purposes or either of them:]

[(i)   for the absolute benefit of my said [husband] [wife] or any person entitled or presumptively entitled to any share of or interest in the capital of my residuary estate [but so that upon the distribution of my residuary estate or any part thereof any capital so paid or applied shall be brought into account by such person]]

[(ii)   by way of loan to my said [husband] [wife] or any person entitled or presumptively entitled to any share of or interest in the capital of my residuary estate upon such conditions as to interest and as to security for repayment and as to the time of repayment and otherwise as my Trustees may think fit [and so that my Trustees shall not be liable for any loss arising from any such loan]]

H9   Power to disregard statutory and equitable rules as to apportionment of income

This clause has the same effect as the traditional and much longer provisions embodied in paragraph 1 of Clause F2.1 and discussed in the notes thereto but with the variation that in Clause H9.1 the operation of the Apportionment Act 1870, as well as the equitable rules, is excluded.

It is thought that this accords with the intention of most testators, to whom it is more natural to regard all receipts in the nature of income accruing after the death as being income available to the life tenant as it would have been to themselves.

Even if the Apportionment Act 1870 were allowed to apply, so that income current at the death would be apportionable as between the estate and the life tenant, amounts so apportioned to the estate are not thereby converted into income of the deceased for income tax purposes (*IRC v Henderson's Executors* (1931) 16

TC 282): for such purpose, payments made after death are wholly income in the hands of the executors.

For these reasons, the Apportionment Act 1870 is usually excluded. However, if the life tenant is likely to be liable to higher rate income tax, exclusion of the Act will increase the income of the life tenant, and may also increase the life tenant's marginal rate of IT. If so, the Act could be allowed to apply, and a legacy given to compensate for the lost income. The amount of such a legacy would be rather a matter of guesswork.

This clause is intended to exclude the Apportionment Act 1870 in all its applications, not only on the death of the testator, or of any life tenant, but also on any change in the presumptive interests of members of a class of contingent beneficiaries, by a person dropping out through failure to attain a vested interest, or by some other person being born (see *Re Joel's Will Trusts* [1967] Ch 14, at 24).

Clause H9.1

All the income from any part of my estate which is actually received after my death [or after the time when any person [becomes or] [ceases to be entitled] [or prospectively entitled] to any beneficial interest in my [residuary] estate] shall be treated as accruing wholly after my death [or after that time as the case may be] without apportionment whatever the period in respect of which it is actually payable to the intent that the Apportionment Act 1870 and the rules of equity relating to apportionments [including those known as the rules in *Howe* v. *Dartmouth* and *Allhusen Whittell* in all their branches] shall for all purposes be wholly excluded in the administration of my estate and of the trusts of this my will

H10   Power to accept receipts for payments to or on behalf of minors

See note 'Minors' to Clause E1.3. The purpose of Clause E1.3 was to enable the executor to deal with a legacy to a minor in the best interests of the minor and with the least possible inconvenience and delay in the administration of the estate.

So far as children are concerned, where a trust arises it may be thought sufficient for the trustees to rely on the statutory powers of maintenance and advancement under TA 1925, ss.31 and 32 respectively (the terms of which are reproduced in Appendix 4). If so, the trustees will have no difficulty in obtaining a good discharge for their payments. Section 31 expressly empowers trustees to pay income to the parent or guardian, if any, 'or otherwise apply' it for maintenance. Section 32 empowers them to 'pay or apply' capital money for a person's advancement or benefit 'in such manner as they may, in their absolute discretion, think fit'.

If it is desired to give the trustee extended powers of *maintenance* (or to alter the age of vesting) and this is done (as in Clause H7.1) by retaining and modifying the provisions of TA 1925, s.31, the provisions of that section as to payment will continue to apply, and will still be adequate.

If it is desired to give extended powers of *advancement,* this could be done in the same way by retaining and modifying TA 1925, s.32, probably by removing proviso (a) in subsection (1). For this Clause H7.1 can be adapted and no separate clause is given. However, the shortcoming of the statutory power is not so much that it is subject to a limit (which may well be thought desirable in itself), as that it does not allow for any provision for payments to a life tenant: s.32 is concerned with advancements, and such a provision is not an advancement. This situation seems to be better dealt with, not by modifying s.32, but by new and express provisions, as in Clause H8.1. Whenever the trustees are given express powers or discretions under which payments may be made for the benefit of minors (as for example under Clauses E4.1, G1.1 and H8.3), express powers as to their discharge for such payments, as in this clause, may be thought desirable and necessary.

If the inclusion of such a power is under consideration with a view only to relieving the trustees of the will from any special responsibility to the beneficiaries in question and, if the interests of those beneficiaries are (apart only from minority) absolute interests, it is for consideration whether this power should be omitted and the trustees left to exercise their statutory power to appoint separate trustees for the minor under AEA 1925, s.42, which is reproduced in Appendix 1.

Clause H10.1

Power in any case where my Trustees have any obligation or discretion under the provisions of my will or under the general law to pay or apply income or capital to or for the benefit of any person who is a minor to discharge that obligation or to exercise that discretion if and whenever they think fit to do so by making payment either to the parent or guardian of the minor or else to the minor personally if of the age of [sixteen]
[   ] years at least and so that their respective receipts shall be a full discharge to my Trustees who shall not be required to see to the application of any income or capital so paid

H11   Power in relation to companies

As to the circumstances in which such powers may be required, see Preliminary Note 4.9 on the family business.

This clause is intended to give a general indication as to the kind of provision which may be required and should be adapted as may be necessary in relation to the particular circumstances.

Although in the absence of any decision on similar wording it is difficult to be certain, it is thought that in most cases the terms of paragraph (1) could safely be left to stand on their own, with only the reservation that by analogy with 'beneficial owner' powers of investment, it would always be expected of trustees acting under such a power that they should act honestly and with ordinary prudence.

Because trustees are otherwise accountable as such for any remuneration received by them as directors if their appointment is procured by virtue of a trust shareholding (see *Re Macadam* [1946] Ch 73; but contrast *Re Gee* [1948] Ch 284). the words in square brackets should be included unless paragraph (2)(i) of the clause is adopted. The wording in that subparagraph is somewhat widened with an excess of caution (see *Re Llewellin's Will Trusts* [1949] Ch 225).

In general the provisions of paragraph (2) should be wide enough to cover most likely requirements. Some draftsmen adopt even more specific and detailed provisions. The risk of possible oversight makes it safer to rely on paragraph (1) alone but, if desired, both can be used in combination.

Clause H11.1

[(1)] In relation to any company of which any shares or securities are for the time being comprised in my residuary estate and any other company which is controlled by any such company my Trustees shall have power (by voting or otherwise) to exercise all rights conferred by the ownership of such shares or securities as fully and freely as if my Trustees were the absolute beneficial owners thereof [and without being liable to account as trustees for any remuneration or benefit obtained by them directly or indirectly in consequence thereof]

[(2)] Further and in particular (and without prejudice to the generality of the foregoing) my Trustees shall have power:

[(i)]   to procure or join in any appointment and to accept any appointment of themselves or any of them or of their nominee or nominees as directors or other officers or employees of the company or of any subsidiary company and to receive and retain for their own advantage any remuneration or other benefit arising or deriving from any such appointment or employment notwithstanding that they are trustees of my will

[(ii)]   to procure or join in any scheme for the reconstruction or amalgamation of the company or of any subsidiary company or in any scheme or modification of rights relating to any such company or its capital or assets in every case with or without a winding up

[(iii)] to subscribe for any shares or securities of the company or of any other company in the exercise of the general powers of investment given by this my will

[(iv)]   to accept any bonus shares or securities issued by the company and in their absolute discretion to determine whether any such shares are income or capital of my residuary estate

[(v)]   to leave the management or conduct of the affairs of the company in the hands of its directors (other than themselves) without themselves being bound or required to intervene in such management or conduct

H12   Power to act although personally interested; power to purchase trust property

It may sometimes be desired to relieve individual trustees from the effects of the general rule of law that a trustee may not profit from his trust. If so, this clause, suitably adapted to the particular circumstances, should be found sufficient for most normal requirements. It should however be used with great caution.

As drafted, the clause may serve either or both of two quite distinct purposes. First, it enables individual trustees to act in some matter in which they might otherwise be precluded from doing because of a separate personal interest. This may be an advantage to the estate (as long as there is at least one other trustee who is disinterested) in that a beneficiary might feel unable to act as a trustee even though it would otherwise have been appropriate for him to do so. Second, it enables such an individual to purchase property from the estate, although this may be to his personal advantage. It would clearly be inequitable (and would also be likely to give rise to a liability to IHT) if the individual concerned were enabled to purchase at an undervalue and any safeguard in the form of a stipulation for purchase at a valuation may give rise to practical difficulties. On the whole, it seems much more sensible to leave such a transaction to be sanctioned by the other beneficiaries. If this is impossible, because of a minority or the possibility of unborn children, it is a matter for serious consideration whether in principle any such transaction should be allowed to take place at all, unless under the safeguard of a public auction. If there are special circumstances, as where the estate includes a business or shareholding or family farm in which some particular beneficiary has a special interest, it is considered that this would be better dealt with by giving an option to purchase or other express provision.

Clause H12.1

Despite any rule of law or equity to the contrary any of my Trustees acting in good faith shall be fully at liberty to enter into any transaction whatsoever concerning the arrangement or disposition of any property for the time being comprised in my [residuary] estate and to exercise any fiduciary power or discretion notwithstanding that he may be in any way personally interested therein [and shall be fully at liberty to purchase any such property for his own account either by private public auction or by private treaty] PROVIDED ALWAYS that in any such case there shall be at least one other of my Trustees [to whom any such personal interest shall first have been disclosed] [and who has no personal interest in the particular transaction] [or purchase] [and PROVIDED FURTHER that in case of a purchase the purchase price shall not be less than the amount of a valuation made for the purpose by a suitably qualified independent valuer]

H13   Power to charge for professional services

If any of the executors and trustees named in the will is a professional person, the power to charge will more usually be embodied in the appointment, as in Clauses B1.1 and B1.3.

If the original appointees are not professional people but it is desired to provide for the possibility that a professional trustee might subsequently be appointed, it may be more convenient to include the power for such a trustee to charge as one of the extended powers conferred on the trustees of the will.

It will be seen that the wording of Clause H13.1 differs from that of Clause B1.1. This has no significance: the choice depends simply on personal preference.

It might be desired in some cases to provide for the possibility that those interested in the estate might wish to appoint a bank or other trust corporation to be a new or additional trustee of the will, as for instance where the testator's appointee dies or otherwise ceases to be available. While provision of this kind is seldom made in practice, it is thought that in appropriate circumstances it might be useful, in case there are minor beneficiaries who are unable to give the necessary consent to the bank's usual terms and conditions, as to charging and otherwise. Clause H13.2 is intended to facilitate such an appointment by giving to those making the appointment a full discretion or, alternatively, requiring consent only from those beneficiaries who are of full age and have vested interests.

In the absence of express entitlement to remuneration by the will, a trustee acting in a professional capacity is entitled to reasonable remuneration out of the trust funds for any services provided all other trustees so agree in writing (TA 2000, s.29(2)). Further (except to the extent the will provides otherwise) such a trustee is entitled to payment in respect of services capable of provision by a lay trustee (TA 2000, s.29(4)); such payment may also be made where, typically, an express clause permits payment of remuneration but (being strictly construed) prevents charging for services a lay trustee could provide (TA 2000, s.28(1), (2)). Taken together these provisions make considerable improvement in the law relating to the ability of a professional trustee to charge for services provided. Nonetheless, as usual, a properly drafted will should continue to provide expressly for the remuneration of all work done by the trustees.

Clause H13.1

Power for any of my Trustees who is a Solicitor [Accountant] or other person engaged in any profession or business to be so employed or act and to charge and be paid all usual professional and other charges for any business transacted or work done by him or his firm in connection with the administration and distribution of my estate or of the trust of my will [whether or not of a professional nature] [whether or not any other person could have done the same personally]

Clause H13.2

Power to make or concur in making any appointment of a trust corporation to be sole trustee or one of the trustees of my will upon such terms and conditions in all respects as may be acceptable to the corporation so appointed [and to every person of full age who has for the time being a vested interest in my residuary estate]

H14   Power of appointing new or additional trustees

The power of appointing a new or additional trustee is normally vested in the continuing trustees or trustee and the personal representative of the last surviving trustee (TA 1925, s.36).

Though it is seldom necessary to do so, it seems desirable that where a life interest arises under a will a surviving wife or husband should always have the direct right to nominate a replacement trustee, even where the wife or husband is already a trustee. This may be of particular value in relation to:

- Clause E4.1 (discretionary trust for spouse and children);
- Clause F3.1 and related clauses (concerned with the family home);
- Clause G1.1 (conferring discretionary powers of variation of the will); and
- Clause H8.1 (concerned with payments from trust capital).

TOLATA 1996 contains provisions whereby, if no person is nominated in the will for appointing new trustees, the beneficiaries of full age and capacity and together absolutely entitled to the trust property can give written directions for the retirement or appointment of a trustee (TOLATA 1996, s.19(1)–(2)). It is always for consideration with the testator whether such a power is desirable given that it is nonetheless only exercisable in the somewhat limited circumstances where the trusts may otherwise be terminated in a situation where *Saunders* v. *Vautier* (1841) 4 Beav 115 would apply. These provisions may, in any event, be excluded if desired (TOLATA 1996, s.21(5)).

Clause H14.1

The power of appointing from time to time a new or additional trustee or trustees of this my will shall be vested in my said [wife] [husband] during [her] [his] life

Clause H14.2

The power given to beneficiaries by section 19 of the Trusts of Land and Appointment of Trustees Act 1996 to direct the appointment and retirement of trustees shall [not] apply to this my will

H15 Powers of trustees to be exercisable only within requirements for an accumulation and maintenance settlement

For the reasons discussed in Preliminary Note 4.7, the danger may arise in some cases that a fund held on trusts which in other respects would have satisfied the requirements for an accumulation and maintenance settlement for IHT purposes, might fail to do so because of the existence of some dispositive power of the trustees which could possibly be exercised outside those requirements. It is thought that the inclusion in the will of this clause should prevent such a possibility.

Use of this clause is therefore recommended in conjunction with any of Clauses F11.1, G1.1, H6.1 or H8.3, or any other express power of advancement or appointment in the will.

As indicated in the notes to those clauses, use of Clause H15.1 would have the effect in some cases of precluding an advancement by way of resettlement. If this result is considered to be undesirable and if the IHT implications are appreciated, this clause would have to be omitted; or else attached only to any other powers to which it might still be relevant.

Clause H15.1

None of the powers and discretions conferred upon or vested in my Trustees (whether by virtue of any of the provisions of this my will or by operation of law) [or so conferred upon or vested in any other person] shall be capable of exercise in any such way as will or may directly or indirectly prevent section 71 of the Inheritance Tax Act 1984 (or any re-enactment or replacement thereof for the time being) from applying or continuing to apply to any property given or held from time to time under the trusts of this my will for the benefit of any of my said [children] [grandchildren] [nephews and nieces] [   ] which is for the time being settled property for the purposes of Inheritance Tax and in which for the time being no interest in possession subsists

I

Conclusion

I1   Testimonium and attestation

Two alternative forms of attestation clause are reproduced here. The second, longer clause has been traditionally used for many years but many draftsmen prefer to use the first short clause which omits nothing of substance. It is generally more convenient to use and is, in particular, easier to memorise for use in case of emergency.

Either form affords equally good prima facie evidence of the due execution of the will in accordance with WA 1837, s.9 (as substituted by AJA 1982, s.17), which is reproduced in Appendix 6 and discussed in Preliminary Note 5.2.

The importance of adopting a sufficient attestation clause is shown by the Non-Contentious Probate Rules 1987, SI 1987/2024, r.12 which is also reproduced in Appendix 6.

The clauses shown here, both of which are in common use, imply that following signature of the will by the testator, both witnesses will have added their signatures, in the presence of the testator and also in one another's presence. This goes beyond the requirements of WA 1837, s.9, but does represent the usual and desirable practice. If the testator and both witnesses have all signed before any of them leaves the room, there should be no risk of non-compliance with the actual requirements of the section. The only possible difficulties in relation to the execution of a will are likely to arise where the testator is elderly, or else is seriously ill or perhaps under partial sedation, as his capacity to make the will and to understand what he and the witnesses are doing in relation to its execution may be open to doubt.

If the will is duly executed and appears on its face to be rational, there is a presumption of law in favour of its validity, but in case any question should arise it is most advisable in such cases to ask the testator's doctor or other medically qualified person to act as a witness. This 'golden if tactless rule' has received strong judicial endorsement in *Kenward* v. *Adams*, *The Times*, 29 November 1975, and in *Re Simpson* (1977) 121 SJ 224. It is perhaps possible that failure to observe it could be held to amount to professional negligence: see Chapter 7. Notes should be taken on the basis of which expert evidence could later be given should this be called for. This precaution is perhaps unnecessary if there is no one who could possibly have any reason to question the will.

As to the formalities of execution, it is equally essential that the testator should have capacity in the sense of being mentally as well as physically 'present'. He must be fully aware of what is being done, both in relation to his own signature (especially where this is made on his behalf) and in relation to the signatures of the witnesses. In particular, it is most important that when the witnesses sign, the testator should be fully capable of seeing them and understanding what they are doing. It is not essential that he should actually see their signatures made, but he must be capable of doing so, and therefore should in fact do so.

Clause I1.1

IN WITNESS whereof I have hereunto set my hand this   day of   20[ ]
SIGNED by the above-named

in our joint presence and then by us in [his] [hers]:

Clause I1.2

SIGNED by the above-named

as and for [his] [her] last will in the presence of us both present together at the same time who at [his] [her] request and in [his] [her] presence and in the presence of each other have hereunto subscribed our names as witnesses:

Codicils

J1　General

A codicil is a document which is duly executed as a testamentary document, and adds to or varies an existing will and/or any previous codicils.

If a will requires amendment, it is better practice to prepare a new will, complete in itself. Where two or more documents have to be read together, there is an increased risk that ambiguities or other difficulties of construction may arise. This is particularly the case where the codicil is prepared hurriedly and without time for proper consideration of its effect, as commonly happens. There is also some risk that a codicil may become separated from the will and lost; to prevent this, it should be endorsed on the will itself, wherever possible.

It is suggested that a will should not normally be amended by a codicil unless there is real urgency or the will is long or complex and the alteration is minor or perfectly simple (involving only the addition of a straightforward gift) or involves the substitution of one straightforward provision or another.

Some examples which may be readily adapted appear in the numbered paragraphs of this clause. If not so adaptable to the particular circumstance, this clause should not be used: a new will should be considered instead.

'In all other respects I confirm my said will'

These words, which are common form, serve to make explicit what is otherwise normally the effect of a codicil. This is to republish the will, and any previous codicils so that these will now take effect and be construed as if actually executed at the date of the present codicil (WA 1837, s.34). This may alter the meaning from what was originally intended, and the terms of the will and any previous codicils must be carefully reconsidered with this in view. In particular, all descriptions of beneficiaries and of the subject matter of specific gifts must be checked to ensure that these still hold good.

Clause J1.1

I   of   DECLARE this to be a [FIRST]
[   ] CODICIL to my WILL dated and made the
                              day of   20[   ]

[[(1)] WHEREAS by my said Will I have appointed [   ] and [   ] to be the
executors and trustees thereof NOW I hereby REVOKE the appointment of the said
[   ] and in [his] [her] place I appoint [   ] to be an
executor and trustee of my said Will jointly with the said [   ]]

[[(2)] I GIVE to [   ] my [   ] in addition to all gifts in [his] [her]
favour contained in my said Will]

[[(3)] I REVOKE the legacy of £   given to [   ] by Clause [   ]
of my said Will [and in substitution for that legacy I GIVE to him [the sum of £   ]
[free of all taxes]]

[[(4)] IN ADDITION to the legacies given by my said Will I GIVE the following further legacies [free of all taxes] namely:]

[[(5)] WHEREAS [   ] one of the residuary legatees named in my
said will has since died NOW I hereby GIVE to [   ] all the share and interest in
my residuary estate which was given in my said Will to the said [   ] [AND
in case the said [   ] shall die in my lifetime then I give the same to
[
                         ] [and   ] [in equal shares]]]

[(6)] [In all other respects I confirm my said Will] IN WITNESS whereof I have hereunto set
my hand this   day of   20[   ]
SIGNED by the above-named

as a [First] [   ] Codicil to [his] [her] Will dated   the
                         day of 20[   ]] [*continue as in Clause* I1.1]

PART III

Appendices

Statutory provisions relating to intestacy

ADMINISTRATION OF ESTATES ACT 1925

* * * * *

s.33 Trust for sale

(1) On the death of a person intestate as to any real or personal estate, that estate shall be held in trust by his personal representatives with the power to sell it.

(2) The personal representatives shall pay out of –

    (a) the ready money of the deceased (so far as not disposed of by his will, if any); and

    (b) any net money arising from disposing of any other part of his estate (after payment of costs),

all such funeral, testamentary and administration expenses, debts and other liabilities as are properly payable thereout having regard to the rules of administration contained in this Part of this Act, and out of the residue of the said money the personal representative shall set aside a fund sufficient to provide for any pecuniary legacies bequeathed by the will (if any) of the deceased.

(3) During the minority of any beneficiary or the subsistence of any life interest and pending the distribution of the whole or any part of the estate of the deceased, the personal representatives may invest the residue of the said money, or so much thereof as may not have been distributed, under the Trustee Act 2000.

(4) The residue of the said money and any investments for the time being representing the same, and any part of the estate of the deceased which remains unsold and is not required for the administration purposes aforesaid, is in this Act referred to as 'the residuary estate of the intestate.'

(5) The income (including net rents and profits of real estate and chattels real after payment of rates, taxes, rent, costs of insurance, repairs and other outgoings properly attributable to income) of so much of the real and personal estate of the deceased as may not be disposed of by his will, if any, or may not be required for the administration purposes aforesaid, may, however such estate is invested, as from the death of the deceased, be treated and applied as income, and for that purpose any necessary apportionment may be made between tenant for life and remainderman.

(6) Nothing in this section affects the rights of any creditor of the deceased or the rights of the Crown in respect of death duties.

(7) Where the deceased leaves a will, this section has effect subject to the provisions contained in the will.

* * * * *

s.41 Powers of personal representative as to appropriation

(1) The personal representative may appropriate any part of the real or personal estate, including things in action, of the deceased in the actual condition or state of investment thereof at the time of appropriation in or towards satisfaction of

any legacy bequeathed by the deceased, or of any other interest or share in his property, whether settled or not, as to the personal representative may seem just and reasonable, according to the respective rights of the persons interested in the property of the deceased:

Provided that –

(i) an appropriation shall not be made under this section so as to affect prejudicially any specific devise or bequest;

(ii) an appropriation of property, whether or not being an investment authorised by law or by the will, if any, of the deceased for the investment of money subject to the trust, shall not (save as hereinafter mentioned) be made under this section except with the following consents:–

   (a) when made for the benefit of a person absolutely and beneficially entitled in possession, the consent of that person;

   (b) when made in respect of any settled legacy share or interest, the consent of either the trustee thereof, if any (not being also the personal representative), or the person who may for the time being be entitled to the income:

If the person whose consent is so required as aforesaid is an infant or is incapable by reason of mental disorder within the meaning of the Mental Health Act 1983, of managing and administering his property and affairs the consent shall be given on his behalf by his parents or parent, testamentary or other guardian or receiver, or if, in the case of an infant, there is no such parent or guardian, by the court on the application of his next friend;

(iii) no consent (save of such trustee as aforesaid) shall be required on behalf of a person who may come into existence after the time of appropriation, or who cannot be found or ascertained at that time;

(iv) if no receiver is acting for a person suffering from mental disorder then, if the appropriation is of an investment authorised by law or by the will, if any, of the deceased for the investment of money subject to the trust, no consent shall be required on behalf of the said person;

(v) if, independently of the personal representative, there is no trustee of a settled legacy share or interest, and no person of full age and capacity entitled to the income thereof, no consent shall be required to an appropriation in respect of such legacy share or interest, provided that the appropriation is of an investment authorised as aforesaid.

(1A) The county court has jurisdiction under proviso (ii) to subsection (1) of this section where the estate in respect of which the application is made does not exceed in amount or value the county court limit.

(2) Any property duly appropriated under the powers conferred by this section shall thereafter be treated as an authorised investment, and may be retained or dealt with accordingly.

(3) For the purposes of such appropriation, the personal representative may ascertain and fix the value of the respective parts of the real and personal estate and the liabilities of the deceased as he may think fit, and shall for that purpose employ a duly qualified valuer in any case where such employment may be necessary; and may make any conveyance (including an assent) which may be requisite for giving effect to the appropriation.

(4) An appropriation made pursuant to this section shall bind all persons interested in the property of the deceased whose consent is not hereby made requisite.

(5) The personal representative shall, in making the appropriation, have regard to the rights of any person who may thereafter come into existence, or who cannot be found or ascertained at the time of appropriation, and of any other person whose consent is not required by this section.

(6) This section does not prejudice any other power of appropriation conferred by law or by the will (if any) of the deceased, and takes effect with any extended powers conferred by the will (if any) of the deceased, and where an appropriation is made under this section, in respect of a settled legacy, share or interest, the property appropriated shall remain subject to all trusts and powers of leasing, disposition, and management or varying investments which would have been applicable thereto or to the legacy, share or interest in respect of which the appropriation is made, if no such appropriation had been made.

(7) If after any real estate has been appropriated in purported exercise of the powers conferred by this section, the person to whom it was conveyed disposes of it or any interest therein, then, in favour of a purchaser, the appropriation shall be deemed to have been made in accordance with the requirements of this section and after all requisite consents, if any, had been given.

(8) In this section, a settled legacy, share or interest includes any legacy, share or interest to which a person is not absolutely entitled in possession at the date of the appropriation, also an annuity, and 'purchaser' means a purchaser for money or money's worth.

(9) This section applies whether the deceased died intestate or not, and whether before or after the commencement of this Act, and extends to property over which a testator exercises a general power of appointment, including the statutory power to dispose of entailed interests, and authorises the setting apart of a fund to answer an annuity by means of the income of that fund or otherwise.

s.42 Power to appoint trustees of infants' property

(1) Where an infant is absolutely entitled under the will or on the intestacy of a person dying before or after the commencement of this Act (in this subsection called 'the deceased') to a devise or legacy, or to the residue of the estate of the deceased, or any share therein, and such devise, legacy, residue or share is not under the will, if any, of the deceased, devised or bequeathed to trustees for the infant, the personal representatives of the deceased may appoint a trust corporation or two or more individuals not exceeding four (whether or not including the personal representatives or one or more of the personal representatives), to be the trustee or trustees of such devise, legacy, residue or share for the infant, and to be trustees of any land devised or any land being or forming part of such residue or share for the purposes of the Settled Land Act 1925, and of the statutory provisions relating to the management of land during a minority, and may execute or do any assurance or thing requisite for vesting such devise, legacy, residue or share in the trustee or trustees so appointed.

On such appointment the personal representatives, as such, shall be discharged from all further liability in respect of such devise, legacy, residue, or share, and the same may be retained in its existing condition or state of investment, or may be converted into money, and such money may be invested in any authorised investment.

(2) Where a personal representative has before the commencement of this Act retained or sold any such devise, legacy, residue or share, and invested the same or the proceeds thereof in any investments in which he was authorised to invest money subject to the trust, then, subject to any order of the court made before such commencement, he shall not be deemed to have incurred any liability on that account, or by reason of not having paid or transferred the money or property into court.

* * * * *

s.46 Succession to real and personal estate on intestacy

(1) The residuary estate of an intestate shall be distributed in the manner or be held on the trusts mentioned in this section, namely:–

   (i) If the intestate leaves a husband or wife, then in accordance with the following Table:

TABLE

If the intestate –	the residuary estate shall be held in trust for the surviving husband or wife absolutely.

(1) leaves –
  (a) no issue, and
  (b) no parent, or brother or sister of the whole blood, or issue of a brother or sister of the whole blood	

(2) leaves issue (whether or not persons mentioned in sub-paragraph (b) above also survive)	the surviving husband or wife shall take the personal chattels absolutely and, in addition, the residuary estate of the intestate (other than the personal chattels) shall stand charged with the payment of a fixed net sum, free of death duties and costs, to the surviving husband or wife with interest thereon from the date of the death at such rate as the Lord Chancellor may specify by order until paid or appropriated, and, subject to providing for that sum and the interest thereon, the residuary estate (other than the personal chattels) shall be held – (a) as to one half upon trust for the surviving husband or wife during his or her life, and, subject to such life interest, on the statutory trusts for the issue of the intestate, and (b) as to the other half, on the statutory trusts for the issue of the intestate.

(3) leaves one or more of the following, that is to say, a parent, a brother or sister of the whole blood, or issue of a brother or sister of the whole blood, but leaves no issue	the surviving husband or wife shall take the personal chattels absolutely and, in addition, the residuary estate of the intestate (other than the personal chattels) shall stand charged with the payment of a fixed net sum, free of death duties and costs, to the surviving husband or wife with interest thereon from the date of the death at such rate as the Lord Chancellor may specify by order until paid or appropriated, and, subject to providing for that sum and the interest thereon, the residuary estate (other than the personal chattels) shall be held –
	
	(a) as to one half in trust for the surviving husband or wife absolutely, and
	
	(b) as to the other half –
	    (i) where the intestate leaves one parent or both parents (whether or not brothers or sisters of the intestate or their issue also survive) in trust for the parent absolutely or, as the case may be, for the two parents in equal shares absolutely
	    (ii) where the intestate leaves no parent, on the statutory trusts for the brothers and sisters of the whole blood of the intestate.

The fixed net sums referred to in paragraphs (2) and (3) of this Table shall be of the amounts provided by or under section 1 of the Family Provision Act 1966

(ii) If the intestate leaves issue but no husband or wife, the residuary estate of the intestate shall be held on the statutory trusts for the issue of the intestate;

(iii) If the intestate leaves no husband or wife and no issue but both parents, then the residuary estate of the intestate shall be held in trust for the father and mother in equal shares absolutely;

(iv) If the intestate leaves no husband or wife and no issue but one parent, then the residuary estate of the intestate shall be held in trust for the surviving father or mother absolutely;

(v) If the intestate leaves no husband or wife and no issue and no parent, then the residuary estate of the intestate shall be held in trust for the following persons living at the death of the intestate, and in the following order and manner, namely:–

First, on the statutory trusts for the brothers and sisters of the whole blood of the intestate; but if no person takes an absolutely vested interest under such trusts; then

Secondly, on the statutory trusts for the brothers and sisters of the half blood of the intestate; but if no person takes an absolutely vested interest under such trusts; then

Thirdly, for the grandparents of the intestate and, if more than one survive the intestate, in equal shares; but if there is no member of this class; then

Fourthly, on the statutory trusts for the uncles and aunts of the intestate (being brothers or sisters of the whole blood of a parent of the intestate); but if no person takes an absolutely vested interest under such trusts; then

Fifthly, on the statutory trusts for the uncles and aunts of the intestate (being brothers or sisters of the half blood of a parent of the intestate).

(vi) In default of any person taking an absolute interest under the foregoing provisions, the residuary estate of the intestate shall belong to the Crown or to the Duchy of Lancaster or to the Duke of Cornwall for the time being, as the case may be, as bona vacantia, and in lieu of any right to escheat.

The Crown or the said Duchy or the said Duke may (without prejudice to the powers reserved by section nine of the Civil List Act 1910, or any other powers), out of the whole or any part of the property devolving on them respectively, provide, in accordance with the existing practice, for dependents, whether kindred or not, of the intestate, and other persons for whom the intestate might reasonably have been expected to make provision.

(1A) The power to make orders under subsection (1) above shall be exercisable by statutory instrument subject to annulment in pursuance of a resolution of either House of Parliament; and any such order may be varied or revoked by a subsequent order made under the power.

(2) A husband and wife shall for all purposes of distribution or division under the foregoing provisions of this section be treated as two persons.

(2A) Where the intestate's husband or wife survived the intestate but died before the end of the period of 28 days beginning with the day on which the intestate died, this section shall have effect as respects the intestate as if the husband or wife had not survived the intestate.

(3) Where the intestate and intestate's husband or wife have died in circumstances rendering it uncertain which of them survived the other and the intestate's husband or wife is by virtue of section one hundred and eighty-four of the Law of Property Act 1925 deemed to have survived the intestate, this section shall, nevertheless, have effect as respects the intestate as if the husband or wife had not survived the intestate.

(4)   The interest payable on the fixed net sum payable to a surviving husband or wife shall be primarily payable out of income.

* * * * *

s.47 Statutory trusts in favour of issue and other classes of relatives of intestate

(1)   Where under this Part of this Act the residuary estate of an intestate, or any part thereof, is directed to be held on the statutory trusts for the issue of the intestate, the same shall be held upon the following trusts, namely:

    (i)   In trust, in equal shares if more than one, for all or any the children or child of the intestate, living at the death of the intestate, who attain the age of [eighteen] years or marry under that age, and for all or any of the issue living at the death of the intestate who attain the age of [eighteen] years or marry under that age of any child of the intestate who predeceases the intestate, such issue to take through all degrees, according to their stocks, in equal shares if more than one, the share which their parent would have taken if living at the death of the intestate, and so that no issue shall take whose parent is living at the death of the intestate and so capable of taking;

    (ii)   The statutory power of advancement, and the statutory provisions which relate to maintenance and accumulation of surplus income, shall apply, but when an infant marries such infant shall be entitled to give valid receipts for the income of the infant's share or interest;

    (iii)   (*Repealed.*)

    (iv)   The personal representatives may permit any infant contingently interested to have the use and enjoyment of any personal chattels in such manner and subject to such conditions (if any) as the personal representatives may consider reasonable, and without being liable to account for any consequential loss.

(2)   If the trusts in favour of the issue of the intestate fail by reason of no child or other issue attaining an absolutely vested interest –

    (a)   the residuary estate of the intestate and the income thereof and all statutory accumulations, if any, of the income thereof, or so much thereof as may not have been paid or applied under any power affecting the same, shall go, devolve and be held under the provisions of this Part of this Act as if the intestate had died without leaving issue living at the death of the intestate;

    (b)   references in this Part of this Act to the intestate 'leaving no issue' shall be construed as 'leaving no issue who attain an absolutely vested interest';

    (c)   references in this Part of this Act to the intestate 'leaving issue' or 'leaving a child or other issue' shall be construed as 'leaving issue who attain an absolutely vested interest'.

(3)   Where under this Part of this Act the residuary estate of an intestate or any part thereof is directed to be held on the statutory trusts for any class of relatives of the intestate, other than issue of the intestate, the same shall be held on trusts corresponding to the statutory trusts for the issue of the intestate (other than the provisions for bringing any money or property into account) as if such trusts (other than as aforesaid) were repeated with the substitution of references to the members or member of that class for references to the children or child of the intestate.

(4)   References in paragraph (i) of subsection (1) of the last foregoing section to the intestate leaving, or not leaving, a member of the class consisting of brothers or sisters of the whole blood of the intestate and issue of brothers or sisters of the whole blood of the intestate shall be construed as references to the intestate leaving, or not leaving, a member of that class who attains an absolutely vested interest.

(5)   (*Repealed.*)

s.47A Right of surviving spouse to have his own life interest redeemed

(1) Where a surviving husband or wife is entitled to a life interest in part of the residuary estate, and so elects, the personal representative shall purchase or redeem the life interest by paying the capital value thereof to the tenant for life, or the persons deriving title under the tenant for life, and the costs of the transaction; and thereupon the residuary estate of the intestate may be dealt with and distributed free from the life interest.

(2) (*Repealed.*)

(3) An election under this section shall only be exercisable if at the time of the election the whole of the said part of the residuary estate consists of property in possession, but, for the purposes of this section, a life interest in property partly in possession and partly not in possession shall be treated as consisting of two separate life interests in those respective parts of the property.

(3A) The capital value shall be reckoned in such manner as the Lord Chancellor may by order direct, and an order under this subsection may include transitional provisions.

(3B) The power to make orders under subsection (3A) above shall be exercisable by statutory instrument subject to annulment in pursuance of a resolution of either House of Parliament; and any such order may be varied or revoked by a subsequent order made under the power.

(4) (*Repealed.*)

(5) An election under this section shall be exercisable only within the period of twelve months from the date on which representation with respect to the estate of the intestate is first taken out:

Provided that if the surviving husband or wife satisfies the court that the limitation to the said period of twelve months will operate unfairly –

(a) in consequence for the representation first taken out being probate of a will subsequently revoked on the ground that the will was invalid, or

(b) in consequence of a question whether a person had an interest in the estate, or as to the nature of an interest in the estate, not having been determined at the time when representation was first taken out, or

(c) in consequence of some other circumstances affecting the administration or distribution of the estate,

the court may extend the said period.

(6) An election under this section shall be exercisable, except where the tenant for life is the sole personal representative, by notifying the personal representative (or, where there are two or more personal representatives of whom one is the tenant for life, all of them except the tenant for life) in writing; and a notification in writing under this subsection shall not be revocable except with the consent of the personal representative.

(7) Where the tenant for life is the sole personal representative an election under this section shall not be effective unless written notice thereof is given to the Senior Registrar of the Family Division of the High Court within the period within which it must be made; and provision may be made by probate rules for keeping a record of such notices and making that record available to the public.

In this subsection the expression 'probate rules' means rules of court made under section 127 of the Supreme Court Act 1981.

(8) An election under this section by a tenant for life who is an infant shall be as valid and binding as it would be if the tenant for life were of age; but the personal representative shall, instead of paying the capital value of the life interest to the tenant for life, deal with it in the same manner as with any other part of the residuary estate to which the tenant for life is absolutely entitled.

(9) In considering for the purposes of the foregoing provisions of this section the question when representation was first taken out, a grant limited to settled land or to trust property shall be left out of account and a grant limited to real estate or to personal

estate shall be left out of account unless a grant limited to the remainder of the estate has previously been made or is made at the same time.

* * * * *

s.55 Definitions
(1) In this Act, unless the context otherwise requires, the following expressions have the meanings hereby assigned to them respectively, that is to say:

* * * * *

(iiiA) 'the County Court limit', in relation to any enactment contained in this Act, means the amount for the time being specified by an Order in Council under section 145 of the County Courts Act 1984 as the county court limit for the purposes of that enactment (or, where no such Order in Council has been made, the corresponding limit specified by Order in Council under section 192 of the County Courts Act 1959);

* * * * *

(x) 'Personal chattels' mean carriages, horses, stable furniture and effects (not used for business purposes), motor cars and accessories (not used for business purposes), garden effects, domestic animals, plate, plated articles, linen, china, glass, books, pictures, prints, furniture, jewellery, articles of household or personal use or ornament, musical and scientific instruments and apparatus, wines, liquors and consumable stores, but do not include any chattels used at the death of the intestate for business purposes nor money or securities for money:

* * * * *

INTESTATES' ESTATES ACT 1952

s.5 Rights of surviving spouse as respects the matrimonial home
The Second Schedule to this Act shall have effect for enabling the surviving husband or wife of a person dying intestate after the commencement of this Act to acquire the matrimonial home.

* * * * *

SCHEDULE 2

RIGHTS OF SURVIVING SPOUSE AS RESPECTS THE MATRIMONIAL HOME

1. (1) Subject to the provisions of this Schedule, where the residuary estate of the intestate comprises an interest in a dwelling-house in which the surviving husband or wife was resident at the time of the intestate's death, the surviving husband or wife may require the personal representative in exercise of the power conferred by section forty-one of the principal Act (and with due regard to the requirements of that section as to valuation) to appropriate the said interest in the dwelling-house in or towards satisfaction of any absolute interest of the surviving husband or wife in the real and personal estate of the intestate.

(2) The right conferred by this paragraph shall not be exercisable where the interest is –

(a) a tenancy which at the date of the death of the intestate was a tenancy which would determine within a period of two years from that date; or

(b) a tenancy which the landlord by notice given after that date could determine within the remainder of that period.

(3) Nothing in subsection (5) of section forty-one of the principal Act (which requires the personal representative, in making an appropriation to any person under that section, to have regard to the rights of others) shall prevent the personal representative from giving effect to the right conferred by this paragraph.

(4) The reference in this paragraph to an absolute interest in the real and personal estate of the intestate includes a reference to the capital value of a life interest which the surviving husband or wife has under this Act elected to have redeemed.

(5) Where part of a building was, at the date of the death of the intestate, occupied as a separate dwelling, that dwelling shall for the purposes of this Schedule be treated as a dwelling-house.

2. Where –

(a) the dwelling-house forms part of a building and an interest in the whole of the building is comprised in the residuary estate; or

(b) the dwelling-house is held with agricultural land and an interest in the agricultural land is comprised in the residuary estate; or

(c) the whole or part of the dwelling-house was at the time of the intestate's death used as a hotel or lodging house; or

(d) a part of the dwelling-house was at the time of the intestate's death used for purposes other than domestic purposes,

the right conferred by paragraph 1 of this Schedule shall not be exercisable unless the court, on being satisfied that the exercise of that right is not likely to diminish the value of assets in the residuary estate (other than the said interest in the dwelling-house) or make them more difficult to dispose of, so orders.

3. (1) The right conferred by paragraph 1 of this Schedule –

(a) shall not be exercisable after the expiration of twelve months from the first taking out of representation with respect to the intestate's estate;

(b) shall not be exercisable after the death of the surviving husband or wife;

(c) shall be exercisable, except where the surviving husband or wife is the sole representative, by notifying the personal representative (or, where there are two or more personal representatives of whom one is the surviving husband or wife, all of them except the surviving husband or wife) in writing.

(2) A notification in writing under paragraph (c) of the foregoing sub-paragraph shall not be revocable except with the consent of the personal representative; but the surviving husband or wife may require the personal representative to have the said interest in the dwelling-house valued in accordance with section forty-one of the principal Act and to inform him or her of the result of that valuation before he or she decides whether to exercise the right.

(3) Subsection (9) of the section forty-seven A added to the principal Act by section two of this Act shall apply for the purposes of the construction of the reference in this paragraph to the first taking out of representation, and the proviso to subsection (5) of that section shall apply for the purpose of enabling the surviving husband or wife to apply for an extension of the period of twelve months mentioned in this paragraph.

4. (1) During the period of twelve months mentioned in paragraph 3 of this Schedule the personal representative shall not without the written consent of the surviving hus-

band or wife sell or otherwise dispose of the said interest in the dwelling-house except in the course of administration owing to want of other assets.

(2) An application to the court under paragraph 2 of this Schedule may be made by the personal representative as well as by the surviving husband or wife, and if, on an application under that paragraph, the court does not order that the right conferred by paragraph 1 of this Schedule shall be exercisable by the surviving husband or wife, the court may authorise the personal representative to dispose of the said interest in the dwelling-house within the said period of twelve months.

(3) Where the court under sub-paragraph (3) of paragraph 3 of this Schedule extends the said period of twelve months, the court may direct that this paragraph shall apply in relation to the extended period as it applied in relation to the original period of twelve months.

(4) This paragraph shall not apply where the surviving husband or wife is the sole personal representative or one of two or more personal representatives.

(5) Nothing in this paragraph shall confer any right on the surviving husband or wife as against a purchaser from the personal representative.

5. (1) Where the surviving husband or wife is one of two or more personal representatives, the rule that a trustee may not be a purchaser of trust property shall not prevent the surviving husband or wife from purchasing out of the estate of the intestate an interest in a dwelling-house in which the surviving husband or wife was resident at the time of the intestate's death.

(2) The power of appropriation under section forty-one of the principal Act shall include power to appropriate an interest in a dwelling-house in which the surviving husband or wife was resident at the time of the intestate's death partly in satisfaction of an interest of the surviving husband or wife in the real and personal estate of the intestate and partly in return for a payment of money by the surviving husband or wife to the personal representative.

6. (1) Where the surviving husband or wife is a person of unsound mind or a defective, a requirement or consent under this Schedule may be made or given on his or her behalf by the committee or receiver, if any, or, where there is no committee or receiver, by the court.

(2) A requirement or consent made or given under this Schedule by a surviving husband or wife who is an infant shall be as valid and binding as it would be if he or she were of age, and, as respects an appropriation in pursuance of paragraph 1 of this Schedule, the provisions of section forty-one of the principal Act as to obtaining the consent of the infant's parent or guardian, or of the court on behalf of the infant, shall not apply.

7. (1) Except where the context otherwise requires, references in this Schedule to a dwelling-house include references to any garden or portion of ground attached to and usually occupied with the dwelling-house or otherwise required for the amenity or convenience of the dwelling-house.

(2) This Schedule shall be construed as one with Part IV of the principal Act.

Statutory provisions relating to family provision

INHERITANCE (PROVISION FOR FAMILY AND DEPENDANTS) ACT 1975

s.1 Application for financial provision from deceased's estate

(1) Where after the commencement of this Act a person dies domiciled in England and Wales and is survived by any of the following persons –

(a) the wife or husband of the deceased;

(b) a former wife or former husband of the deceased who has not remarried;

(ba) any person (not being a person included in paragraph (a) or (b) above) to whom subsection (1A) below applies;

(c) a child of the deceased;

(d) any person (not being a child of the deceased) who, in the case of any marriage to which the deceased was at any time a party, was treated by the deceased as a child of the family in relation to that marriage;

(e) any person (not being a person included in the foregoing paragraphs of this subsection) who immediately before the death of the deceased was being maintained, either wholly or partly, by the deceased;

that person may apply to the court for an order under section 2 of this Act on the ground that the disposition of the deceased's estate effected by his will or the law relating to intestacy, or the combination of his will and that law, is not such as to make reasonable financial provision for the applicant.

(1A) This subsection applies to a person if the deceased died on or after 1st January 1996 and, during the whole of the period of two years ending immediately before the date when the deceased died, the person was living –

(a) in the same household as the deceased, and

(b) as the husband or wife of the deceased.

(2) In this Act 'reasonable financial provision' –

(a) in the case of an application made by virtue of subsection (1)(a) above by the husband or wife of the deceased (except where the marriage with the deceased was the subject of a decree of judicial separation and at the date of death the decree was in force and the separation was continuing), means such financial provision as it would be reasonable in all the circumstances of the case for a husband or wife to receive, whether or not that provision is required for his or her maintenance;

(b) in the case of any other application made by virtue of subsection (1) above, means such financial provision as it would be reasonable in all the circumstances of the case for the applicant to receive for his maintenance.

(3) For the purposes of subsection (1)(e) above, a person shall be treated as being maintained by the deceased, either wholly or partly, as the case may be, if the deceased, otherwise than for full valuable consideration, was making a substantial

contribution in money or money's worth towards the reasonable needs of that person.

s.2 Powers of court to make orders

(1) Subject to the provisions of this Act, where an application is made for an order under this section, the court may, if it is satisfied that the disposition of the deceased's estate effected by his will or the law relating to intestacy, or the combination of his will and that law, is not such as to make reasonable financial provision for the applicant, make any one or more of the following orders –

    (a) an order for the making to the applicant out of the net estate of the deceased of such periodical payments and for such term as may be specified in the order;

    (b) an order for the payment to the applicant out of that estate of a lump sum of such amount as may be so specified;

    (c) an order for the transfer to the applicant out such property comprised in that estate as may be so specified;

    (d) an order for the settlement for the benefit of the applicant of such property comprised in that estate as may be so specified;

    (e) an order for the acquisition out of property comprised in that estate of such property as may be so specified and for the transfer of the property so acquired to the applicant or for the settlement thereof for his benefit;

    (f) an order varying any ante-nuptial or post-nuptial settlement (including such a settlement made by will) made on the parties to a marriage to which the deceased was one of the parties, the variation being for the benefit of the surviving party to that marriage, or any child of that marriage, or any person who was treated by the deceased as a child of the family in relation to that marriage.

(2) An order under subsection (1)(a) above providing for the making out of the net estate of the deceased of periodical payments may provide for –

    (a) payments of such amount as may be specified in the order,

    (b) payments equal to the whole of the income of the net estate or of such portion thereof as may be so specified,

    (c) payments equal to the whole of the income of such part of the net estate as the court may direct to be set aside or appropriated for the making out of the income thereof of payments under this section,

or may provide for the amount of the payments or any of them to be determined in any other way the court thinks fit.

(3) Where an order under section (1)(a) above provides for the making of payments of an amount specified in the order, the order may direct that such part of the net estate as may be so specified shall be set aside or appropriated for the making out of the income thereof of those payments; but no larger part of the net estate shall be so set aside or appropriated than is sufficient, at the date or the order, to produce by the income thereof the amount required for the making of those payments.

(4) An order under this section may contain such consequential and supplemental provisions as the court thinks necessary or expedient for the purpose of giving effect to the order or for the purpose of securing that the order operates fairly as between one beneficiary of the estate of the deceased and another and may, in particular, but without prejudice to the generality of this subsection –

    (a) order any person who holds any property which forms part of the net estate of the deceased to make such payment or transfer such property as may be specified in the order;

    (b) vary the disposition of the deceased's estate effected by the will or the law relating to intestacy, or by both the will and the law relating to intestacy, in such manner as the court thinks fair and reasonable having regard to the provisions of the order and all the circumstances of the case;

(c)   confer on the trustees of any property which is the subject of an order under this section such powers as appear to the court to be necessary or expedient.

s.3 Matters to which court is to have regard in exercising powers under s.2

(1)   Where an application is made for an order under section 2 of this Act, the court shall, in determining whether the disposition of the deceased's estate effected by his will or the law relating to intestacy, or the combination of his will and that law, is such as to make reasonable financial provision for the applicant and, if the court considers that reasonable financial provision has not been made, in determining whether and in what manner it shall exercise its powers under that section, have regard to the following matters, that is to say –

(a)   the financial resources and financial needs which the applicant has or is likely to have in the foreseeable future;

(b)   the financial resources and financial needs which any other applicant for an order under section 2 of this Act has or is likely to have in the foreseeable future;

(c)   the financial resources and financial needs which any beneficiary of the estate of the deceased has or is likely to have in the foreseeable future;

(d)   any obligations and responsibilities which the deceased had towards any applicant for an order under the said section 2 or towards any beneficiary of the estate of the deceased;

(e)   the size and nature of the net estate of the deceased;

(f)   any physical or mental disability of any applicant for an order under the said section 2 or any beneficiary of the estate of the deceased;

(g)   any other matter, including the conduct of the applicant or any other person, which in the circumstances of the case the court may consider relevant.

(2)   Without prejudice to the generality of paragraph (g) of subsection (1) above, where an application for an order under section 2 of this Act is made by virtue of section 1(1)(a) or 1(1)(b) of this Act, the court shall, in addition to the matters specifically mentioned in paragraphs (a) to (f) of that subsection, have regard to –

(a)   the age of the applicant and the duration of the marriage;

(b)   the contribution made by the applicant to the welfare of the family of the deceased, including any contribution made by looking after the home or caring for the family;

and in the case of an application by the wife or husband of the deceased, the court shall also, unless at the date of death a decree of judicial separation was in force and the separation was continuing, have regard to the provision which the applicant might reasonably have expected to receive if on the day on which the deceased died the marriage, instead of being terminated by death, had been terminated by a decree of divorce.

(2A) Without prejudice to the generality of paragraph (g) of subsection (1) above, where an application for an order under section 2 of this Act is made by virtue of section 1(1)(ba) of this Act, the court shall, in addition to the matters specifically mentioned in paragraphs (a) to (f) of that subsection, have regard to –

(a)   the age of the applicant and the length of the period during which the applicant lived as the husband or wife of the deceased and in the same household as the deceased;

(b)   the contribution made by the applicant to the welfare of the family of the deceased, including any contribution made by looking after the home or caring for the family.

(3)   Without prejudice to the generality of paragraph (g) of subsection (1) above, where an application for an order under section 2 of this Act is made by virtue of section

1(1)(c) or 1(1)(d) of this Act, the court shall, in addition to the matters specifically mentioned in paragraphs (a) to (f) of that subsection, have regard to the manner in which the applicant was being or in which he might expect to be educated or trained, and where the application is made by virtue of section 1(1)(d) the court shall also have regard –

(a) to whether the deceased had assumed any responsibility for the applicant's maintenance and, if so, to the extent to which and the basis upon which the deceased assumed that responsibility and to the length of time for which the deceased discharged that responsibility;

(b) to whether in assuming and discharging that responsibility the deceased did so knowing that the applicant was not his own child;

(c) to the liability of any other person to maintain the applicant.

(4) Without prejudice to the generality of paragraph (g) of subsection (1) above, where an application for an order under section 2 of this Act is made by virtue of section 1(1)(e) of this Act, the court shall, in addition to the matters specifically mentioned in paragraphs (a) to (f) of that subsection, have regard to the extent to which and the basis upon which the deceased assumed responsibility for the maintenance of the applicant, and to the length of time for which the deceased discharged that responsibility.

(5) In considering the matters to which the court is required to have regard under this section, the court shall take into account the facts as known to the court at the date of the hearing.

(6) In considering the financial resources of any person for the purposes of this section the court shall take into account his earning capacity and in considering the financial needs of any person for the purposes of this section the court shall take into account his financial obligations and responsibilities.

s.4 Time-limit for applications

An application for an order under section 2 of this Act shall not, except with the permission of the court, be made after the end of the period of six months from the date on which representation with respect to the estate of the deceased is first taken out.

s.5 Interim orders

(1) Where on an application for an order under section 2 of this Act it appears to the court –

(a) that the applicant is in immediate need of financial assistance, but it is not yet possible to determine what order (if any) should be made under that section; and

(b) that property forming part of the net estate of the deceased is or can be made available to meet the need of the applicant;

the court may order that, subject to such conditions or restrictions, if any, as the court may impose and to any further order of the court, there shall be paid to the applicant out of the net estate of the deceased such sum or sums and (if more than one) at such intervals as the court thinks reasonable; and the court may order that, subject to the provisions of this Act, such payments are to be made until such date as the court may specify, not being later than the date on which the court either makes an order under the said section 2 or decides not to exercise its powers under that section.

(2) Subsections (2), (3) and (4) of section 2 of this Act shall apply in relation to an order under this section as they apply in relation to an order under that section.

(3) In determining what order, if any, should be made under this section the court shall, so far as the urgency of the case admits, have regard to the same matters as those to which the court is required to have regard under section 3 of this Act.

(4) An order made under section 2 of this Act may provide that any sum paid to the applicant by virtue of this section shall be treated to such an extent and in such manner as may be provided by that order as having been paid on account of any payment provided for by that order.

s.6 Variation, discharge, etc of orders for periodical payments

(1) Subject to the provisions of this Act, where the court has made an order under section 2(1)(a) of this Act (in this section referred to as 'the original order') for the making of periodical payments to any person (in this section referred to as 'the original recipient'), the court, on an application under this section, shall have power by order to vary or discharge the original order or to suspend any provision of it temporarily and to revive the operation of any provision so suspended.

(2) Without prejudice to the generality of subsection (1) above, an order made on an application for the variation of the original order may –

   (a) provide for the making out of any relevant property of such periodical payments and for such term as may be specified in the order to any person who has applied, or would but for section 4 of this Act be entitled to apply, for an order under section 2 of this Act (whether or not, in the case of any application, an order was made in favour of the applicant);

   (b) provide for payment out of any relevant property of a lump sum of such amount as may be so specified to the original recipient or to any such person as is mentioned in paragraph (a) above;

   (c) provide for the transfer of the relevant property, or such part thereof as may be so specified, to the original recipient or to any such person as is so mentioned.

(3) Where the original order provides that any periodical payments payable thereunder to the original recipient are to cease on the occurrence of an event specified in the order (other than the remarriage of a former wife or former husband) or on the expiration of a period so specified, then, if, before the end of the period of six months from the date of the occurrence of that event or of the expiration of that period, an application is made for an order under this section, the court shall have power to make any order which it would have had power to make if the application had been made before the date (whether in favour of the original recipient or any such person as is mentioned in subsection (2)(a) above and whether having effect from that date or from such later date as the court may specify).

(4) Any reference in this section to the original order shall include a reference to an order made under this section and any reference in this section to the original recipient shall include a reference to any person to whom periodical payments are required to be made by virtue of an order under this section.

(5) An application under this section may be made by any of the following persons, that is to say –

   (a) any person who by virtue of section 1(1) of this Act has applied, or would but for section 4 of this Act be entitled to apply, for an order under section 2 of this Act,

   (b) the personal representatives of the deceased,

   (c) the trustees of any relevant property, and

   (d) any beneficiary of the estate of the deceased.

(6) An order under this section may only affect –

   (a) property the income of which is at the date of the order applicable wholly or in part for the making of periodical payments to any person who has applied for an order under this Act, or

   (b) in the case of an application under subsection (3) above in respect of payments which have ceased to be payable on the occurrence of an event or the expiration of a period, property the income of which was so applicable immediately before the occurrence of that event or the expiration of that period, as the case may be,

and any such property as is mentioned in paragraph (a) or (b) above is in subsections (2) and (5) above referred to as 'relevant property'.

(7) In exercising the powers conferred by this section the court shall have regard to all the circumstances of the case, including any change in any of the matters to which the court was required to have regard when making the order to which the application relates.

(8) Where the court makes an order under this section, it may give such consequential directions as it thinks necessary or expedient having regard to the provisions of the order.

(9) No such order as is mentioned in section 2(1)(d), (e) or (f), 9, 10 or 11 of this Act shall be made on an application under this section.

(10) For the avoidance of doubt it is hereby declared that, in relation to an order which provides for the making of periodical payments which are to cease on the occurrence of an event specified in the order (other than the remarriage of a former wife or former husband) or on the expiration of a period so specified, the power to vary an order includes power to provide for the making of periodical payments after the expiration of that period or the occurrence of that event.

s.7 Payment of lump sums by instalments

(1) An order under section 2(1)(b) or 6(2)(b) of this Act for the payment of a lump sum may provide for the payment of that sum by instalments of such amount as may be specified in the order.

(2) Where an order is made by virtue of subsection (1) above, the court shall have power, on an application made by the person to whom the lump sum is payable, by the personal representatives of the deceased or by the trustees of the property out of which the lump sum is payable, to vary that order by varying the number of instalments payable, the amount of any instalment and the date on which any instalment becomes payable.

Property available for financial provision

s.8 Property treated as part of 'net estate'

(1) Where a deceased person has in accordance with the provisions of any enactment nominated any person to receive any sum of money or other property on his death and that nomination is in force at the time of his death, that sum of money, after deducting therefrom any inheritance tax payable in respect thereof, or that other property, to the extent of the value thereof at the date of the death of the deceased after deducting therefrom any inheritance tax so payable, shall be treated for the purposes of this Act as part of the net estate of the deceased; but this subsection shall not render any person liable for having paid that sum or transferred that other property to the person named in the nomination in accordance with the directions given in the nomination.

(2) Where any sum of money or other property is received by any person as a donatio mortis causa made by a deceased person, that sum of money, after deducting therefrom any inheritance tax payable thereon, or that other property, to the extent of the value thereof at the date of the death of the deceased after deducting therefrom any inheritance tax so payable, shall be treated for the purposes of this Act as part of the net estate of the deceased; but this subsection shall not render any person liable for having paid that sum or transferred that other property in order to give effect to that donatio mortis causa.

(3) The amount of inheritance tax to be deducted for the purposes of this section shall not exceed the amount of that tax which has been borne by the person nominated by

the deceased or, as the case may be, the person who has received a sum of money or other property as a donatio mortis causa.

s.9 Property held on a joint tenancy

(1) Where a deceased person was immediately before his death beneficially entitled to a joint tenancy of any property, then, if, before the end of the period of six months from the date on which representation with respect to the estate of the deceased was first taken out, an application is made for an order under section 2 of this Act, the court for the purpose of facilitating the making of financial provision for the applicant under this Act may order that the deceased's severable share of that property, at the value thereof immediately before his death, shall, to such extent as appears to the court to be just in all the circumstances of the case, be treated for the purposes of this Act as part of the net estate of the deceased.

(2) In determining the extent to which any severable share is to be treated as part of the net estate of the deceased by virtue of an order under subsection (1) above, the court shall have regard to any inheritance tax payable in respect of that severable share.

(3) Where an order is made under subsection (1) above, the provisions of this section shall not render any person liable for anything done by him before the order was made.

(4) For the avoidance of doubt it is hereby declared that for the purposes of this section there may be a joint tenancy of a chose in action.

Powers of court in relation to transactions intended to defeat applications for financial provision

s.10 Dispositions intended to defeat applications for financial provision

(1) Where an application is made to the court for an order under section 2 of the Act, the applicant may, in the proceedings on that application, apply to the court for an order under subsection (2) below.

(2) Where on an application under subsection (1) above the court is satisfied –

   (a) that, less than six years before the date of the death of the deceased, the deceased with the intention of defeating an application for financial provision under this Act made a disposition, and

   (b) that full valuable consideration for that disposition was not given by the person to whom or for the benefit of whom the disposition was made (in this section referred to as 'the donee') or by any other person, and

   (c) that the exercise of the powers conferred by this section would facilitate the making of financial provision for the applicant under this Act,

then, subject to the provisions of this section and of sections 12 and 13 of this Act, the court may order the donee (whether or not at the date of the order he holds any interest in the property disposed of to him or for his benefit by the deceased) to provide, for the purpose of the making of that financial provision, such sum of money or other property as may be specified in the order.

(3) Where an order is made under subsection (2) above as respects any disposition made by the deceased which consisted of the payment of money to or for the benefit of the the donee, the amount of any sum of money or the value of any property ordered to be provided under that subsection shall not exceed the amount of the payment made by the deceased after deducting therefrom any inheritance tax borne by the donee in respect of that payment.

(4) Where an order is made under subsection (2) above as respects any disposition made by the deceased which consisted of the transfer of property (other than a sum of money) to or for the benefit of the donee, the amount of any sum of money or the value of any property ordered to be provided under that subsection shall not exceed the value at the date of the death of the deceased of the property disposed of by him

to or for the benefit of the donee (or if that property has been disposed of by the person to whom it was transferred by the deceased, the value at the date of that disposal thereof) after deducting therefrom any inheritance tax borne by the donee in respect of the transfer of that property by the deceased.

(5) Where an application (in this subsection referred to as 'the original application') is made for an order under subsection (2) above in relation to any disposition, then, if on an application under this subsection by the donee or by any applicant for an order under section 2 of this Act the court is satisfied –

(a) that, less than six years before the date of the death of the deceased, the deceased with the intention of defeating an application for financial provision under this Act made a disposition other than the disposition which is the subject of the original application, and

(b) that full valuable consideration for that other disposition was not given by the person to whom or for the benefit of whom that other disposition was made or by any other person,

the court may exercise in relation to the person to whom or for the benefit of whom that other disposition was made the powers which the court would have had under subsection (2) above if the original application had been made in respect of that other disposition and the court had been satisfied as to the matters set out in paragraphs (a), (b) and (c) of that subsection; and where any application is made under this subsection, any reference in this section (except in subsection (2)(b)) to the donee shall include a reference to the person to whom or for the benefit of whom that other disposition was made.

(6) In determining whether and in what manner to exercise its powers under this section, the court shall have regard to the circumstances in which any disposition was made and any valuable consideration which was given therefor, the relationship, if any, of the donee to the deceased, the conduct and financial resources of the donee and all the other circumstances of the case.

(7) In this section 'disposition' does not include –

(a) any provision in a will, any such nomination as is mentioned in section 8(1) of this Act or any donatio mortis causa, or

(b) any appointment of property made, otherwise than by will, in the exercise of a special power of appointment,

but, subject to these exceptions, includes any payment of money (including the payment of a premium under a policy of assurance) and any conveyance, assurance, appointment or gift of property of any description, whether made by an instrument or otherwise.

(8) The provisions of this section do not apply to any disposition made before the commencement of this Act.

s.11 Contracts to leave property by will

(1) Where an application is made to a court for an order under section 2 of this Act, the applicant may, in the proceedings on that application, apply to the court for an order under this section.

(2) Where on an application under subsection (1) above the court is satisfied –

(a) that the deceased made a contract by which he agreed to leave by his will a sum of money or other property to any person or by which he agreed that a sum of money or other property would be paid or transferred to any person out of his estate, and

(b) that the deceased made that contract with the intention of defeating an application for financial provision under this Act, and

(c) that when the contract was made full valuable consideration for that contract was not given or promised by the person with whom or for the benefit of whom the contract was made (in this section referred to as 'the donee') or by any other person, and

(d) that the exercise of the powers conferred by this section would facilitate the making of financial provision for the applicant under this Act,

then, subject to the provisions of this section and of sections 12 and 13 of this Act, the court may make any one or more of the following orders, that is to say –

(i) if any money has been paid or any other property has been transferred to or for the benefit of the donee in accordance with the contract, an order directing the donee to provide, for the purpose of the making of that financial provision, such sum of money or other property as may be specified in the order;

(ii) if the money or all the money has not been paid or the property or all the property has not been transferred in accordance with the contract, an order directing the personal representatives not to make any payment or transfer any property, or not to make any further payment or transfer any further property, as the case may be, in accordance therewith or directing the personal representatives only to make such payment or transfer such property as may be specified in the order.

(3) Notwithstanding anything in subsection (2) above, the court may exercise its powers thereunder in relation to any contract made by the deceased only to the extent that the court considers that the amount of any sum of money paid or to be paid or the value of any property transferred or to be transferred in accordance with the contract exceeds the value of any valuable consideration given or to be given for that contract, and for this purpose the court shall have regard to the value of property at the date of the hearing.

(4) In determining whether and in what manner to exercise its powers under this section, the court shall have regard to the circumstances in which the contract was made, the relationship, if any, of the donee to the deceased, the conduct and financial resources of the donee and all the other circumstances of the case.

(5) Where an order has been made under subsection (2) above in relation to any contract, the rights of any person to enforce that contract or to recover damages or to obtain other relief for the breach thereof shall be subject to any adjustment made by the court under section 12(3) of this Act and shall survive to such extent only as is consistent with giving effect to the terms of that order.

(6) The provisions of this section do not apply to a contract made before the commencement of this Act.

s.12 Provisions supplementary to ss.10 and 11

(1) Where the exercise of any of the powers conferred by section 10 or 11 of this Act is conditional on the court being satisfied that a disposition or contract was made by a deceased person with the intention of defeating an application for financial provision under this Act, that condition shall be fulfilled if the court is of the opinion that, on a balance or probabilities, the intention of the deceased (though not necessarily his sole intention) in making the disposition or contract was to prevent an order for financial provision being made under this Act or to reduce the amount of the provision which might otherwise be granted by an order thereunder.

(2) Where an application is made under section 11 of this Act with respect to any contract made by the deceased and no valuable consideration was given or promised by any person for that contract then, notwithstanding anything in subsection (1) above, it shall be presumed, unless the contrary is shown, that the deceased made that contract with the intention of defeating an application for financial provision under this Act.

(3) Where the court makes an order under section 10 or 11 of this Act it may give such consequential directions as it thinks fit (including directions requiring the making of any payment or the transfer of any property) for giving effect to the order or for securing a fair adjustment of the rights of the persons affected thereby.

(4) Any power conferred on the court by the said section 10 or 11 to order the donee, in

relation to any disposition or contract, to provide any sum of money or other property shall be exercisable in like manner in relation to the personal representative of the donee, and –

(a) any reference in section 10(4) to the disposal of property by the donee shall include a reference to disposal by the personal representative of the donee, and
(b) any reference in section 10(5) to an application by the donee under that subsection shall include a reference to an application by the personal representative of the donee;

but the court shall not have power under the said section 10 or 11 to make an order in respect of any property forming part of the estate of the donee which has been distributed by the personal representative; and the personal representative shall not be liable for having distributed any such property before he has notice of the making of an application under the said section 10 or 11 on the ground that he ought to have taken into account the possibility that such an application would be made.

s.13 Provisions as to trustees in relation to ss.10 and 11

(1) Where an application is made for –

(a) an order under section 10 of this Act in respect of a disposition made by the deceased to any person as a trustee, or
(b) an order under section 11 of this Act in respect of any payment made or property transferred, in accordance with a contract made by the deceased, to any person as a trustee,

the powers of the court under the said section 10 or 11 to order that trustee to provide a sum of money or other property shall be subject to the following limitation (in addition, in a case of an application under section 10, to any provision regarding the deduction of inheritance tax) namely, that the amount of any sum of money or the value of any property ordered to be provided –

(i)   in the case of an application in respect of a disposition which consisted of the payment of money or an application in respect of the payment of money in accordance with a contract, shall not exceed the aggregate of so much of that money as is at the date of the order in the hands of the trustee and the value at that date of any property which represents that money or is derived therefrom and is at that date in the hands of the trustee;
(ii) in the case of an application in respect of a disposition which consisted of the transfer of property (other than a sum of money) or an application in respect of the transfer of property (other than a sum of money) in accordance with a contract, shall not exceed the aggregate of the value at the date of the order of so much of that property as is at that date in the hands of the trustee and the value at that date of any property which represents the first mentioned property or is derived therefrom and is at that date in the hands of the trustee.

(2) Where any such application is made in respect of a disposition made to any person as a trustee or in respect of any payment made or property transferred in pursuance of a contract to any person as a trustee, the trustee shall not be liable for having distributed any money or other property on the ground that he ought to have taken into account the possibility that such an application would be made.

(3) Where any such application is made in respect of a disposition made to any person as a trustee or in respect of any payment made or property transferred in accordance with a contract to any person as a trustee, any reference in the said section 10 or 11 to the donee shall be construed as including a reference to the trustee or trustees for

the time being of the trust in question and any reference in subsection (1) or (2) above to a trustee shall be construed in the same way.

Special provisions relating to cases of divorce, separation, etc

s.14 Provision as to cases where no financial relief was granted in divorce proceedings, etc

(1) Where, within twelve months from the date on which a decree of divorce or nullity of marriage has been made absolute or a decree of judicial separation has been granted, a party to the marriage dies and –

    (a) an application for a financial provision order under section 23 of the Matrimonial Causes Act 1973 or a property adjustment order under section 24 of that Act has not been made by the other party to that marriage, or

    (b) such an application has been made but the proceedings thereon have not been determined at the time of the death of the deceased,

then, if an application for an order under section 2 of this Act is made by that other party, the court shall, notwithstanding anything in section 1 or section 3 of this Act, have power, if it thinks it just to do so, to treat that party for the purposes of that application as if the decree of divorce or nullity of marriage had not been made absolute or the decree of judicial separation had not been granted, as the case may be.

(2) This section shall not apply in relation to a decree of judicial separation unless at the date of the death of the deceased the decree was in force and the separation was continuing.

s.15 Restriction imposed in divorce proceedings, etc on application under this Act

(1) On the grant of a decree of divorce, a decree of nullity of marriage or a decree of judicial separation or at any time thereafter the court, if it considers it just to do so, may, on the application of either party to the marriage, order that the other party to the marriage shall not on the death of the applicant be entitled to apply for an order under section 2 of this Act.

    In this subsection 'the court' means the High Court or, where a county court has jurisdiction by virtue of Part V of the Matrimonial and Family Proceedings Act 1984, a county court.

(2) In the case of a decree of divorce or nullity of marriage an order may be made under subsection (1) above before or after the decree is made absolute, but if it is made before the decree is made absolute it shall not take effect unless the decree is made absolute.

(3) Where an order made under subsection (1) above on the grant of a decree of divorce or nullity of marriage has come into force with respect to a party to a marriage, then, on the death of the other party to that marriage, the court shall not entertain any application for an order under section 2 of this Act made by the first-mentioned party.

(4) Where an order made under subsection (1) above on the grant of a decree of judicial separation has come into force with respect to any party to a marriage, then, if the other party to that marriage dies while the decree is in force and the separation is continuing, the court shall not entertain any application for an order under section 2 of this Act made by the first-mentioned party.

s.15A Restriction imposed in proceedings under Matrimonial and Family Proceedings Act 1984 on application under this Act

(1) On making an order under section 17 of the Matrimonial and Family Proceedings Act 1984 (orders for financial provision and property adjustment following overseas divorces, etc) the court, if it considers it just to do so, may, on the application of either party to the marriage, order that the other party to the marriage shall not on the death of the applicant be entitled to apply for an order under section 2 of this Act.

In this subsection 'the court' means the High Court or, where a county court has jurisdiction by virtue of Part V of the Matrimonial and Family Proceedings Act 1984, a county court.

(2) Where an order under subsection (1) above has been made with respect to a party to a marriage which has been dissolved or annulled, then, on the death of the other party to that marriage, the court shall not entertain an application under section 2 of this Act made by the first-mentioned party.

(3) Where an order under subsection (1) above has been made with respect to a party to a marriage the parties to which have been legally separated, then, if the other party to the marriage dies while the legal separation is in force, the court shall not entertain an application under section 2 of this Act made by the first-mentioned party.

s.16 Variation and discharge of secured periodical payments orders made under Matrimonial Causes Act 1973

(1) Where an application for an order under section 2 of this Act is made to the court by any person who was at the time of the death of the deceased entitled to payments from the deceased under a secured periodical payments order made under the Matrimonial Causes Act 1973, then, in the proceedings on that application, the court shall have power, if an application is made under this section by that person or by the personal representative of the deceased, to vary or discharge that periodical payments order or to revive the operation of any provision thereof which has been suspended under section 31 of that Act.

(2) In exercising the powers conferred by this section the court shall have regard to all the circumstances of the case, including any order which the court proposes to make under section 2 or section 5 of this Act and any change (whether resulting from the death of the deceased or otherwise) in any of the matters to which the court was required to have regard when making the secured periodical payments order.

(3) The powers exercisable by the court under this section in relation to an order shall be exercisable also in relation to any instrument executed in pursuance of the order.

s.17 Variation and revocation of maintenance agreements

(1) Where an application for an order under section 2 of this Act is made to the court by any person who was at the time of the death of the deceased entitled to payments from the deceased under a maintenance agreement which provided for the continuation of payments under the agreement after the death of the deceased, then, in the proceedings on that application, the court shall have power, if an application is made under this section by that person or by the personal representative of the deceased, to vary or revoke that agreement.

(2) In exercising the powers conferred by this section the court shall have regard to all the circumstances of the case, including any order which the court proposes to make under section 2 or section 5 of this Act and any change (whether resulting from the death of the deceased or otherwise) in any of the circumstances in the light of which the agreement was made.

(3) If a maintenance agreement is varied by the court under this section the like consequences shall ensue as if the variation had been made immediately before the death of the deceased by agreement between the parties and for valuable consideration.

(4) In this section 'maintenance agreement', in relation to a deceased person, means any agreement made, whether in writing or not and whether before or after the commencement of this Act, by the deceased with any person with whom he entered into a marriage, being an agreement which contained provisions governing the rights and liabilities towards one another when living separately of the parties to that marriage (whether or not the marriage has been dissolved or annulled) in respect of the making or securing of payments or the disposition or use of any property, including such rights and liabilities with respect to the maintenance or education of any child,

whether or not a child of the deceased or a person who was treated by the deceased as a child of the family in relation to that marriage.

s.18 Availability of court's powers under this Act in applications under ss.31 and 36 of the Matrimonial Causes Act 1973

(1) Where –

(a) a person against whom a secured periodical payment order was made under the Matrimonial Causes Act 1973 has died and an application is made under section 31(6) of that Act for the variation or discharge of that order or for the revival of the operation of any provision thereof which has been suspended, or

(b) a party to a maintenance agreement within the meaning of section 34 of that Act has died, the agreement being one which provides for the continuation of payments thereunder after the death of one of the parties, and an application is made under section 36(1) of that Act for the alteration of the agreement under section 35 thereof,

the court shall have power to direct that the application made under the said section 31(6) or 36(1) shall be deemed to have been accompanied by an application for an order under section 2 of this Act.

(2) Where the court gives a direction under subsection (1) above it shall have power, in the proceedings on the application under the said section 31(6) or 36(1), to make any order which the court would have had power to make under the provisions of this Act if the application under the said section 31(6) or 36(1), as the case may be, had been made jointly with an application for an order under the said section 2; and the court shall have power to give such consequential directions as may be necessary for enabling the court to exercise any of the powers available to the court under this Act in the case of an application for an order under section 2.

(3) Where an order made under section 15(1) of this Act is in force with respect to a party to a marriage, the court shall not give a direction under subsection (1) above with respect to any application made under the said section 31(6) or 36(1) by that party on the death of the other party.

Miscellaneous and supplementary provisions

s.19 Effect, duration and form of orders

(1) Where an order is made under section 2 of this Act then for all purposes, including the purposes of the enactments relating to inheritance tax, the will or the law relating to intestacy, or both the will and the law relating to intestacy, as the case may be, shall have effect and be deemed to have had effect as from the deceased's death subject to the provisions of the order.

(2) Any order made under section 2 or 5 of this Act in favour of –

(a) an applicant who was the former husband or former wife of the deceased, or

(b) an applicant who was the husband or wife of the deceased in a case where the marriage with the deceased was the subject of a decree of judicial separation and at the date of death the decree was in force and the separation was continuing,

shall, in so far as it provides for the making of periodical payments, cease to have effect on the remarriage of the applicant, except in relation to any arrears due under the order on the date of the remarriage.

(3) A copy of every order made under this Act other than an order made under section 15(1) of this Act shall be sent to the principal registry of the Family Division for entry and filing, and a memorandum of the order shall be endorsed on, or permanently annexed to, the probate or letters of administration under which the estate is being administered.

s.20 Provisions as to personal representatives

(1) The provisions of this Act shall not render the personal representative of a deceased person liable for having distributed any part of the estate of the deceased, after the end of the period of six months from the date on which representation with respect to the estate of the deceased is first taken out, on the ground that he ought to have taken into account the possibility –

    (a) that the court might permit the making of an application for an order under section 2 of this Act after the end of that period, or

    (b) that, where an order has been made under the said section 2, the court might exercise in relation thereto the powers conferred on it by section 6 of this Act,

but this subsection shall not prejudice any power to recover, by reason of the making of an order under this Act, any part of the estate so distributed.

(2) Where the personal representative of a deceased person pays any sum directed by an order under section 5 of this Act to be paid out of the deceased's net estate, he shall not be under any liability by reason of that estate not being sufficient to make the payment, unless at the time of making the payment he has reasonable cause to believe that the estate is not sufficient.

(3) Where a deceased person entered into a contract by which he agreed to leave by his will any sum of money or other property to any person or by which he agreed that a sum of money or other property would be paid or transferred to any person out of his estate, then, if the personal representative of the deceased has reason to believe that the deceased entered into the contract with the intention of defeating an application for financial provision under this Act, he may, notwithstanding anything in that contract, postpone the payment of that sum of money or the transfer of that property until the expiration of the period of six months from the date on which representation with respect to the estate of the deceased is first taken out or, if during that period an application is made for an order under section 2 of this Act, until the determination of the proceedings on that application.

ss.21, 22 *(Repealed.)*

s.23 Determination of date on which representation was first taken out

In considering for the purposes of this Act when representation with respect to the estate of a deceased person was first taken out, a grant limited to settled land or to trust property shall be left out of account, and a grant limited to real estate or to personal estate shall be left out of account unless a grant limited to the remainder of the estate has previously been made or is made at the same time.

s.24 Effect of this Act on s.46(1)(vi) of Administration of Estates Act 1925

Section 46(1)(vi) of the Administration of Estates Act 1925, in so far as it provides for the devolution of property on the Crown, the Duchy of Lancaster or the Duke of Cornwall as bona vacantia, shall have effect subject to the provisions of this Act.

s.25 Interpretation

(1) In this Act –

    'beneficiary', in relation to the estate of a deceased person, means –

        (a) a person who under the will of the deceased or under the law relating to intestacy is beneficially interested in the estate or would be so interested if an order had not been made under this Act, and

        (b) a person who has received any sum of money or other property which by virtue of section 8(1) or 8(2) of this Act is treated as part of the net estate of the deceased or would have received that sum or other property if an order had not been made under this Act;

'child' includes an illegitimate child and a child en ventre sa mere at the death of the deceased;

'the court' unless the context otherwise requires means the High Court, or where a county court has jurisdiction by virtue of section 22 of this Act, a county court;

'former wife' or 'former husband' means a person whose marriage with the deceased was during the lifetime of the deceased either –

(a) dissolved or annulled by a decree of divorce or a decree of nullity of marriage granted under the law of any part of the British Islands, or

(b) dissolved or annulled in any country or territory outside the British Islands by a divorce or annulment which is entitled to be recognised as valid by the law of England and Wales;

'net estate', in relation to a deceased person, means –

(a) all property of which the deceased had power to dispose by his will (otherwise than by virtue of a special power of appointment) less the amount of his funeral, testamentary and administration expenses, debts and liabilities, including any inheritance tax payable out of his estate on his death;

(b) any property in respect of which the deceased held a general power of appointment (not being a power exercisable by will) which has not been exercised;

(c) any sum of money or other property which is treated for the purposes of this Act as part of the net estate of the deceased by virtue of section 8(1) or (2) of this Act;

(d) any property which is treated for the purposes of this Act as part of the net estate of the deceased by virtue of an order made under section 9 of the Act;

(e) any sum of money or other property which is, by reason of a disposition or contract made by the deceased, ordered under section 10 or 11 of this Act to be provided for the purpose of the making of financial provision under this Act;

'property' includes any chose in action;

'reasonable financial provision' has the meaning assigned to it by section 1 of this Act;

'valuable consideration' does not include marriage or a promise of marriage;

'will' includes codicil.

(2) For the purposes of paragraph (a) of the definition of 'net estate' in subsection (1) above a person who is not of full age and capacity shall be treated as having power to dispose by will of all property of which he would have had power to dispose by will if he had been of full age and capacity.

(3) Any reference in this Act to provision out of the net estate of a deceased person includes a reference to provision extending to the whole of that estate.

(4) For the purposes of this Act any reference to a wife or husband shall be treated as including a reference to a person who in good faith entered into a void marriage with the deceased unless either –

(a) the marriage of the deceased and that person was dissolved or annulled during the lifetime of the deceased and the dissolution or annulment is recognised by the law of England and Wales, or

(b) that person has during the lifetime of the deceased entered into a later marriage.

(5) Any reference in this Act to remarriage or to a person who has remarried includes a reference to a marriage which is by law void or voidable or to a person who has entered into such a marriage, as the case may be, and a marriage shall be treated for the purposes of this Act as a remarriage, in relation to any party thereto, notwithstanding that the previous marriage of that party was void or voidable.

(6) Any reference in this Act to an order or decree made under the Matrimonial Causes Act 1973 or under any section of that Act shall be construed as including a reference

to an order or decree which is deemed to have been made under that Act or under that section thereof, as the case may be.

(7) Any reference in this Act to any enactment is a reference to that enactment as amended by or under any subsequent enactment.

s.26 Consequential amendments, repeals and transitional provisions

(1) (*Amending clause.*)

(2) Subject to the provisions of this section, the enactments specified in the Schedule to this Act are hereby repealed to the extent specified in the third column of the Schedule.

(3) The repeal of the said enactment shall not affect their operation in relation to any application made thereunder (whether before or after the commencement of this Act) with reference to the death of any person who died before the commencement of this Act.

(4) Without prejudice to the provisions of section 39 of the Interpretation Act 1889 (which relates to the effect of repeals) nothing in any repeal made by this Act shall affect any order made or direction given under any enactment repealed by this Act, and, subject to the provisions of this Act, every such order or direction (other than an order made under section 4A of the Inheritance (Family Provision) Act 1938 or section 28A of the Matrimonial Causes Act 1965) shall, if it is in force at the commencement of this Act or is made by virtue of subsection (2) above, continue in force as if it had been made under section 2(1)(a) of this Act, and for the purposes of section 6(7) of this Act the court in exercising its powers under that section in relation to an order continued in force by this subsection shall be required to have regard to any change in any of the circumstances to which the court would have been required to have regard when making that order if the order had been made with reference to the death of any person who died after the commencement of this Act.

s.27 Short title, commencement and extent

(1) This Act may be cited as the Inheritance (Provision for Family and Dependants) Act 1975.

(2) This Act does not extend to Scotland or Northern Ireland.

(3) This Act shall come into force on 1st April 1976.

INHERITANCE TAX ACT 1984

* * * * *

s.146 Inheritance (Provision for Family and Dependants) Act 1975

(1) Where an order is made under section 2 of the Inheritance (Provision for Family and Dependants) Act 1975 ('the 1975 Act') in relation to any property forming part of the net estate of a deceased person, then, without prejudice to section 19(1) of that Act, the property shall for the purposes of this Act be treated as if it had on his death devolved subject to the provisions of the order.

(2) Where an order is made under section 10 of the 1975 Act requiring a person to provide any money or other property by reason of a disposition made by the deceased, then –

(a) if that disposition was a chargeable transfer and the personal representatives of the deceased make a claim for the purpose –

(i) tax paid or payable on the value transferred by that chargeable transfer (whether or not by the claimants) shall be repaid to them by the Board or, as the case may be, shall not be payable, and

      (ii)   the rate or rates of tax applicable to the transfer of value made by the deceased on his death shall be determined as if the values previously transferred by chargeable transfers made by him were reduced by that value;

    (b) the money or property shall be included in the deceased's estate for the purpose of the transfer of value made by him on his death.

(3) Where the money or other property ordered to be provided under section 10 of the 1975 Act is less than the maximum permitted by that section, subsection (2)(a) above shall have effect in relation to such part of the value there mentioned as is appropriate.

(4) The adjustment in consequence of the provisions of this section or of section 19(1) of the 1975 Act of the tax payable in respect of the transfer of value made by the deceased on this death shall not affect –

    (a) the amount of any deduction to be made under section 8 of that Act in respect of tax borne by the person mentioned in subsection (3) of that section, or

    (b) the amount of tax to which regard is to be had under section 9(2) of that Act;

and where a person is ordered under that Act to make a payment or transfer property by reason of his holding property treated as part of the deceased's net estate under section 8 or 9 and tax borne by him is taken into account for the purposes of the order, any repayment of that tax shall be made to the personal representatives of the deceased and not to that person.

(5) Tax repaid under paragraph (a)(i) of subsection (2) above shall be included in the deceased's estate for the purposes of the transfer of value made by him on his death; and tax repaid under that paragraph or under subsection (4) above shall form part of the deceased's net estate for the purposes of the 1975 Act.

(6) Anything which is done in compliance with an order under the 1975 Act or occurs on the coming into force of such an order and which would (apart from this subsection) constitute an occasion on which tax is chargeable under any provision, other than section 79, of Chapter III of Part III of this Act, shall not constitute such an occasion; and where an order under the 1975 Act provides for property to be settled or for the variation of a settlement, and (apart from this subsection) tax would be charged under section 52(1) above on the coming into force of the order, section 52(1) shall not apply.

(7) In subsections (2)(a) and (5) above references to tax include references to interest on tax.

(8) Where an order is made staying or dismissing proceedings under the 1975 Act on terms set out in or scheduled to the order, this section shall have effect as if any of those terms which could have been included in an order under section 2 or 10 of that Act were provisions of such an order.

(9) In this section any reference to, or to any provision of, the 1975 Act includes a reference to, or to the corresponding provision of, the Inheritance (Provision for Family and Dependants) (Northern Ireland) Order 1979.

Statutory provisions relating to variations and disclaimers

INHERITANCE TAX ACT 1984

* * * * *

s.17 Changes in distribution of deceased's estate, etc

None of the following is a transfer of value –

    (a) a variation or disclaimer to which section 142(1) below applies;

    (b) a transfer to which section 143 below applies;

    (c) an election by a surviving spouse under section 47A of the Administration of Estates Act 1925;

    (d) the renunciation of a claim to legitim within the period mentioned in section 147(6) below.

* * * * *

Changes in distribution of deceased's estate, etc

s.142 Alteration of dispositions taking effect on death

(1) Where within the period of two years after a person's death –

    (a) any of the dispositions (whether effected by will, under the law relating to intestacy or otherwise) of the property comprised in his estate immediately before his death are varied, or

    (b) the benefit conferred by any of those dispositions is disclaimed,

by any instrument in writing made by the persons or any of the persons who benefit or would benefit under the dispositions, this Act shall apply as if the variation had been effected by the deceased or, as the case may be, the disclaimed benefit had never been conferred.

(2) Subsection (1) above shall not apply to a variation unless the instrument contains a statement, made by all the relevant persons, to the effect that they intend the subsection to apply to the variation.

(2A) For the purposes of subsection (2) above the relevant persons are –

    (a) the person or persons making the instrument, and

    (b) where the variation results in additional tax being payable, the personal representatives.

Personal representatives may decline to make a statement under subsection (2) above only if no, or no sufficient, assets are held by them in that capacity for discharging the additional tax.

(3) Subsection (1) above shall not apply to a variation or disclaimer made for any consideration in money or money's worth other than consideration consisting of the making, in respect of another of the dispositions, of a variation or disclaimer to which that subsection applies.

(4) Where a variation to which subsection (1) above applies results in property being held in trust for a person for a period which ends not more than two years after the death, this Act shall apply as if the disposition of the property that takes effect at the end of the period had had effect from the beginning of the period; but this subsection shall not affect the application of this Act in relation to any distribution or application of property occurring before that disposition takes effect.

(5) For the purposes of subsection (1) above the property comprised in a person's estate includes any excluded property but not any property to which he is treated as entitled by virtue of section 49(1) above or section 102 of the Finance Act 1986.

(6) Subsection (1) above applies whether or not the administration of the estate is complete or the property concerned has been distributed in accordance with the original dispositions.

(7) In the application of subsection (4) above to Scotland, property which is subject to a proper liferent shall be deemed to be held in trust for the liferenter.

s.143 Compliance with testator's request

Where a testator expresses a wish that property bequeathed by his will should be transferred by the legatee to other persons, and the legatee transfers any of the property in accordance with that wish within the period of two years after the death of the testator, this Act shall have effect as if the property transferred had been bequeathed by the will to the transferee.

s.144 Distribution etc from property settled by will

(1) This section applies where property comprised in a person's estate immediately before his death is settled by his will and, within the period of two years after his death and before any interest in possession has subsisted in the property, there occurs –

(a) an event on which tax would (apart from this section) be chargeable under any provision, other than section 64 or 79, of Chapter III of Part III of this Act, or

(b) an event on which tax would be so chargeable but for section 75 or 76 above or paragraph 16(1) of Schedule 4 to this Act.

(2) Where this section applies by virtue of an event within paragraph (a) of subsection (1) above, tax shall not be charged under the provision in question on that event; and in every case in which this section applies in relation to an event, this Act shall have effect as if the will had provided that on the testator's death the property should be held as it is held after the event.

s.145 Redemption of surviving spouse's life interest

Where an election is made by a surviving spouse under section 47A of the Administration of Estates Act 1925, this Act shall have effect as if the surviving spouse, instead of being entitled to the life interest, had been entitled to a sum equal to the capital value mentioned in that section.

* * * * *

TAXATION OF CHARGEABLE GAINS ACT 1992

s.62 Death: general provisions

* * * * *

(6) Subject to subsections (7) and (8) below, where within the period of 2 years after a person's death any of the dispositions (whether effected by will, under the law relating

to intestacy or otherwise) of the property of which he was competent to dispose are varied, or the benefit conferred by any of those dispositions is disclaimed, by an instrument in writing made by the persons or any of the persons who benefit or would benefit under the dispositions –

(a)   the variation or disclaimer shall not constitute a disposal for the purposes of this Act, and

(b)   this section shall apply as if the variation had been effected by the deceased or, as the case may be, the disclaimed benefit had never been conferred.

(7) Subsection (6) above does not apply to a variation unless the instrument contains a statement by the persons making the instrument to the effect that they intend the subsection to apply to the variation.

(8) Subsection (6) above does not apply to a variation or disclaimer made for any consideration in money or money's worth other than consideration consisting of the making of a variation or disclaimer in respect of another of the dispositions.

(9) Subsection (6) above applies whether or not the administration of the estate is complete or the property has been distributed in accordance with the original dispositions.

(10) In this section references to assets of which a deceased person was competent to dispose are references to assets of the deceased which (otherwise than in right of a power of appointment or of the testamentary power conferred by statute to dispose of entailed interests) he could, if of full age and capacity, have disposed of by his will, assuming that all the assets were situated in England and, if he was not domiciled in the United Kingdom, that he was domiciled in England, and include references to his severable share in any assets to which, immediately before his death, he was beneficially entitled as a joint tenant.

* * * * *

APPENDIX 4

Statutory provisions relating to powers of trustees

TRUSTEE ACT 1925

* * * * *

s.19 Power to insure

(1) A trustee may –

    (a) insure any property which is subject to the trust against risks of loss or damage due to any event, and

    (b) pay the premiums out of the trust funds.

(2) In the case of property held on a bare trust, the power to insure is subject to any direction given by the beneficiary or each of the beneficiaries –

    (a) that any property specified in the direction is not to be insured;

    (b) that any property specified in the direction is not to be insured except on such conditions as may be so specified.

(3) Property is held on a bare trust if it is held on trust for –

    (a) a beneficiary who is full age and capacity and absolutely entitled to the property subject to the trust, or

    (b) beneficiaries each of whom is of full age and capacity and who (taken together) are absolutely entitled to the property subject to the trust.

* * * * *

Maintenance, Advancement and Protective Trusts

s.31 Power to apply income for maintenance and to accumulate surplus income during a minority

(1) Where any property is held by trustees in trust for any person for any interest whatsoever, whether vested or contingent, then, subject to any prior interests or charges affecting that property –

    (i) during the infancy of any such person, if his interest so long continues, the trustees may, at their sole discretion, pay to his parent or guardian, if any, or otherwise apply for or towards his maintenance, education, or benefit, the whole or such part, if any, of the income of that property as may, in all the circumstances, be reasonable, whether or not there is –

        (a) any other fund applicable to the same purpose; or

        (b) any person bound by law to provide for his maintenance or education; and

    (ii) if such person on attaining the age of eighteen years has not a vested interest in such income, the trustees shall thenceforth pay the income of that property and of any accretion thereto under subsection (2) of this section to him, until he either attains a vested interest therein or dies, or until failure of his interest:

Provided that, in deciding whether the whole or any part of the income of the property is during a minority to be paid or applied for the purposes aforesaid, the trustees shall have regard to the age of the infant and his requirements and generally to the circumstances of the case, and in particular to what other income, if any, is applicable for the same purposes; and where trustees have notice that the income of more than one fund is applicable for those purposes, then, so far as practicable, unless the entire income of the funds is paid or applied as aforesaid or the court otherwise directs, a proportionate part only of the income of each fund shall be so paid or applied.

(2) During the infancy of any such person, if his interest so long continues, the trustees shall accumulate all the residue of that income in the way of compound interest by investing the same and the resulting income thereof from time to time in authorised investments, and shall hold those accumulations as follows –

    (i)   If any such person –

        (a)   attains the age of eighteen years, or marries under that age, and his interest in such income during his infancy or until his marriage is a vested interest; or

        (b)   on attaining the age of eighteen years or on marriage under that age becomes entitled to the property from which such income arose in fee simple, absolute or determinable, or absolutely, or for an entailed interest;

the trustees shall hold the accumulations in trust for such person absolutely, but without prejudice to any provision with respect thereto contained in any settlement by him made under any statutory powers during his infancy, and so that the receipt of such person after marriage, and though still an infant, shall be a good discharge; and

    (ii) In any other case the trustees shall, notwithstanding that such person had a vested interest in such income, hold the accumulations as an accretion to the capital of the property from which such accumulations arose, and as one fund with such capital for all purposes, and so that, if such property is settled land, such accumulations shall be held upon the same trusts as if the same were capital money arising therefrom;

but the trustees may, at any time during the infancy of such person if his interest so long continues, apply those accumulations, or any part thereof, as if they were income arising in the then current year.

(3) This section applies in the case of a contingent interest only if the limitation or trust carries the intermediate income of the property, but it applies to a future or contingent legacy by the parent of, or a person standing in loco parentis to, the legatee, if and for such period as, under the general law, the legacy carries interest for the maintenance of the legatee, and in any such case as last aforesaid the rate of interest shall (if the income available is sufficient, and subject to any rules of court to the contrary) be five pounds per centum per annum.

(4) This section applies to a vested annuity in like manner as if the annuity were the income of property held by trustees in trust to pay the income thereof to the annuitant for the same period for which the annuity is payable, save that in any case accumulations made during the infancy of the annuitant shall be held in trust for the annuitant or his personal representatives absolutely.

(5) This section does not apply where the instrument, if any, under which the interest arises came into operation before the commencement of this Act.

s.32 Power of advancement

(1) Trustees may at any time or times pay or apply any capital money subject to a trust, for the advancement or benefit, in such manner as they may, in their absolute discretion, think fit, of any person entitled to the capital of the trust property or of any share thereof, whether absolutely or contingently on his attaining any specified age or on the occurrence of any other event, or subject to a gift over on his death under specified age or on the occurrence of any other event, and whether in possession or in remainder or reversion, and such payment or application may be made notwithstanding that the interest of such person is liable to be defeated by the exercise of a power of appointment or revocation, or to be diminished by the increase of the class to which he belongs:

Provided that –

    (a) the money so paid or applied for the advancement or benefit of any person shall not exceed altogether in amount one-half of the presumptive or vested share or interest of that person in the trust property; and

    (b) if that person is or becomes absolutely and indefeasibly entitled to a share in the trust property the money so paid or applied shall be brought into account as part of such share; and

    (c) no such payment or application shall be made so as to prejudice any person entitled to any prior life or other interest, whether vested or contingent, in the money paid or applied unless such person is in existence and of full age and consents in writing to such payment or application.

(2) This section does not apply to capital money arising under the Settled Land Act 1925.

(3) This section does not apply to trusts constituted or created before the commencement of this Act.

* * * * *

TRUSTEE ACT 2000

PART I

THE DUTY OF CARE

s.1 The duty of care

(1) Whenever the duty under this subsection applies to a trustee, he must exercise such care and skill as is reasonable in the circumstances having regard in particular –

    (a) to any special knowledge or experience that he has or holds himself out as having, and

    (b) if he acts as trustee in the course of a business or profession, to any special knowledge or experience that it is reasonable to expect of a person acting in the course of that kind of business or profession.

(2) In this Act the duty under subsection (1) is called 'the duty of care'.

s.2 Application of duty of care

Schedule 1 makes provision about when the duty of care applies to a trustee.

PART II

INVESTMENT

s.3 General power of investment

(1) Subject to the provisions of this Part, a trustee may make any kind of investment that he could make if he were absolutely entitled to the assets of the trust.

(2) In this Act the power under subsection (1) is called 'the general power of investment'.

(3) The general power of investment does not permit a trustee to make investments in land other than in loans secured on land (but see also section 8).

(4) A person invests in a loan secured on land if he has rights under any contract under which –

(a) one person provides another with credit, and

(b) the obligation of the borrower to repay is secured on land.

(5) 'Credit' includes any cash loan or other financial accommodation.

(6) 'Cash' includes money in any form.

s.4 Standard investment criteria

(1) In exercising any power of investment, whether arising under this Part or otherwise, a trustee must have regard to the standard investment criteria.

(2) A trustee must from time to time review the investments of the trust and consider whether, having regard to the standard investment criteria, they should be varied.

(3) The standard investment criteria, in relation to a trust, are –

(a) the suitability to the trust of investments of the same kind as any particular investment proposed to be made or retained and of that particular investment as an investment of that kind, and

(b) the need for diversification of investments of the trust, in so far as is appropriate to the circumstances of the trust.

s.5 Advice

(1) Before exercising any power of investment, whether arising under this Part or otherwise, a trustee must (unless the exception applies) obtain and consider proper advice about the way in which, having regard to the standard investment criteria, the power should be exercised.

(2) When reviewing the investments of the trust, a trustee must (unless the exception applies) obtain and consider proper advice about whether, having regard to the standard investment criteria, the investments should be varied.

(3) The exception is that a trustee need not obtain such advice if he reasonably concludes that in all the circumstances it is unnecessary or inappropriate to do so.

(4) Proper advice is the advice of a person who is reasonably believed by the trustee to be qualified to give it by his ability in and practical experience of financial and other matters relating to the proposed investment.

s.6 Restriction or exclusion of this Part etc

(1) The general power of investment is –

(a) in addition to powers conferred on trustees otherwise than by this Act, but

(b) subject to any restriction or exclusion imposed by the trust instrument or by any enactment or any provision of subordinate legislation.

(2) For the purposes of this Act, an enactment or a provision of subordinate legislation is not to be regarded as being, or as being part of, a trust instrument.

(3) In this Act 'subordinate legislation' has the same meaning as in the Interpretation Act 1978.

s.7 Existing trusts

(1) This Part applies in relation to trusts whether created before or after its commencement.

(2) No provision relating to the powers of a trustee contained in a trust instrument made before 3rd August 1961 is to be treated (for the purposes of section 6(1)(b)) as restricting or excluding the general power of investment.

(3) A provision contained in a trust instrument made before the commencement of this Part which –

(a) has effect under section 3(2) of the Trustee Investments Act 1961 as a power to invest under that Act, or

(b) confers power to invest under that Act,

is to be treated as conferring the general power of investment on a trustee.

PART III

ACQUISITION OF LAND

s.8 Power to acquire freehold and leasehold land

(1) A trustee may acquire freehold or leasehold land in the United Kingdom –

(a) as an investment,

(b) for occupation by a beneficiary, or

(c) for any other reason.

(2) 'Freehold or leasehold land' means –

(a) in relation to England and Wales, a legal estate in land,

(b) in relation to Scotland –

(i) the estate or interest of the proprietor of the dominium utile or, in the case of land not held on feudal tenure, the estate or interest of the owner, or

(ii) a tenancy, and

(c) in relation to Northern Ireland, a legal estate in land, including land held under a fee farm grant.

(3) For the purpose of exercising his functions as a trustee, a trustee who acquires land under this section has all the powers of an absolute owner in relation to the land.

s.9 Restriction or exclusion of this Part etc

The powers conferred by this Part are –

(a) in addition to powers conferred on trustees otherwise than by this Part, but

(b) subject to any restriction or exclusion imposed by the trust instrument or by any enactment or any provision of subordinate legislation.

s.10 Existing trusts

(1) This Part does not apply in relation to –

(a) a trust of property which consists of or includes land which (despite section 2 of the Trusts of Land and Appointment of Trustees Act 1996) is settled land, or

(b) a trust to which the Universities and College Estates Act 1925 applies.

(2) Subject to subsection (1), this Part applies in relation to trusts whether created before or after its commencement.

PART IV

AGENTS, NOMINEES AND CUSTODIANS

Agents

s.11 Power to employ agents

(1) Subject to the provisions of this Part, the trustees of a trust may authorise any person to exercise any or all of their delegable functions as their agent.

(2) In the case of a trust other than a charitable trust, the trustees' delegable functions consist of any function other than –

  (a) any function relating to whether or in what way any assets of the trust should be distributed,

  (b) any power to decide whether any fees or other payment due to be made out of the trust funds should be made out of income or capital,

  (c) any power to appoint a person to be a trustee of the trust, or

  (d) any power conferred by any other enactment or the trust instrument which permits the trustees to delegate any of their functions or to appoint a person to act as a nominee or custodian.

(3) In the case of a charitable trust, the trustees' delegable functions are –

  (a) any function consisting of carrying out a decision that the trustees have taken;

  (b) any function relating to the investment of assets subject to the trust (including, in the case of land held as an investment, managing the land and creating or disposing of an interest in the land);

  (c) any function relating to the raising of funds for the trust otherwise than by means of profits of a trade which is an integral part of carrying out the trust's charitable purpose;

  (d) any other function prescribed by an order made by the Secretary of State.

(4) For the purposes of subsection (3)(c) a trade is an integral part of carrying out a trust's charitable purpose if, whether carried on in the United Kingdom or elsewhere, the profits are applied solely to the purposes of the trust and either –

  (a) the trade is exercised in the course of the actual carrying out of a primary purpose of the trust, or

  (b) the work in connection with the trade is mainly carried out by beneficiaries of the trust.

(5) The power to make an order under subsection (3)(d) is exercisable by statutory instrument which shall be subject to annulment in pursuance of a resolution of either House of Parliament.

* * * * *

PART V

REMUNERATION

s.28 Trustee's entitlement to payment under trust instrument

(1) Except to the extent (if any) to which the trust instrument makes inconsistent provision, subsections (2) to (4) apply to a trustee if –

(a) there is a provision in the trust instrument entitling him to receive payment out of trust funds in respect of services provided by him to or on behalf of the trust, and

(b) the trustee is a trust corporation or is acting in a professional capacity.

(2) The trustee is to be treated as entitled under the trust instrument to receive payment in respect of services even if they are services which are capable of being provided by a lay trustee.

(3) Subsection (2) applies to a trustee of a charitable trust who is not a trust corporation only –

(a) if he is not a sole trustee, and

(b) to the extent that a majority of the other trustees have agreed that it should apply to him.

(4) Any payments to which the trustee is entitled in respect of services are to be treated as remuneration for services (and not as a gift) for the purposes of –

(a) section 15 of the Wills Act 1837 (gifts to an attesting witness to be void), and

(b) section 34(3) of the Administration of Estates Act 1925 (order in which estate to be paid out).

(5) For the purposes of this Part, a trustee acts in a professional capacity if he acts in the course of a profession or business which consists of or includes the provision of services in connection with –

(a) the management or administration of trusts generally or a particular kind of trust, or

(b) any particular aspect of the management or administration of trusts generally or a particular kind of trust,

and the services he provides to or on behalf of the trust fall within that description.

(6) For the purposes of this Part, a person acts as a lay trustee if he –

(a) is not a trust corporation, and

(b) does not act in a professional capacity.

s.29 Remuneration of certain trustees

(1) Subject to subsection (5), a trustee who –

(a) is a trust corporation, but

(b) is not a trustee of a charitable trust,

is entitled to receive reasonable remuneration out of the trust funds for any services that the trust corporation provides to or on behalf of the trust.

(2) Subject to subsection (5), a trustee who –

(a) acts in a professional capacity, but

(b) is not a trust corporation, a trustee of a charitable trust or a sole trustee,

is entitled to receive reasonable remuneration out of the trust funds for any services that he provides to or on behalf of the trust if each other trustee has agreed in writing that he may be remunerated for the services.

(3) 'Reasonable remuneration' means, in relation to the provision of services by a trustee, such remuneration as is reasonable in the circumstances for the provision of those services to or on behalf of that trust by that trustee and for the purposes of subsection (1) includes, in relation to the provision of services by a trustee who is an authorised institution under the Banking Act 1987 and provides the services in that capacity, the institution's reasonable charges for the provision of such services.

(4) A trustee is entitled to remuneration under this section even if the services in question are capable of being provided by a lay trustee.

(5) A trustee is not entitled to remuneration under this section if any provision about his entitlement to remuneration has been made –

(a) by the trust instrument, or

(b) by any enactment or any provision of subordinate legislation.

(6) This section applies to a trustee who has been authorised under a power conferred by Part IV or the trust instrument –

(a) to exercise functions as an agent of the trustees, or

(b) to act as a nominee or custodian,

as it applies to any other trustee.

s.30 Remuneration of trustees of charitable trusts

(1) The Secretary of State may by regulations make provision for the remuneration of trustees of charitable trusts who are trust corporations or act in a professional capacity.

(2) The power under subsection (1) includes power to make provision for the remuneration of a trustee who has been authorised under a power conferred by Part IV or any other enactment or any provision of subordinate legislation, or by the trust instrument –

(a) to exercise functions as an agent of the trustees, or

(b) to act as a nominee or custodian.

(3) Regulations under this section may –

(a) make different provision for different cases;

(b) contain such supplemental, incidental, consequential and transitional provision as the Secretary of State considers appropriate.

(4) The power to make regulations under this section is exercisable by statutory instrument, but no such instrument shall be made unless a draft of it has been laid before Parliament and approved by a resolution of each House of Parliament.

s.31 Trustees' expenses

(1) A trustee –

(a) is entitled to be reimbursed from the trust funds, or

(b) may pay out of the trust funds,

expenses properly incurred by him when acting on behalf of the trust.

(2) This section applies to a trustee who has been authorised under a power conferred by Part IV or any other enactment or any provision of subordinate legislation, or by the trust instrument –

(a) to exercise functions as an agent of the trustees, or

(b) to act as a nominee or custodian,

as it applies to any other trustee.

s.32 Remuneration and expenses of agents, nominees and custodians

(1) This section applies if, under a power conferred by Part IV or any other enactment or any provision of subordinate legislation, or by the trust instrument, a person other than a trustee has been –

(a) authorised to exercise functions as an agent of the trustees, or

(b) appointed to act as a nominee or custodian.

(2) The trustees may remunerate the agent, nominee or custodian out of the trust funds for services if –

(a) he is engaged on terms entitling him to be remunerated for those services, and

(b) the amount does not exceed such remuneration as is reasonable in the circumstances for the provision of those services by him to or on behalf of that trust.

(3) The trustees may reimburse the agent, nominee or custodian out of the trust funds for any expenses properly incurred by him in exercising functions as an agent, nominee or custodian.

s.33 Application

(1) Subject to subsection (2), sections 28, 29, 31 and 32 apply in relation to services provided to or on behalf of, or (as the case may be) expenses incurred on or after their commencement on behalf of, trusts whenever created.

(2) Nothing in section 28 or 29 is to be treated as affecting the operation of –

 (a) section 15 of the Wills Act 1837, or
 (b) section 34(3) of the Administration of Estates Act 1925,

in relation to any death occurring before the commencement of section 28 or (as the case may be) section 29.

* * * * *

s.35 Personal representatives

(1) Subject to the following provisions of this section, this Act applies in relation to a personal representative administering an estate according to the law as it applies to a trustee carrying out a trust for beneficiaries.

(2) For this purpose this Act is to be read with the appropriate modifications and in particular –

 (a) references to the trust instrument are to be read as references to the will,
 (b) references to a beneficiary or to beneficiaries, apart from the reference to a beneficiary in section 8(1)(b), are to be read as references to a person or the persons interested in the due administration of the estate, and
 (c) the reference to a beneficiary in section 8(1)(b) is to be read as a reference to a person who under the will of the deceased or under the law relating to intestacy is beneficially interested in the estate.

(3) Remuneration to which a personal representative is entitled under section 28 or 29 is to be treated as an administration expense for the purposes of –

 (a) section 34(3) of the Administration of Estates Act 1925 (order in which estate to be paid out), and
 (b) any provision giving reasonable administration expenses priority over the preferential debts listed in Schedule 6 to the Insolvency Act 1986.

(4) Nothing in subsection (3) is to be treated as affecting the operation of the provisions mentioned in paragraphs (a) and (b) of that subsection in relation to any death occurring before the commencement of this section.

* * * * *

TRUSTS OF LAND AND APPOINTMENT OF TRUSTEES ACT 1996

PART I

TRUSTS OF LAND

* * * * *

Settlements and trusts for sale as trusts of land

s.2 Trusts in place of settlements

(1) No settlement created after the commencement of this Act is a settlement for the purposes of the Settled Land Act 1925; and no settlement shall be deemed to be made under that Act after that commencement.

(2) Subsection (1) does not apply to a settlement created on the occasion of an alteration in any interest in, or of a person becoming entitled under, a settlement which –

  (a) is in existence at the commencement of this Act, or
  (b) derives from a settlement within paragraph (a) or this paragraph.

(3) But a settlement created as mentioned in subsection (2) is not a settlement for the purposes of the Settled Land Act 1925 if provision to the effect that it is not is made in the instrument, or any of the instruments, by which it is created.

(4) Where at any time after the commencement of this Act there is in the case of any settlement which is a settlement for the purposes of the Settled Land Act 1925 no relevant property which is, or is deemed to be, subject to the settlement, the settlement permanently ceases at that time to be a settlement for the purposes of that Act.

   In this subsection 'relevant property' means land and personal chattels to which section 67(1) of the Settled Land Act 1925 (heirlooms) applies.

(5) No land held on charitable, ecclesiastical or public trusts shall be or be deemed to be settled land after the commencement of this Act, even if it was or was deemed to be settled land before that commencement.

(6) Schedule 1 has effect to make provision consequential on this section (including provision to impose a trust in circumstances in which, apart from this section, there would be a settlement for the purposes of the Settled Land Act 1925 (and there would not otherwise be a trust)).

* * * * *

s.4 Express trusts for sale as trusts of land

(1) In the case of every trust for sale of land created by a disposition there is to be implied, despite any provision to the contrary made by the disposition, a power for the trustees to postpone sale of the land; and the trustees are not liable in any way for postponing sale of the land, in the exercise of their discretion, for an indefinite period.

(2) Subsection (1) applies to a trust whether it is created, or arises, before or after the commencement of this Act.

(3) Subsection (1) does not affect any liability incurred by trustees before that commencement.

* * * * *

Consents and consultation

s.10 Consents

(1) If a disposition creating a trust of land requires the consent of more than two persons to the exercise by the trustees of any function relating to the land, the consent of any two of them to the exercise of the function is sufficient in favour of a purchaser.

(2) Subsection (1) does not apply to the exercise of a function by trustees of land held on charitable, ecclesiastical or public trusts.

(3) Where at any time a person whose consent is expressed by a disposition creating a trust of land to be required to the exercise by the trustees of any function relating to the land is not of full age –

    (a) his consent is not, in favour of a purchaser, required to the exercise of the function, but

    (b) the trustees shall obtain the consent of a parent who has parental responsibility for him (within the meaning of the Children Act 1989) or of a guardian of his.

s.11 Consultation with beneficiaries

(1) The trustees of land shall in the exercise of any function relating to land subject to the trust –

    (a) so far as practicable, consult the beneficiaries of full age and beneficially entitled to an interest in possession in the land, and

    (b) so far as consistent with the general interest of the trust, give effect to the wishes of those beneficiaries, or (in case of dispute) of the majority (according to the value of their combined interests)

(2) Subsection (1) does not apply –

    (a) in relation to a trust created by a disposition in so far as provision that it does not apply is made by the disposition,

    (b) in relation to a trust created or arising under a will made before the commencement of this Act, or

    (c) in relation to the exercise of the power mentioned in section 6(2).

(3) Subsection (1) does not apply to a trust created before the commencement of this Act by a disposition, or a trust created after that commencement by reference to such a trust, unless provision to the effect that it is to apply is made by a deed executed –

    (a) in a case in which the trust was created by one person and he is of full capacity, by that person, or

    (b) in a case in which the trust was created by more than one person, by such of the persons who created the trust as are alive and of full capacity.

(4) A deed executed for the purposes of subsection (3) is irrevocable.

Right of beneficiaries to occupy trust land

s.12 The right to occupy

(1) A beneficiary who is beneficially entitled to an interest in possession in land subject to a trust of land is entitled by reason of his interest to occupy the land at any time if at that time –

    (a) the purposes of the trust include making the land available for his occupation (or for the occupation of beneficiaries of a class of which he is a member or of beneficiaries in general), or

    (b) the land is held by the trustees so as to be so available.

(2) Subsection (1) does not confer on a beneficiary a right to occupy land if it is either unavailable or unsuitable for occupation by him.

(3) This section is subject to section 13.

s.13 Exclusion and restriction of right to occupy

(1) Where two or more beneficiaries are (or apart from this subsection would be) entitled under section 12 to occupy land, the trustees of land may exclude or restrict the entitlement of any one or more (but not all) of them.

(2) Trustees may not under subsection (1) –

(a) unreasonably exclude any beneficiary's entitlement to occupy land, or

(b) restrict any such entitlement to an unreasonable extent.

(3) The trustees of land may from time to time impose reasonable conditions on any beneficiary in relation to his occupation of land by reason of his entitlement under section 12.

(4) The matters to which trustees are to have regard in exercising the powers conferred by this section include –

(a) the intentions of the person or persons (if any) who created the trust,

(b) the purposes for which the land is held, and

(c) the circumstances and wishes of each of the beneficiaries who is (or apart from any previous exercise by the trustees of those powers would be) entitled to occupy the land under section 12.

(5) The conditions which may be imposed on a beneficiary under subsection (3) include, in particular, conditions requiring him –

(a) to pay any outgoings or expenses in respect of the land, or

(b) to assume any other obligation in relation to the land or to any activity which is or is proposed to be conducted there.

(6) Where the entitlement of any beneficiary to occupy land under section 12 has been excluded or restricted, the conditions which may be imposed on any other beneficiary under subsection (3) include, in particular, conditions requiring him to –

(a) make payments by way of compensation to the beneficiary whose entitlement has been excluded or restricted, or

(b) forgo any payment or other benefit to which he would otherwise be entitled under the trust so as to benefit that beneficiary.

(7) The powers conferred on trustees by this section may not be exercised –

(a) so as prevent any person who is in occupation of land (whether or not by reason of an entitlement under section 12) from continuing to occupy the land, or

(b) in a manner likely to result in any such person ceasing to occupy the land,

unless he consents or the court has given approval.

(8) The matters to which the court is to have regard in determining whether to give approval under subsection (7) include the matters mentioned in subsection (4)(a) to (c).

* * * * *

s.18 Application of Part to personal representatives

(1) The provisions of this Part relating to trustees, other than sections 10, 11 and 14, apply to personal representatives, but with appropriate modifications and without prejudice to the functions of personal representatives for the purposes of administration.

(2) The appropriate modifications include –

(a) the substitution of references to persons interested in the due administration of the estate for references to beneficiaries, and

(b) the substitution of references to the will for references to the disposition creating the trust.

(3) Section 3(1) does not apply to personal representatives if the death occurs before the commencement of this Act.

PART II

APPOINTMENT AND RETIREMENT OF TRUSTEES

s.19 Appointment and retirement of trustee at instance of beneficiaries

(1) This section applies in the case of a trust where –
  (a) there is no person nominated for the purpose of appointing new trustees by the instrument, if any, creating the trust, and
  (b) the beneficiaries under the trust are of full age and capacity and (taken together) are absolutely entitled to the property subject to the trust.

(2) The beneficiaries may give a direction or directions of either or both of the following descriptions –
  (a) a written direction to a trustee or trustees to retire from the trust, and
  (b) a written direction to the trustees or trustee for the time being (or, if there are none, to the personal representative of the last person who was a trustee) to appoint by writing to be a trustee or trustees the person or persons specified in the direction.

(3) Where –
  (a) a trustee has been given a direction under subsection (2)(a),
  (b) reasonable arrangements have been made for the protection of any rights of his in connection with the trust,
  (c) after he has retired there will be either a trust corporation or at least two persons to act as trustees to perform the trust, and
  (d) either another person is to be appointed to be a new trustee on his retirement (whether in compliance with a direction under subsection (2)(b) or otherwise) or the continuing trustees by deed consent to his retirement,

he shall make a deed declaring his retirement and shall be deemed to have retired and be discharged from the trust.

(4) Where a trustee retires under subsection (3) he and the continuing trustees (together with any new trustee) shall (subject to any arrangements for the protection of his rights) do anything necessary to vest the trust property in the continuing trustees (or the continuing and new trustees).

(5) This section has effect subject to the restrictions imposed by the Trustee Act 1925 on the number of trustees.

* * * * *

Statutory provisions relating to accumulation and maintenance settlements

INHERITANCE TAX ACT 1984

* * * * *

s.71 Accumulation and maintenance trusts

(1) Subject to subsection (2) below, this section applies to settled property if –

    (a) one or more persons (in this section referred to as beneficiaries) will, on or before attaining a specified age not exceeding twenty-five, become beneficially entitled to it or to an interest in possession in it, and

    (b) no interest in possession subsists in it and the income from it is to be accumulated so far as not applied for the maintenance, education or benefit of a beneficiary.

(2) This section does not apply to settled property unless either –

    (a) not more than twenty-five years have elapsed since the commencement of the settlement or, if it was later, since the time (or latest time) when the conditions stated in paragraphs (a) and (b) of subsection (1) above became satisfied with respect to the property, or

    (b) all the persons who are or have been beneficiaries are or were either –

        (i) grandchildren of a common grandparent, or

        (ii) children, widows or widowers of such grandchildren who were themselves beneficiaries but died before the time when, had they survived, they would have become entitled as mentioned in subsection (1)(a) above.

(3) Subject to subsections (4) and (5) below, there shall be a charge to tax under this section –

    (a) where settled property ceases to be property to which this section applies, and

    (b) in a case in which paragraph (a) above does not apply, where the trustees make a disposition as a result of which the value of settled property to which this section applies is less than it would be but for the disposition.

(4) Tax shall not be charged under this section –

    (a) on a beneficiary's becoming beneficially entitled to, or to an interest in possession in, settled property on or before attaining the specified age, or

    (b) on the death of a beneficiary before attaining the specified age.

(5) Subsections (3) to (8) and (10) of section 70 above shall apply for the purposes of this section as they apply for the purposes of that section (with the substitution of a reference to subsection (3)(b) above for the reference in section 70(4) to section 70(2)(b)).

(6) Where the conditions stated in paragraphs (a) and (b) of subsection (1) above were satisfied on 15th April 1976 with respect to property comprised in a settlement which commenced before that day, subsection (2)(a) above shall have effect with the substitution of a reference to that day for the reference to the commencement of the settle-

ment, and the condition stated in subsection (2)(b) above shall be treated as satisfied if –

    (a)   it is satisfied in respect of the period beginning with 15th April 1976, or

    (b)   it is satisfied in respect of the period beginning with 1st April 1977 and either there was no beneficiary living on 15th April 1976 or the beneficiaries on 1st April 1977 included a living beneficiary, or

    (c)   there is no power under the terms of the settlement whereby it could have become satisfied in respect of the period beginning with 1st April 1977, and the trusts of the settlement have not been varied at any time after 15th April 1976.

(7) In subsection (1) above 'persons' includes unborn persons; but the conditions stated in that subsection shall be treated as not satisfied unless there is or has been a living beneficiary.

(8) For the purposes of this section a person's children shall be taken to include his illegitimate children, his adopted children and his stepchildren.

APPENDIX 6

Amendments to Wills Act 1837 and other provisions as to rectification, interpretation and execution of wills

ADMINISTRATION OF JUSTICE ACT 1982

* * * * *

PART IV

WILLS

Amendments of Wills Act 1837

s.17 Relaxation of formal requirements for making wills

The following section shall be substituted for section 9 of the Wills Act 1837 –

'**s.9 Signing and attestation of wills**

No will shall be valid unless –

    (a)   it is in writing, and signed by the testator, or by some other person in his presence and by his direction; and

    (b)   it appears that the testator intended by his signature to give effect to the will; and

    (c)   the signature is made or acknowledged by the testator in the presence of two or more witnesses present at the same time; and

    (d)   each witness either –

        (i)   attests and signs the will; or

        (ii)   acknowledges his signature,

in the presence of the testator (but not necessarily in the presence of any other witness),

but no form of attestation shall be necessary.'

s.18 Effect of marriage or its termination on wills

(1)   The following section shall be substituted for section 18 of the Wills Act 1837 –

'**s.18 Wills to be revoked by marriage, except in certain cases**

    (1)   Subject to subsections (2) to (4) below, a will shall be revoked by the testator's marriage.

    (2)   A disposition in a will in exercise of a power of appointment shall take effect notwithstanding the testator's subsequent marriage unless the property so appointed would in default of appointment pass to his personal representatives.

(3)   Where it appears from a will that at the time it was made the testator was expecting to be married to a particular person and that he intended that the will should not be revoked by the marriage, the will shall not be revoked by his marriage to that person.

(4)   Where it appears from a will that at the time it was made the testator was expecting to be married to a particular person and that he intended that a disposition in the will should not be revoked by his marriage to that person, –

   (a)   that disposition shall take effect notwithstanding the marriage; and

   (b)   any other disposition in the will shall take effect also, unless it appears from the will that the testator intended the disposition to be revoked by the marriage.'

(2)   The following section shall be inserted after that section –

's.18A Effect of dissolution or annulment of marriage on wills

(1)   Where, after a testator has made a will, a decree of a court dissolves or annuls his marriage or declares it void, –

   (a)   the will shall take effect as if any appointment of the former spouse as an executor or as the executor and trustee of the will were omitted; and

   (b)   any devise or bequest to the former spouse shall lapse,

except in so far as a contrary intention appears by the will.

(2)   Subsection (1)(b) above is without prejudice to any right of the former spouse to apply for financial provision under the Inheritance (Provision for Family and Dependants) Act 1975.

(3)   Where –

   (a)   by the terms of a will an interest in remainder is subject to a life interest; and

   (b)   the life interest lapses by virtue of subsection (1)(b) above,

the interest in remainder shall be treated as if it had not been subject to the life interest and, if it was contingent upon the termination of the life interest, as if it had not been so contingent.'

s.19 Gifts to children etc who predecease testator

The following section shall be substituted for section 33 of the Wills Act 1837 –

's.33 Gifts to children or other issue who leave issue living at the testator's death shall not lapse

(1)   Where –

   (a)   a will contains a devise or bequest to a child or remoter descendant of the testator; and

   (b)   the intended beneficiary dies before the testator, leaving issue; and

   (c)   issue of the intended beneficiary are living at the testator's death,

then, unless a contrary intention appears by the will, the devise or bequest shall take effect as a devise or bequest to the issue living at the testator's death.

(2)   Where –

   (a)   a will contains a devise or bequest to a class of persons consisting of children or remoter descendants of the testator; and

   (b)   a member of the class dies before the testator, leaving issue; and

   (c)   issue of that member are living at the testator's death,

then, unless a contrary intention appears by the will, the devise or bequest shall take effect as if the class included the issue of its deceased member living at the testator's death.

(3) Issue shall take under this section through all degrees, according to their stock, in equal shares if more than one, any gift or share which their parent would have taken and so that no issue shall take whose parent is living at the testator's death and so capable of taking.

(4) For the purposes of this section –

   (a) the illegitimacy of any person is to be disregarded; and
   (b) a person conceived before the testator's death and born living thereafter is to be taken to have been living at the testator's death.'

Rectification and interpretation of wills

s.20 Rectification

(1) If a court is satisfied that a will is so expressed that it fails to carry out the testator's intentions, in consequence –

   (a) of a clerical error; or
   (b) of a failure to understand his instructions,

   it may order that the will shall be rectified so as to carry out his intentions.

(2) An application for an order under this section shall not, except with the permission of the court, be made after the end of the period of six months from the date on which representation with respect to the estate of the deceased is first taken out.

(3) The provisions of this section shall not render the personal representatives of a deceased person liable for having distributed any part of the estate of the deceased, after the end of the period of six months from the date on which representation with respect to the estate of the deceased is first taken out, on the ground that they ought to have taken into account the possibility that the court might permit the making of an application for an order under this section after the end of that period; but this subsection shall not prejudice any power to recover, by reason of the making of an order under this section, any part of the estate so distributed.

(4) In considering for the purposes of this section when representation with respect to the estate of a deceased person was first taken out, a grant limited to settled land or to trust property shall be left out of account, and a grant limited to real estate or to personal estate shall be left out of account unless a grant limited to the remainder of the estate has previously been made or is made at the same time.

s.21 Interpretation of wills – general rules as to evidence

(1) This section applies to a will –

   (a) in so far as any part of it is meaningless;
   (b) in so far as the language used in any part of it is ambiguous on the face of it;
   (c) in so far as evidence, other than evidence of the testator's intention, shows that the language used in any part of it is ambiguous in the light of surrounding circumstances.

(2) In so far as this section applies to a will extrinsic evidence, including evidence of the testator's intention, may be admitted to assist in its interpretation.

s.22 Presumption as to effect of gifts to spouses

Except where a contrary intention is shown it shall be presumed that if a testator devises or bequeaths property to his spouse in terms which in themselves would give an absolute interest to the spouse, but by the same instrument purports to give his issue an interest in the same property, the gift to the spouse is absolute notwithstanding the purported gift to the issue.

* * * * *

NON-CONTENTIOUS PROBATE RULES 1987, SI 1987/2024

* * * * *

r.12 Evidence as to due execution of will

(1) Subject to paragraphs (2) and (3) below, where a will contains no attestation clause or the attestation clause is insufficient, or where it appears to the district judge or registrar that there is doubt about the due execution of the will, he shall before admitting it to proof require an affidavit as to due execution from one or more of the attesting witnesses or, if no attesting witness is conveniently available, from any other person who was present when the will was executed; and if the district judge or registrar, after considering the evidence, is satisfied that the will was not duly executed, he shall refuse probate and mark the will accordingly.

(2) If no affidavit can be obtained in accordance with paragraph (1) above, the district judge or registrar may accept evidence on affidavit from any person he may think fit to show that the signature on the will is in the handwriting of the deceased, or of any other matter which may raise a presumption in favour of due execution of the will, and may if he thinks fit require that notice of the application be given to any person who may be prejudiced by the will.

(3) A district judge or registrar may accept a will for proof without evidence as aforesaid if he is satisfied that the distribution of the estate is not thereby affected.

* * * * *

Statutory provisions relating to family law and guardianship

FAMILY LAW REFORM ACT 1987

* * * * *

PART I

GENERAL PRINCIPLE

s.1 General principle

(1) In this Act and enactments passed and instruments made after the coming into force of this section, references (however expressed) to any relationship between two persons shall, unless the contrary intention appears, be construed without regard to whether or not the father and mother of either of them, or the father and mother of any person through whom the relationship is deduced, have or had been married to each other at any time.

(2) In this Act and enactments passed after the coming into force of this section, unless the contrary intention appears –

    (a) references to a person whose father and mother were married to each other at the time of his birth include; and

    (b) references to a person whose father and mother were not married to each other at the time of his birth do not include,

references to any person to whom subsection (3) below applies, and cognate references shall be construed accordingly.

(3) This subsection applies to any person who –

    (a) is treated as legitimate by virtue of section 1 of the Legitimacy Act 1976;

    (b) is a legitimated person within the meaning of section 10 of that Act;

    (c) is an adopted person within the meaning of Chapter 4 of Part I of the Adoption and Children Act 2002; or

    (d) is otherwise treated in law as legitimate.

(4) For the purpose of construing references falling within subsection (2) above, the time of a person's birth shall be taken to include any time during the period beginning with –

    (a) the insemination resulting in his birth; or

    (b) where there was no such insemination, his conception,

and (in either case) ending with his birth.

* * * * *

PART III

PROPERTY RIGHTS

s.18 Succession on intestacy

(1) In Part IV of the Administration of Estates Act 1925 (which deals with the distribution of the estate of an intestate), references (however expressed) to any relationship between two persons shall be construed in accordance with section 1 above.

(2) For the purpose of subsection (1) above and that Part of that Act, a person whose father and mother were not married to each other at the time of his birth shall be presumed not to have been survived by his father, or by any person related to him only through his father, unless the contrary is shown.

(3) In section 50(1) of that Act (which relates to the construction of documents), the reference to Part IV of that Act, or to the foregoing provisions of that Part, shall in relation to an instrument inter vivos made, or a will or codicil coming into operation, after the coming into force of this section (but not in relation to instruments inter vivos made or wills or codicils coming into operation earlier) be construed as including references to this section.

(4) This section does not affect any rights under the intestacy of a person dying before the coming into force of this section.

s.19 Dispositions of property

(1) In the following dispositions, namely –

(a) dispositions inter vivos made on or after the date on which this section comes into force; and

(b) dispositions by will or codicil where the will or codicil is made on or after that date,

references (whether express or implied) to any relationship between two persons shall be construed in accordance with section 1 above.

(2) It is hereby declared that the use, without more, of the word 'heir' or 'heirs' or any expression purporting to create an entailed interest in real or personal property does not show a contrary intention for the purposes of section 1 as applied by subsection (1) above.

(3) In relation to the dispositions mentioned in subsection (1) above, section 33 of the Trustee Act 1925 (which specifies the trust implied by a direction that income is to be held on protective trusts for the benefit of any person) shall have effect as if any reference (however expressed) to any relationship between two persons were construed in accordance with section 1 above.

(4) Where under any disposition of real or personal property, any interest in such property is limited (whether subject to any preceding limitation or charge or not) in such a way that it would, apart from this section, devolve (as nearly as the law permits) along with a dignity or title of honour, then –

(a) whether or not the disposition contains an express reference to the dignity or title of honour; and

(b) whether or not the property or some interest in the property may in some event become severed from it,

nothing in this section shall operate to sever the property or any interest in it from the dignity or title, but the property or interest shall devolve in all respects as if this section had not been enacted.

(5) This section is without prejudice to section 42 of the Adoption Act 1976 (construction of dispositions in cases of adoption).

(6) In this section 'disposition' means a disposition, including an oral disposition, of real or personal property whether inter vivos or by will or codicil.

(7) Notwithstanding any rule of law, a disposition made by will or codicil executed before the date on which this section comes into force shall not be treated for the purposes of this section as made on or after that date by reason only that the will or codicil is confirmed by a codicil executed on or after that date.

s.20 No special protection for trustees and personal representatives

Section 17 of the Family Law Reform Act 1969 (which enables trustees and personal representatives to distribute property without having ascertained that no person whose parents were not married to each other at the time of his birth, or who claims through such a person, is or may be entitled to an interest in the property) shall cease to have effect.

s.21 Entitlement to grant of probate etc

(1) For the purpose of determining the person or persons who would in accordance with probate rules be entitled to a grant of probate or administration in respect of the estate of a deceased person, the deceased shall be presumed, unless the contrary is shown, not to have been survived –

    (a) by any person related to him whose father and mother were not married to each other at the time of his birth; or

    (b) by any person whose relationship with him is deduced through such a person as is mentioned in paragraph (a) above.

(2) In this section 'probate rules' means rules of court made under section 127 of the Supreme Court Act 1981.

(3) This section does not apply in relation to the estate of a person dying before the coming into force of this section.

CHILDREN ACT 1989

PART I

INTRODUCTORY

s.1 Welfare of the child

(1) When a court determines any question with respect to –

    (a) the upbringing of a child; or

    (b) the administration of a child's property or the application of any income arising from it,

the child's welfare shall be the court's paramount consideration.

(2) In any proceedings in which any question with respect to the upbringing of a child arises, the court shall have regard to the general principle that any delay in determining the question is likely to prejudice the welfare of the child.

(3) In the circumstances mentioned in subsection (4), a court shall have regard in particular to –

    (a) the ascertainable wishes and feelings of the child concerned (considered in the light of his age and understanding);

    (b) his physical, emotional and educational needs;

    (c) the likely effect on him of any change in his circumstances;

    (d) his age, sex, background and any characteristics of his which the court considers relevant;

    (e) any harm which he has suffered or is at risk of suffering;

    (f) how capable each of his parents, and any other person in relation to whom the court considers the question to be relevant, is of meeting his needs;

(g) the range of powers available to the court under this Act in the proceedings in question.

(4) The circumstances are that –

    (a) the court is considering whether to make, vary or discharge a section 8 order, and the making, variation or discharge of the order is opposed by any party to the proceedings; or

    (b) the court is considering whether to make, vary or discharge a special guardianship order or an order under Part IV.

(5) Where a court is considering whether or not to make one or more orders under this Act with respect to a child, it shall not make the order or any of the orders unless it considers that doing so would be better for the child than making no order at all.

s.2 Parental responsibility for children

(1) Where a child's father and mother were married to each other at the time of his birth, they shall each have parental responsibility for the child.

(2) Where a child's father and mother were not married to each other at the time of his birth –

    (a) the mother shall have parental responsibility for the child;

    (b) the father shall have parental responsibility for the child if he has acquired it (and has not ceased to have it) in accordance with the provisions of this Act.

(3) References in this Act to a child whose father and mother were, or (as the case may be) were not, married to each other at the time of his birth must be read with section 1 of the Family Law Reform Act 1987 (which extends their meaning).

(4) The rule of law that a father is the natural guardian of his legitimate child is abolished.

(5) More than one person may have parental responsibility for the same child at the same time.

(6) A person who has parental responsibility for a child at any time shall not cease to have that responsibility solely because some other person subsequently acquires parental responsibility for the child.

(7) Where more than one person has parental responsibility for a child, each of them may act alone and without the other (or others) in meeting that responsibility; but nothing in this Part shall be taken to affect the operation of any enactment which requires the consent of more than one person in a matter affecting the child.

(8) The fact that a person has parental responsibility for a child shall not entitle him to act in any way which would be incompatible with any order made with respect to the child under this Act.

(9) A person who has parental responsibility for a child may not surrender or transfer any part of that responsibility to another but may arrange for some or all of it to be met by one or more persons acting on his behalf.

(10) The person with whom any such arrangement is made may himself be a person who already has parental responsibility for the child concerned.

(11) The making of any such arrangement shall not affect any liability of the person making it which may arise from any failure to meet any part of his parental responsibility for the child concerned.

s.3 Meaning of 'parental responsibility'

(1) In this Act 'parental responsibility' means all the rights, duties, powers, responsibilities and authority which by law a parent of a child has in relation to the child and his property.

(2) It also includes the rights, powers and duties which a guardian of the child's estate (appointed, before the commencement of section 5, to act generally) would have had in relation to the child and his property.

(3) The rights referred to in subsection (2) include, in particular, the right of the guardian

to receive or recover in his own name, for the benefit of the child, property of whatever description and wherever situated which the child is entitled to receive or
recover.

(4) The fact that a person has, or does not have, parental responsibility for a child shall
not affect –

    (a) any obligation which he may have in relation to the child (such as a statutory
duty to maintain the child); or

    (b) any rights which, in the event of the child's death, he (or any other person) may
have in relation to the child's property.

(5) A person who –

    (a) does not have parental responsibility for a particular child; but

    (b) has care of the child,

may (subject to the provisions of this Act) do what is reasonable in all the circumstances
of the case for the purpose of safeguarding or promoting the child's welfare.

s.4 Acquisition of parental responsibility by father

(1) Where a child's father and mother were not married to each other at the time of his
birth the father shall acquire parental responsibility for the child if –

    (a) he becomes registered as the child's father under any of the enactments specified
in subsection (1A);

    (b) he and the child's mother make an agreement (a 'parental responsibility agreement')
providing for him to have parental responsibility for the child; or

    (c) the court, on his application, orders that he shall have parental responsibility for
the child.

(1A) The enactments referred to in subsection (1)(a) are –

    (a) paragraphs (a), (b) and (c) of section 10(1) and of section 10A(1) of the Births
and Deaths Registration Act 1953;

    (b) paragraphs (a), (b)(i) and (c) of section 18(1), and sections 18(2)(b) and
20(1)(a) of the Registration of Births, Deaths and Marriages (Scotland) Act 1965;
and

    (c) sub-paragraphs (a), (b) and (c) of Article 14(3) of the Births and Deaths
Registration (Northern Ireland) Order 1976.

(1B) The Lord Chancellor may by order amend subsection (1A) so as to add further enactments to the list in that subsection.

(2) No parental responsibility agreement shall have effect for the purposes of this Act
unless –

    (a) it is made in the form prescribed by regulations made by the Lord Chancellor;
and

    (b) where regulations are made by the Lord Chancellor prescribing the manner in
which such agreements must be recorded, it is recorded in the prescribed
manner.

(2A) A person who has acquired parental responsibility under subsection (1) shall cease to
have that responsibility only if the court so orders.

(3) The court may make an order under subsection (2A) on the application –

    (a) of any person who has parental responsibility for the child; or

    (b) with the leave of the court, of the child himself,

subject, in the case of parental responsibility acquired under subsection (1)(c), to
section 12(4).

s.4A Acquisition of parental responsibility by step-parent

(1) Where a child's parent ('parent A') who has parental responsibility for the child is married to a person who is not the child's parent ('the step-parent') –

    (a) parent A or, if the other parent of the child also has parental responsibility for the child, both parents may by agreement with the step-parent provide for the step-parent to have parental responsibility for the child; or

    (b) the court may, on the application of the step-parent, order that the step-parent shall have parental responsibility for the child.

(2) An agreement under subsection (1)(a) is also a 'parental responsibility agreement', and section 4(2) applies in relation to such agreements as it applies in relation to parental responsibility agreements under section 4.

(3) A parental responsibility agreement under subsection (1)(a), or an order under subsection (1)(b), may only be brought to an end by an order of the court made on the application –

    (a) of any person who has parental responsibility for the child; or

    (b) with the leave of the court, of the child himself.

(4) The court may only grant leave under subsection (3)(b) if it is satisfied that the child has sufficient understanding to make the proposed application.

s.5 Appointment of guardians

(1) Where an application with respect to a child is made to the court by any individual, the court may by order appoint that individual to be the child's guardian if –

    (a) the child has no parent with parental responsibility for him; or

    (b) a residence order has been made with respect to the child in favour of a parent, guardian or special guardian of his who has died while the order was in force.

    (c) paragraph (b) does not apply, and the child's only or last surviving special guardian dies.

(2) The power conferred by subsection (1) may also be exercised in any family proceedings if the court considers that the order should be made even though no application has been made for it.

(3) A parent who has parental responsibility for his child may appoint another individual to be the child's guardian in the event of his death.

(4) A guardian of a child may appoint another individual to take his place as the child's guardian in the event of his death; and a special guardian of a child may appoint another individual to be the child's guardian in the event of his death.

(5) An appointment under subsection (3) or (4) shall not have effect unless it is made in writing, is dated and is signed by the person making the appointment or –

    (a) in the case of an appointment made by a will which is not signed by the testator, is signed at the direction of the testator in accordance with the requirements of section 9 of the Wills Act 1837; or

    (b) in any other case, is signed at the direction of the person making the appointment, in his presence and in the presence of two witnesses who each attest the signature.

(6) A person appointed as a child's guardian under this section shall have parental responsibility for the child concerned.

(7) Where –

    (a) on the death of any person making an appointment under subsection (3) or (4), the child concerned has no parent with parental responsibility for him; or

    (b) immediately before the death of any person making such an appointment, a residence order in his favour was in force with respect to the child or he was the child's only (or last surviving) special guardian,

the appointment shall take effect on the death of that person.

(8) Where, on the death of any person making an appointment under subsection (3) or
    (4) –

    (a) the child concerned has a parent with parental responsibility for him; and
    (b) subsection (7)(b) does not apply,

    the appointment shall take effect when the child no longer has a parent who has
    parental responsibility for him.

(9) Subsections (1) and (7) do not apply if the residence order referred to in paragraph
    (b) of those subsections was also made in favour of a surviving parent of the child.

(10) Nothing in this section shall be taken to prevent an appointment under subsection (3)
     or (4) being made by two or more persons acting jointly.

(11) Subject to any provision made by rules of court, no court shall exercise the High
     Court's inherent jurisdiction to appoint a guardian of the estate of any child.

(12) Where rules of court are made under subsection (11) they may prescribe the circum-
     stances in which, and conditions subject to which, an appointment of such a guardian
     may be made.

(13) A guardian of a child may only be appointed in accordance with the provisions of this
     section.

s.6 Guardians: revocation and disclaimer

(1) An appointment under section 5(3) or (4) revokes an earlier such appointment
     (including one made in an unrevoked will or codicil) made by the same person in
     respect of the same child, unless it is clear (whether as the result of an express provi-
     sion in the later appointment or by any necessary implication) that the purpose of the
     later appointment is to appoint an additional guardian.

(2) An appointment under section 5(3) or (4) (including one made in an unrevoked will
     or codicil) is revoked if the person who made the appointment revokes it by a writ-
     ten and dated instrument which is signed –

    (a) by him; or
    (b) at his direction, in his presence and in the presence of two witnesses who each
         attest the signature.

(3) An appointment under section 5(3) or (4) (other than one made in a will or codicil)
     is revoked if, with the intention of revoking the appointment, the person who made
     it –

    (a) destroys the instrument by which it was made; or
    (b) has some other person destroy that instrument in his presence.

(3A) An appointment under section 5(3) or (4) (including one made in an unrevoked will
     or codicil) is revoked if the person appointed is the spouse of the person who made
     the appointment and either –

    (a) a decree of a court of civil jurisdiction in England and Wales dissolves or annuls
         the marriage, or
    (b) the marriage is dissolved or annulled and the divorce or annulment is entitled to
         recognition in England and Wales by virtue of Part II of the Family Law Act
         1986,

    unless a contrary intention appears by the appointment.

(4) For the avoidance of doubt, an appointment under section 5(3) or (4) made in a will
     or codicil is revoked if the will or codicil is revoked.

(5) A person who is appointed as a guardian under section 5(3) or (4) may disclaim his
     appointment by an instrument in writing signed by him and made within a reason-
     able time of his first knowing that the appointment has taken effect.

(6) Where regulations are made by the Lord Chancellor prescribing the manner in which
     such disclaimers must be recorded, no such disclaimer shall have effect unless it is
     recorded in the prescribed manner.

(7) Any appointment of a guardian under section 5 may be brought to an end at any time by order of the court –

    (a) on the application of any person who has parental responsibility for the child;

    (b) on the application of the child concerned, with leave of the court; or

    (c) in any family proceedings, if the court considers that it should be brought to an end even though no application has been made.

* * * * *

SCHEDULE 14

* * * * *

GUARDIANS

Existing guardians to be guardians under this Act

12. (1) Any appointment of a person as guardian of a child which –
    (a) was made –

        (i) under sections 3 to 5 of the Guardianship of Minors Act 1971;

        (ii) under section 38(3) of the Sexual Offences Act 1956; or

        (iii) under the High Court's inherent jurisdiction with respect to children; and

    (b) has taken effect before the commencement of section 5,

    shall (subject to sub-paragraph (2)) be deemed, on and after the commencement of section 5, to be an appointment made and having effect under that section.

    (2) Where an appointment of a person as guardian of a child has effect under section 5 by virtue of sub-paragraph (1)(a)(ii), the appointment shall not have effect for a period which is longer than any period specified in the order.

Appointment of guardian not yet in effect

13. Any appointment of a person to be a guardian of a child –

    (a) which was made as mentioned in paragraph 12(1)(a)(i); but

    (b) which, immediately before the commencement of section 5, had not taken effect,

    shall take effect in accordance with section 5 (as modified, where it applies, by paragraph 8(2)).

Persons deemed to be appointed as guardians under existing wills

14. For the purposes of the Wills Act 1837 and of this Act any disposition by will and testament or devise of the custody and tuition of any child, made before the commencement of section 5 and paragraph 1 of Schedule 13, shall be deemed to be an appointment by will of a guardian of the child.

* * * * *

Will Forms

It is the policy of this book to offer a collection of particular precedent clauses from which a complete draft may be readily compiled to meet the individual circumstances of any particular case. This is still considered to be the most economical presentation, and the most convenient format for the storage of material on a database.

However, the following three complete will forms are included, to supplement the precedent clauses. Although there should never be any such thing as a 'standard' will form, these forms may be found acceptable for generalised use in a number of straightforward cases, with or without modification, and may be conveniently used as 'common form' material, for that purpose.

WILL 1 ABSOLUTE GIFT TO WIDOW, IF SHE SURVIVES BY 28 DAYS; FAILING WHICH, UPON TRUST FOR CHILDREN; SOLICITOR TRUSTEES BEING APPOINTED IN THAT EVENT

THIS IS THE LAST WILL AND TESTAMENT

of me   of

in the County of

1   I HEREBY REVOKE all former wills and testamentary dispositions made by me.
2   IF and only if my wife   survives me by twenty-eight clear days I DEVISE AND BEQUEATH all my real and personal property whatsoever and wheresoever unto my said Wife absolutely and appoint her sole Executrix hereof
3   IF my said wife fails to attain a vested interest hereunder (but not otherwise) the following clauses shall have effect in substitution for Clause 2 above
4   I APPOINT   and   of Solicitors (hereinafter called 'my Trustees' which expression where the context admits includes any trustee hereof for the time being) to be the Executors and Trustees hereof
5   (1) I GIVE DEVISE AND BEQUEATH all my real and personal property not otherwise specifically disposed of to my Trustees upon the following trusts
    (2) MY TRUSTEES shall pay and discharge therefrom all my debts and funeral testamentary and administration expenses
    (3) MY TRUSTEES shall hold the balance of my said real and personal property remaining after such payments (hereinafter called 'my residuary estate') upon the beneficial trusts and with and subject to the powers and provisions hereinafter contained
6   MY TRUSTEES shall hold my residuary estate Upon Trust for such of my children as shall be living at my death and shall attain the age of twenty-one years and if more than one in equal shares absolutely Provided Always that if any child of mine shall die without having attained a vested interest hereunder leaving a child or children living at my death then any such child or children (meaning in either case a grandchild or grandchildren of mine) as shall attain the age of eighteen years shall take by substitution and in equal shares if more than one per stirpes the share of my residuary estate which such deceased child of mine would have taken had he or she survived and attained a vested interest
7   MY TRUSTEES shall have power to invest trust money and to vary and transpose investments from time to time with the same full and unrestricted freedom in their choice of investments as if they were a sole absolute beneficial owner
8   BY WAY OF EXTENSION of the powers conferred upon them by law:
    (1) My Trustees may exercise the powers as to application of income conferred by section 31 of the Trustee Act 1925 without regard to the restrictions in the proviso to subsection (1) of that section
    (2) My Trustees may exercise the power of advancement conferred by section 32 of the Trustee Act 1925 without regard to the restriction in paragraph (a) of subsection (1) of that section
9   I Declare that any Executor or Trustee of this my Will who is or shall be a Solicitor or engaged in any other profession or business shall be entitled to charge and be paid his usual professional or other charges for work done by him or his firm in the execution or otherwise in relation to the trusts hereof including any work or business which he might be as a Trustee required to do or transact in person

AS WITNESS my hand this   day of   20[   ]

SIGNED by the above-named

                           in

our joint presence and then

by us in his:

WILL 2   TAX-SAVING WILL OF MARRIED WOMAN, LEAVING BULK OF ESTATE IN TRUST FOR CHILDREN IN ANY EVENT

THIS IS THE LAST WILL AND TESTAMENT

of me   of   in the County of

Wife of

1   I HEREBY REVOKE all former wills and testamentary dispositions

2   I APPOINT   and   of   in the County of (hereinafter called 'my Trustees' which expression where the context admits includes any trustees hereof for the time being) to be the executors and trustees hereof

3   I GIVE to my husband   absolutely all my personal chattels as defined by section 55(1)(x) of the Administration of Estates Act 1925

4   SUBJECT TO payment thereout of my debts and funeral and testamentary expenses and all legacies given hereby or by any codicil hereto I give to my Trustees all my real and personal property not otherwise specifically disposed of Upon Trust for such of my children as shall be living at my death and if more than one in equal shares absolutely Provided Always that if any child of mine shall die in my lifetime leaving a child or children living at my death who shall attain the age of twenty-five years such last mentioned child or children shall take by substitution and if more than one in equal shares per stirpes the share of my estate which his her or their parent would have taken if he or she had survived to attain a vested interest

5   The following powers and discretions shall be exercisable by my Trustees in addition to their powers and discretions under the general law:

(1) Power to invest money and to vary or transpose investments from time to time with the same full and unrestricted freedom in their choice of investments as if my Trustees were a sole absolute beneficial owner

(2) Power to exercise the statutory powers as to application of income conferred by section 31 of the Trustee Act 1925 without regard to the restrictions in the proviso to subsection (1) of that section

(3) Power to exercise the statutory power of advancement conferred by section 32 of the Trustee Act 1925 without regard to the restriction in paragraph (a) of subsection (1) of that section

(4) Power in any case where my Trustees have any obligation or discretion under the provisions of my will or under the general law to pay or apply income or capital to or for the benefit of any person who is a minor to discharge that obligation or to exercise that discretion if and whenever they think fit to do so by making payment either to the parent or guardian of the minor or else to the minor personally if of the age of sixteen years at least and so that their respective receipts shall be a full discharge to my Trustees who shall not be required to see to the application of any income or capital so paid

(5) Power for any of my Trustees who is a Solicitor or other person engaged in any profession or business to be so employed or act and to charge and be paid all usual professional and other charges for any business transacted or work done by him or his firm in connection with the administration and distribution of my estate or the trusts of my will whether or not of a professional nature and whether or not any person could have done the same personally

IN WITNESS whereof I have hereunto set my hand this

day of   20[   ]

SIGNED by the above-named

                              in

our joint presence and then

by us in hers:

WILL 3   TAX-SAVING WILL, CREATING TRUST FUND BY WAY OF SETTLED LEGACY FOR CHILDREN, WITHIN THE NIL RATE OF IHT; RESIDUE TO WIDOW FOR LIFE AND, SUBJECT THERETO, IN TRUST FOR CHILDREN

THIS IS THE LAST WILL AND TESTAMENT

of me   of   in the County of

1   I HEREBY REVOKE all former wills and testamentary dispositions
2   I APPOINT   and   of   in the County of (hereinafter called 'my Trustees' which expression where the context admits includes any trustee hereof for the time being) to be the executors and trustees hereof
3   I GIVE to my wife   absolutely all my personal chattels as defined by section 55(1)(x) of the Administration of Estates Act 1925
4   (1) I GIVE to my Trustees such a sum as can be transferred on my death without being chargeable to Inheritance Tax (disregarding any exemption or relief) at any rate above the nil rate of tax Upon such and the like Trusts for the benefit of my children and issue as are declared in respect of my residuary estate by Clause 6(2) below but as if my said Wife   had predeceased me
     (2) In relation to the trusts of this gift my Trustees shall have all such and the like powers and discretions hereinafter conferred upon them or otherwise applicable in relation to my residuary estate as are for the time being capable of being exercised in relation to this gift
5   (1) I GIVE to my Trustees all my real and personal property not otherwise specifically disposed of Upon the following Trusts
     (2) My Trustees shall pay and discharge therefrom all my debts (including any debt which is a charge on any property in which at the time of my death I have a beneficial interest) and funeral and testamentary expenses and all tax payable by reason of my death
     (3) My Trustees shall hold the balance of my said real and personal property remaining after such payments (hereinafter called 'my residuary estate') Upon the beneficial Trusts and with and subject to the powers and provisions hereinafter declared and contained
6   MY TRUSTEES shall hold my residuary estate Upon the following Trusts:
     (1) Upon Trust to pay the income thereof to my said Wife during her life and subject thereto
     (2) Upon Trust for such of my children as shall be living at my death and who shall have attained or shall attain the age of eighteen years and if more than one in equal shares absolutely Provided Always that if any child of mine shall die in my lifetime leaving a child or children living at my death who shall attain the age of twenty-five years such last-mentioned child or children shall take by substitution and if more than one in equal shares per stirpes the share of my residuary estate which his or her or their parent would have taken if he or she had survived to attain a vested interest and Provided Further that if any child of mine shall die in my lifetime leaving no child who shall attain a vested interest under the foregoing proviso but such deceased child of mine shall leave a widow or widower living at my death then such widow or widower shall take by substitution the share of my residuary estate which such deceased child of mine would have taken if he or she had survived to attain a vested interest
7   The following powers and discretions shall be exercisable by my Trustees in addition to their powers and discretions under the general law:

(1) Power to treat all income from any part of my estate which is actually received after my death or after the time when any person becomes or ceases to be entitled or prospectively entitled to any beneficial interest in my residuary estate as accruing wholly after my death or after that time as the case may be without apportionment whatever the period in respect of which it is actually payable to the intent that the Apportionment Act 1870 and the rules in *Howe* v. *Dartmouth* and *Allhusen* v. *Whittell* in all their branches shall for all purposes be wholly excluded in the administration of my estate and of the trusts of this my will

(2) Power in the administration and execution of any of the trusts hereof to make any such appropriation as is authorised by section 41 of the Administration of Estates Act 1925 but without being required to obtain any such consents as are referred to in that section

(3) Power to insure against loss or damage by fire or from any other insurable risk any property for the time being comprised in my residuary estate to any amount and to pay all premiums for any such insurance at their discretion out of the income or capital of my residuary estate and so that any money received under any such insurance shall be applicable at their discretion either in or towards making good the loss or damage in respect of which it was received or otherwise as if it were proceeds of sale of the property insured

(4) Power to invest trust money and to vary and transpose investments from time to time with the same full and unrestricted freedom in their choice of investments as if my Trustees were a sole absolute beneficial owner

(5) Power to apply trust money at any time and from time to time in the purchase or in the improvement of any freehold or leasehold dwelling house within the United Kingdom and to permit any such dwelling house to be used as a residence by my said Wife upon such terms and conditions as in their absolute discretion my Trustees from time to time think fit to require

(6) Power at any time to effect any policy of insurance of whatever nature upon the lives of any of the beneficiaries and to pay or apply any part of the capital or income (including accumulations of income) of my residuary estate in or towards the payment of any premium for effecting or maintaining any such policy or to borrow from any person or corporation (including any one or more of themselves) the whole or any part of the moneys required for the payment of any such premium whether or not the loan is secured upon the whole or any part of my residuary estate and upon such terms as to interest repayment and otherwise as my Trustees shall see fit to agree to the intent that my Trustees shall hold any such policy and the proceeds thereof and all moneys arising therefrom as an accretion to the capital of my residuary estate

(7) Power at any time and from time to time to pay or apply capital money from my residuary estate to any extent up to a maximum of one half to my said Wife or for her benefit as my Trustees in their absolute discretion may think fit

(8) Power to exercise the statutory powers as to application of income conferred by section 31 of the Trustee Act 1925 without regard to the restrictions in the proviso to subsection (1) of that section

(9) Power to exercise the statutory power of advancement conferred by section 32 of the Trustee Act 1925 without regard to the restriction in paragraph (a) of subsection (1) of that section

(10) Power in any case where my Trustees have any obligation or discretion under the provisions of my will or under the general law to pay or apply income or capital to or for the benefit of any person who is a minor to discharge that obligation or to exercise that discretion if and whenever they think fit to do so by making payment either to the parent or guardian of the minor or else to the minor personally if of the age of sixteen years at least and so that their respective receipts shall be a full discharge to my Trustees who shall not be required to see to the application of any income or capital so paid

(11) Power for any of my Trustees who is a Solicitor or other person engaged in any profession or business to be so employed or act and to charge and be paid all usual professional and other charges for any business transacted or work by him or his firm in connection with the administration and distribution of my estate or the trusts of my will whether or not of a professional nature and whether or not any person could have done the same personally

8   None of the powers and discretions conferred upon or vested in my Trustees (whether by virtue of any of the provisions of this my will or by operation of law) shall be capable of exercise in any way such as will or may directly or indirectly prevent section 71 of the Inheritance Act 1984 (or any re-enactment or replacement thereof for the time being) from applying or continuing to apply to any property given or held from time to time under the trusts of this my will for the benefit of any of my said children or their children widows or widowers which is for the time being settled property for the purposes of Inheritance Tax and in which for the time being no interest in possession subsists

9   The power of appointing from time to time a new or additional trustee or trustees of this my will shall be vested in my said Wife during her life

10   I Declare that the foregoing provisions of my will are made and the dispositions of my estate therein contained shall have effect only (if at all) subject to the overriding powers and discretions which I hereby confer upon my Trustees but so that all such powers and discretions shall be exercisable only (if at all) with the consent of my said Wife that is to say:

(1)   During the period of twenty-three months following my death (or so much of that period during which any part of my estate continues to be subject to the trusts and powers of my will) my Trustees shall accumulate the income of my residuary estate (or so much thereof as is not from time to time applied for the maintenance education or benefit of any person pursuant to the provisions of paragraph (2) of this Clause) and shall hold such accumulations by way of addition to the capital of my residuary estate

(2)   During the period aforesaid my Trustees shall have power at any time and from time to time and whenever they may in their absolute and uncontrolled discretion think fit to pay or apply the whole or any part or parts of the income or of the capital or of the income and the capital of my residuary estate to or for the benefit of all or any one or more exclusively of the others or other of the following persons that is to say my said Wife and any of my children and any widow widower or child born during the lifetime of the survivor of myself and my said Wife of any child of mine who may predecease such survivor

(3)   If any of my Trustees is or may become personally interested as a beneficiary in the exercise of (or omission to exercise) any or all of the powers and discretions hereby conferred upon my Trustees generally he may from time to time join in exercising that power or any such discretion as if he were not so interested and may nevertheless retain for his own use any benefit which in good faith he may derive in consequence thereof as if he were not a trustee

(4)   My Trustees may exercise any or all of the powers and discretions hereby conferred upon them at any time after my death and in particular whether or not probate of my will has been granted and whether or not the administration of my estate has (subject to any exercise of any of the said powers and discretions) been completed

(5)   Notwithstanding the fiduciary nature of the powers and discretions hereby conferred on my Trustees I further Declare that my Trustees may at any time wholly or in part release the same but without prejudice to any payment or application of capital or income previously made by them thereunder

IN WITNESS whereof I have hereunto set my hand this

day of   20[   ]

SIGNED by the above-named   ⎫

                        in   ⎬

our joint presence and then   ⎭

by us in his:

Index

Gifts

  absolute gift

    dispositions of residue 89–91, 98–100

    family home 31

    grandchildren, to 98–9

    matrimonial home 67–8

    nephews and nieces, to 99–100

    personal chattels 60

    private residence 67–8

    surviving spouse, to 89–91

  ademption 67, 72

  bank account 65–6

  building society account 65–6

  choses in action 65–6

  family home

    absolute gift 31

    gifts in trust 31–2, 68–70

    limited interest 32

    terms of occupation 32–3

  household effects 61–3

  interests in land 67–73

  investment property 71–3

  jewellery 61–3

  legatee's choice 61–3

  life policy 65–6

  local authority bond 65–6

  marriage, in consideration of 15

  pecuniary legacies *see* Pecuniary legacies

  personal chattels *see* Personal chattels

  precatory trusts 38, 64–5

  private residence

    absolute gift 67–8

    previously settled under SLA 1925 70–1

    in trust 68–70

  reservation, subject to 17

  shared gifts 61, 62

    basis of division 62

  stocks and shares 66–7

  substitutions 44–5, 62

    dispositions of residue 94, 98, 99

    stocks and shares 66–7

  variation or disclaimer xii, 36–7, 158–60

Grandchildren

  dispositions of residue 98–9

  pecuniary legacies 74–6, 77–8

Guardians, appointment of 58–9, 185–7

House *see* Family home; Investment property; Matrimonial home; Private residence

Household effects 61–3

Illegitimacy 47

Income tax xii, 11

  contingent or vested interests 29–31

  variation or disclaimer 37

  see also Taxation

Inheritance tax

  accumulation and maintenance trusts 24–8, 44, 115, 123–4, 174–5

    age of vesting 25, 27

    interest in possession 25

    overriding discretionary trusts 26

    subsisting interest in possession 26–7

    variation of dispositions after death 27–8

  advances out of capital 116

  agricultural property 15

  annual exemption 15

  anti-avoidance provisions xii, 16, 17–18

  burden of tax 18–20

  business property 15

  contemporaneous deaths 23

  discretionary trusts 16, 78–81

  election to redeem life interest on intestacy 38

  estate duty, and 17–18

  estate planning 11

  family businesses 15

  family, dispositions for maintenance of 15

  family home

    excluded from survivor's estate 33–4

    terms of occupation 32–3

  family provision, law of 10

  farms 15

  flat rate 13, 14

  gifts in consideration of marriage 15

  investment property 72

  lifetime transfers, exempt and potentially exempt 15–18

  limited interest, with remainders 95

  matrimonial home 82–3

  mitigation of tax 12–18